ROUTLEDGE LIBRARY EDITIONS
BROADCASTING

Volume 34

TELECOMMUNICATIONS IN DEVELOPING COUNTRIES

TELECOMMUNICATIONS IN DEVELOPING COUNTRIES

The Challenge from Brazil

MICHAEL HOBDAY

LONDON AND NEW YORK

First published in 1990 by Routledge

This edition first published in 2024
by Routledge
4 Park Square, Milton Park, Abingdon, Oxon OX14 4RN

and by Routledge
605 Third Avenue, New York, NY 10158

Routledge is an imprint of the Taylor & Francis Group, an informa business

© 1990 Michael Hobday

All rights reserved. No part of this book may be reprinted or reproduced or utilised in any form or by any electronic, mechanical, or other means, now known or hereafter invented, including photocopying and recording, or in any information storage or retrieval system, without permission in writing from the publishers.

Trademark notice: Product or corporate names may be trademarks or registered trademarks, and are used only for identification and explanation without intent to infringe.

British Library Cataloguing in Publication Data
A catalogue record for this book is available from the British Library

ISBN: 978-1-032-59391-3 (Set)
ISBN: 978-1-032-62352-8 (Volume 34) (hbk)
ISBN: 978-1-032-62357-3 (Volume 34) (pbk)
ISBN: 978-1-032-62355-9 (Volume 34) (ebk)

DOI: 10.4324/9781032623559

Publisher's Note
The publisher has gone to great lengths to ensure the quality of this reprint but points out that some imperfections in the original copies may be apparent.

Disclaimer
The publisher has made every effort to trace copyright holders and would welcome correspondence from those they have been unable to trace.

Telecommunications in Developing Countries
The Challenge from Brazil

Michael Hobday

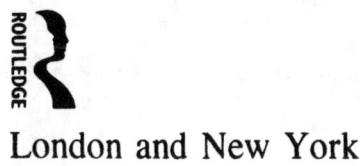

London and New York

First published 1990 by Routledge
11 New Fetter Lane, London EC4P 4EE

Simultaneously published in the USA and Canada
by Routledge
a division of Routledge, Chapman and Hall, Inc.
29 West 35th Street, New York, NY 10001

© 1990 Michael Hobday

Printed in Great Britain by
Biddles Ltd, Guildford and King's Lynn

All rights reserved. No part of this book may be reprinted or reproduced or utilized in any form or by any electronic, mechanical, or other means, now known or hereafter invented, including photocopying and recording, or in any information storage or retrieval system, without permission in writing from the publishers.

British Library Cataloguing in Publication Data

Hobday, Michael
   Telecommunications in developing countries : the
   challenge from Brazil.
   1. Brazil. Telecommunications series
   I. Title
   384'.0981
   ISBN 0-415-00156-0

Library of Congress Cataloging-in-Publication Data

Hobday, Michael.
   Telecommunications in developing countries : the challenge from
  Brazil / Michael Hobday.
     p. cm.
   Includes bibliographical references.
   ISBN 0-415-00156-0
   1. Telecommunication – Brazil. 2. Telecommunication equipment
industry – Brazil. 3. Telecommunication and state – Brazil.
4. Brazil – Economic policy. I. Title.
HE7994.H63 1990
384'.0981 – dc20   89-39367
                                                                  CIP

For Lilian Cissie Mary

CONTENTS

List of Figures	ix
List of Tables	xi
Foreword by Professor Christopher Freeman	xv
Acknowledgements	xvii
Introduction	1
Chapter 1. 'Schumpeterian Learning' - A New Approach to Technology Diffusion and the Developing Countries	11
Chapter 2. The Impact of Microelectronics on the International Telecommunications Industry	35
Chapter 3. Developing Countries: The Potential for Technological Leapfrogging	60
Chapter 4. The Expansion of Brazil's New Communications Infrastructure	88
Chapter 5. Technology Diffusion Through Brazilian Research and Development in Digital Telecommunications	111
Chapter 6. The Technological Integration of the Multinational Subsidiaries	149
Chapter 7. Technological Accumulation and Economic Crisis - The Emergence of a Brazilian Telecommunications Industry	169
Conclusions	194

Contents

Appendix 1   203
Bibliographical References   208
Index   218

LIST OF FIGURES

1.1 The Diffusion Path of an Innovation
    Under Conditions of Increased Demand   20

4.1 Organisational Chart of the Brazilian
    Ministry of Communications 1982   92

5.1 Research and Development at TELEBRAS   117

5.2 Technological Capabilities Required in
    Telecommunications Activities, Electro-
    mechanical and Microelectronic   144

6.1 Ericsson do Brasil: Organisation of
    Technology Directorate - 1983   157

LIST OF TABLES

2.1 Shares of Major Telecommunications Product Lines in World Sales 1980-1985 (estimated) — 37

2.2 Estimates of Research and Development Costs of Digital Switching Systems (billions of dollars) — 39

2.3 Estimated Regional Markets for Telecommunications Equipment (shipments in billions of dollars - 1979 prices) — 46

2.4 Sales of Major Telecommunications Equipment Manufacturers, 1982 and 1983 (current prices) — 48

2.5 Recent Major Joint Ventures and Acquisitions Involving Leading Telecommunications Companies by Firm and Product Area — 52

3.1 Selected Telecommunications and Economic Indicators - Latin America circa 1980 — 79

3.2 Telecommunications Equipment Markets in the Latin American Region (millions of dollars) — 81

3.3 Multinational Corporation Suppliers of Telephone Exchange Equipment in Latin America — 84

4.1 Royalties on Technology Remitted from Ericsson do Brasil to L.M. Ericsson, 1972-1977 (Swedish crowns) — 95

4.2 Employment, Sales and Profits of Ericsson do Brasil, 1971-1980 — 96

Tables

4.3	Quantities and Densities of Telephones in Brazil - Selected Years 1948-1984	99
4.4	Investments in the TELEBRAS System, 1976-1983 (current US dollars)	100
4.5	Selected Brazilian Informatics and Telematics Services	104
5.1	The Distribution of Research and Development Activities in Telecommunications According to the CPqD/TELEBRAS Plan	115
5.2	Investment in Research and Development by TELEBRAS, 1977-1984 (millions of dollars, current prices)	119
5.3	Human Resources of CPqD, circa 1983	120
5.4	Major Programmes and Projects under CPqD	121
5.5	Patents Registered by CPqD, 1976-1984	127
5.6	Officially Registered Patents and Technology Transfer Agreements by Firms with TELEBRAS	129
5.7	Official National and International Technical Collaboration Agreements between CPqD and Technology Suppliers	132
5.8	Technological Characterisation of Microelectronic and Electromechanical Telecommunications	142
6.1	Principal Activities of the Major Telecommunications Multinationals in Brazil - Approximate Starting Dates	151
6.2	Participation by Brazilian Shareholders in Ordinary Shares and in Total Capital in Telecommunications Multinationals, circa 1984	152
6.3	Research and Development Expenditures and Employment by the Major Telecommunications Multinational Subsidiaries, 1973-1983 (millions of dollars, current prices)	154
6.4	Commercial Balance of the Telecommunications Equipment Supply Sector, 1975-1983 (millions of dollars, current prices)	155

Tables

6.5 Equipment and Component Imports and
    Exports by Ericsson do Brasil, 1975-1983
    (millions of dollars, free on board,
    current prices)   158

6.6 Nippon Electric Company Equipment and
    Component Exports, 1979-1983 (thousands
    of dollars, current prices)   162

6.7 Indicators of Research and Development
    Intensity of Four Leading Telecommunications
    Manufacturers in Brazil, 1983   163

7.1 Brazil's Telecommunications Equipment
    Supply Market, 1975-1983 (billions of
    dollars, current prices)   171

7.2 The Top 20 Major Firms in the Telecom-
    munications Equipment Supply Industry,
    1982 and 1983 (thousands of dollars,
    current prices)   174

7.3 Size Profile of Brazilian Telecom-
    munications Firms by Sales Groupings
    for 1983 (millions of dollars, current
    prices)   178

7.4 Cost Comparisons of Brazilian Telecom-
    munications Equipment and Internationally
    Available Similar Selected Major Products,
    1983 (average current prices, dollars)   184

7.5 Selected Economic Performance Indicators
    of the TELEBRAS Telecommunications Operating
    System, 1972-1982 (prices in constant 1977
    cruzeiros, millions)   188

FOREWORD

This is an important book for three major reasons. First of all, it deals with technological and industrial developments in one of the most interesting and exciting countries in the world. Far too little is known about Brazil in Europe and North America, even though it is by far the largest country in Latin America and already a giant in the world economy. It is not generally realised that, despite her acute problems of poverty and indebtedness, Brazil has made rapid progress in many advanced industries such as aircraft, machine tools, computers and - as Mike Hobday's book so clearly demonstrates - telecommunications.

Secondly, the book shows the crucial importance of infrastructural investment and technology policies for any Third World country which aspires to catch up with the established industrial countries. The contemporary wave of technical change is above all based on a combination of microelectronics, computerisation and telecommunications. These technologies are transforming every branch of manufacturing and services and affect every function within the firm including office administration, as well as design, development, marketing and production. They also create the possibility of establishing entirely new industries and services, based on data banks and value-added networks of various kinds. All of these developments depend on an adequate telecommunications infrastructure. The successful development of this Brazilian infrastructure, as described by Mike Hobday in this book, required a combination of industrial and technology policies, which has major implications for the Third World generally.

Finally, there are important lessons from this experience, not only for the newly industrialising countries, but also for the established industrial countries. The simplistic recipe of de-regulation

Foreword

and privatisation is not in itself an adequate basis for telecommunications policy in any country.

Mike Hobday brings to his task a combination of theoretical insights into the process of development, with much practical experience in the electronics industry and field-work in Brazil. This combination of sympathetic understanding of Third World problems with deep knowledge and familiarity with the technology and the economics has produced a very stimulating and informative book.

Professor Christopher Freeman
Science Policy Research Unit
University of Sussex

ACKNOWLEDGEMENTS

I would like to thank Kurt Hoffman for his help and friendly advice during the preparation of this book, for arranging for me to carry out the research within Brazil and for being a constant source of ideas and constructive criticism. I owe a large debt to Sylvia Meli for encouraging me to go to university and for her ruthless criticisms of my shoddy work. Norman Clark's interest and encouragement were always appreciated. There are also a large number of people in Brazil who, under no obligation, helped me to find my feet and carry out the research. Although it would be impossible to name them all here, I should like especially to thank Claudio Barbosa for his kindness and support throughout my stay in Brazil. Finally, I would like to express my appreciation to Charlotte Huggett, without whose help this book would never have seen the light of day. Naturally, I accept full responsibility for the contents.

Michael Hobday
Science Policy Research Unit
University of Sussex
Falmer
Brighton BN1 9RF
Sussex, UK

INTRODUCTION

The need for an efficient, modern, telecommunications (telecoms) infrastructure is now widely recognised as crucial to economic development. However, in the volumes of literature concerning communications and economic development almost no attention has been paid to the problems and opportunities facing developing countries (DCs) in acquiring telecoms technology or in manufacturing the equipment which goes to form the telecoms infrastructure.(1) Until very recently the issues of manufacturing and technological progress in telecoms have fallen outside the realm of academic investigation. Problems of technology transfer and local industrial development have largely been dealt with by government agencies responsible for telecoms policy in the DCs, the international institutions responsible for telecoms regulation, and the multinational corporations (MNCs) who have traditionally supplied most DCs with equipment and technology. In recent years, however, a surge of interest in matters of telecoms technology and DCs has arisen. This awareness comes not only from the 'traditional' actors mentioned above, but also from a wide variety of economists, journalists and governments in the developed and developing countries alike. Nineteen eighty-three was designated 'World Telecommunications Year' by the United Nations. In 1982 the powerful regulatory body, the International Telecommunications Union (ITU), for the first time in its long history recognised the vital role of telecoms in the economic and social progress of all countries (International Telecommunications Union, 1984, p. 1). At the same time the World Bank began to review its lending policy on telecoms, the OECD began a major joint study with the ITU on matters of telecoms and economic development, and an independent worldwide commission was set up to investigate a wide range of issues centring on telecoms and the progress of the Third World.

Introduction

An interesting question to ask is why, all of a sudden, so much interest has been focused on telecoms and economic development? According to the international agencies promoting the issues, it is the gross inequality between the developed and developing nations in telecoms infrastructure. They point out that in the advanced countries the telecoms sector is looked upon as an engine of economic growth, a major source of employment and a vital infrastructure for economic activities of almost all kinds (International Telecommunications Union, 1984, p. 1). In contrast, the DCs are largely excluded from the centres of technological and economic activity in telecoms, and only account for a minor share of the world's infrastructural resources. This is certainly true. However, the north-south relations of inequality are neither new, nor specific to telecoms. Cynics might argue that the very fact that the DCs are, by definition, installing and expanding their basic telecoms networks means that DC markets are enormously important to the multinationals who dominate the international markets. Given that the advanced countries already have their basic networks installed, this 'new compassion' for the plight of the Third World might simply be an excuse for the advanced countries and, in particular, the transnational corporations to strengthen their grip on the growing Third World markets. But again, even if this were the case, these issues are neither new nor peculiar to telecoms and one must therefore look further afield to explain the current focus of international attention.

This book argues that the new factor which has galvanised interest and awareness in telecoms is the emergence and diffusion of microelectronic technology. One of the aims of this study is to show how this specific technological form has profoundly and irrevocably transformed the telecoms industry. During the latter half of the 1970s and into the 1980s adoption of digital, microelectronic technology has altered the nature of telecoms products, the processes by which they are manufactured, the size and growth of the international telecoms market, the nature and forms of corporate competition, the role of government policy in promoting technological change and supporting local equipment makers, and so on. Many of these changes are closely associated with the pivotal role telecoms play in providing the infrastructure for the information-intensive activities based on microelectronics. Also, as social and economic activities become more and more dependent on information technology (IT), telecoms are seen as one of the crucial 'leading-edge' technologies, leading the transition to the so-called 'information society' of the future.(2)

Almost inevitably, these changes have led to a whole new series of problems, opportunities and challenges for DCs. In many respects the changing economic and technological environment facing the DCs demands an understanding of the particular characteristics of the technology itself. An appreciation of how modern telecoms technology differs from the previous electromechanical technology is essential to an understanding of the opportunities facing DCs in their attempts to install telecoms networks, and in some cases to produce and design equipment locally. Does technological change threaten a widening of the technology gap between the developed and developing countries? Or does the new technology offer the advantages of 'leapfrogging' earlier forms of technology and gaining the benefits of going directly to a more advanced technological form? Is the technology more or less appropriate to the needs of the DCs, however defined? Are digital products easier or more difficult to develop and manufacture? Other questions concern the effects of technological change on the possibilities of technology transfer to the DCs, and the ability of governments to bargain with the MNCs. Will the sophisticated nature of digital technology lead to a worsening position on the part of the DCs, or conversely does it offer new market opportunities for import substitution and local industrial development?

These questions are not only challenging in their own right, but they also challenge current methods of economic analysis and ways of thinking about technology and DCs. Conventional economic analysis, for the large part, has treated technological change as 'exogenous' to the economic system. Outside conventional, neoclassical economics, some significant advances have been made in conceptualising the relationships between technology and the economic system. There can be little doubt, for example, that the work of Nelson and Winter, Rosenberg, Freeman and other so-called neotechnology or neo-Schumpeterian (3) writers have greatly enriched our understanding of technology in economics. But these advances have rarely been extended to analysing DCs, and consequently there is little in the way of existing theory and methodology to approach the subject.

Similarly, if we turn to the field of development economics there exists a corresponding lack of attention to the issues of how technological advance in the developed countries might affect DCs. While there exists a body of empirical literature

Introduction

concerning the acquisition of technological capabilities by DCs, and a great deal of study into the relations of dependence which may occur as a result of technology transfer, there is remarkably little study into how technological change in the advanced countries may affect economic opportunity in the DCs. When a major technological upheaval, or discontinuity, occurs as it has done in telecoms, presumably the conditions for technology transfer and local development will change. Is it not likely that the whole network of economic relations between the advanced countries and the developing nations will alter? Unfortunately there are few guidelines on how the subject can or should be approached.

It is quite likely that this general lack of understanding about technology and the DCs has acted to fuel the speculation about telecoms and the DCs. In a very short period of time technological change has thrown the historically cemented economic relations between the developed and developing countries in telecoms into confusion. Certainly, there exists a remarkable degree of uncertainty over the prospects facing individual DCs in this area. The final Report of the Independent Commission for World Wide Telecommunications Development, mentioned above, is understandably inconclusive about the prospects and problems facing the DCs. To address the problem the Commission recommended that a new centre for telecoms development was to be set up in 1985 to research into experiences of DCs in telecoms, and to help governments to formulate effective industrial, technological and infrastructural policies (International Telecommunications Union, 1984, Chapter 8).

From the point of view of economic investigation, the telecoms sector offers a unique opportunity to analyse how the transition to microelectronic technology may affect the economic relations between the DCs and the developed countries. The telecoms equipment industry is the only major world industry which has undergone an almost complete transformation from one based on electromechanical technology to one based on microelectronics. In other rapidly growing areas of IT such as computing and informatics we have no previous industrial counterpart sufficiently similar to make a historical comparison. These industries were generated out of the new technology itself and therefore cannot provide the necessary contrast. Conversely, the telecoms industry is an old, well-established industry dating back to the late nineteenth century. Other traditional economic sectors such as the automotive and garments industries, however, cannot provide such a rich

Introduction

source of historical analysis. These industries are at a far earlier stage in the adoption and diffusion of microelectronics.(4) Beyond informed speculation it is impossible to predict how the current changes in technology will affect their industrial future, and therefore they cannot provide the necessary historical comparison. The telecoms equipment industry therefore provides a unique opportunity to make a direct contrast between the new technology and the old, and to investigate how the transition has so far affected specific DCs.(5)

Equally important from a practical policy point of view is whether or not specific DCs are actually in a position to respond positively to technological change. Can government action help to prevent any possible widening of the technology gap and avoid a deterioration in comparative advantage? Or, in a more positive manner, can governments successfully manage the technology gap in such a way as to gain any economic advantages that the new technology has to offer? Can the technology gap actually be exploited in terms of avoiding the high technology investment costs incurred by the MNC manufacturers and following a low cost strategy of adapting and improving the technology? Conversely, is it entirely outside the capacity of individual governments to orchestrate technological change in an economically beneficial way? It may be that the conditions in particular DCs prevent any room for positive policy responses, and that particular difficulties inherent in microelectronic technology mitigate against capability accumulation by the DCs. From this point of view too, the telecoms sector provides a potentially rich and valuable case for study.

Objectives of the Study

Given the state of change and uncertainty facing the DCs in telecoms the aim of this book is to analyse the historical development of the telecoms sector in Brazil from the perspective of the transition from electromechanical to microelectronic technology. Brazil is an extremely interesting case to study as it is unique among the larger DCs in having decided to invest heavily in microelectronic-based telecoms as early as the mid-1970s. This means that unlike the large majority of DCs Brazil already has almost a decade of experience in dealing with many of the issues discussed above. In the mid-1970s the Brazilian Ministry of Communications (MINICOM) took the conscious decision to examine the possibility of installing modern digital telecoms systems and to develop locally the technology needed for the

Introduction

expansion of the network. MINICOM decided to eliminate dependence on foreign technology sources as far as possible, to begin controlling the industrial activities of the MNCs, and also to establish a domestic, Brazilian telecoms equipment supply industry.

To support these ambitious objectives the government set up a research and development (R&D) centre to generate technology, and to identify, marshal and deploy the existing technological resources available within the country. In retrospect, the aim of the government was to establish Brazil's first major industrial and technological base in digital technology.

With hindsight, Brazil was attempting to 'leapfrog' intermediate forms of electromechanical technology and move directly to microelectronic technology. At the time, however, the main concern of MINICOM was to expand and upgrade the local telecoms network, and to reduce what was becoming a costly dependence on the small oligopoly of multinational equipment suppliers. By the early 1970s virtually the entire Brazilian telecoms industry was owned and controlled by four MNCs. As shown later, Brazil had no organised R&D capabilities, no significant local industry and a wholly inadequate telecoms infrastructure. Brazil's experience in wrestling with these problems, and the structural changes which occurred during this crucial period, should therefore provide useful insights into the problems of technological accumulation with microelectronics.

As noted earlier, the prospects facing other DCs in acquiring telecoms technology will vary according to many economic, technological and historical factors specific to individual economies. Nevertheless, Brazil's experience may well prove useful to other larger developing economies such as India, China and Malaysia, who have expressed similar desires for their own telecoms sectors.(6)

To help guide the study Chapter 1 begins by outlining the broad theoretical framework for the investigation. Two separate approaches to technology are brought together to provide this framework: the learning approach to technological acquisition in the DCs, and a branch of neo-Schumpeterian theory known as diffusion theory. Two conceptual arguments are made: first, that the concept of learning 'fits' naturally within, and benefits from, the diffusion approach to technological advance and transition; second, that in its own right the concept of learning adds a missing dimension to present diffusion studies and enriches the approach. In amalgamating these two

Introduction

approaches the concept of 'Schumpeterian learning' is introduced. This is done to provide a methodology for systematically analysing the dynamics of the diffusion of technology, at the firm, inter-firm, sectoral and macroeconomic levels. While these 'mechanisms' of technological change are not totally ignored in diffusion studies, they tend to be implicitly assumed, rather than explicitly analysed and researched.

Given that, by definition, the DCs are largely separated from the 'centres of gravity' of international technological advance and development, then they must depend to a large extent on the diffusion of technology from the developed economies. An explicit analysis of the mechanisms by which technology diffusion occurs at the microeconomic, sectoral, government and macroeconomic levels is clearly important to the field of development economics. However, the main reason for introducing this new concept of Schumpeterian learning is to use it as a scheme for analysing Brazil's progress in acquiring telecoms technology, and more generally to throw some light on the prospects for DCs in assimilating IT.

In order to understand the international economic environment within which Brazil and other DCs are confronting technological change, Chapter 2 focuses upon the international telecoms industry. Although many factors are linked to the present restructuring of the world telecoms industry including government telecoms regulatory policy and the entrance of Japanese corporations into several telecoms market segments, Chapter 2 argues that the current upheavals can best be understood from the point of view of changes in product and process technologies. In turn these changes can be traced to the new technological opportunities presented by microelectronic technology. One of the main reasons for the observed, intensifying, global competition is the driving force of technological 'convergence'. Technological convergence in products and processes based on semiconductor, microelectronic technology explain many of the observed patterns of market growth, corporate behaviour, the erosion of traditional market boundaries and so forth.

Chapter 3 examines the overall economic position facing DCs in the field of telecoms. The potential for DCs to 'leapfrog' older forms of technology is assessed and contrasted with the current concerns over the possibility of a widening of the technology gap between the developed and developing countries. Most observers in the broader field of microelectronic innovation and the Third World are

Introduction

pessimistic about the future for DCs in IT.(7) The main concerns focus on the possible shift in comparative advantage away from the DCs, as automation and semi-automation technologies encourage the MNCs to relocate production facilities back to the advanced countries and closer to the markets they serve (sometimes called the 'northward drift'). Other related problems concern the likelihood of new detrimental forms of technological dependence occurring as the DCs become more and more reliant on the major MNCs who dominate the international IT markets. Behind this worry is the proposition that the new technology confronts the DCs with severe, perhaps insurmountable, barriers in terms of skills and factor endowments. Some authors even forecast a widening of the technology gap, with the Third World increasingly excluded from economic activities based on microelectronics and the technological frontier moving further and further away from the grasp of the DCs.

In direct contrast with these views others suggest that the intensely competitive international market conditions place the DCs in a favourable position, both to purchase microelectronic products and to bargain with the MNCs for the transfer of technology and manufacturing facilities. Chapter 3 attempts to assess these issues from the point of view of the telecoms industry, and briefly outlines the conditions facing Latin America in terms of MNC competition and the technological move towards digital systems. This chapter therefore 'sets the stage' for the Brazilian study, both in terms of the central economic issues to focus upon and the importance of the Brazilian market within the broader regional context.

The rest of the book presents the results of detailed field research carried out in Brazil during the period September 1983 to September 1984. During the course of the research more than 50 detailed interviews were conducted and data were collected from the major segments of the telecoms industry including (a) those responsible for formulating and executing industrial policy in various government departments and the telecoms administration TELEBRAS, (b) directors and engineers of the government R&D centre for telecoms, (c) representatives of the state operating companies which provide the telecoms services and (d) a sample of the multinational and national firms in the equipment supply industry. The aim of the interview programme was to supplement the quantitative data obtained during the research with a qualitative understanding of Brazil's achievements, and failures, in the telecoms area.

Introduction

Chapter 4 begins by tracing the historical progress of Brazil's telecoms sector up to the early 1970s, and concludes with a brief account of the industrial, technological and infrastructural position at that time. From this starting point Chapter 4 then assesses Brazil's performance in expanding and upgrading the national telecoms network since the early 1970s. Close attention is paid to whether Brazil succeeded in 'leapfrogging' earlier forms of telecoms infrastructure in such a way as to meet the forthcoming demands of IT.

Chapter 5 is a case study of the government R&D centre in telecoms. Here, the opportunity is taken to make a detailed analysis of the mechanisms of technological development with microelectronic-based technology at both the engineering and management levels. The main purpose is to gain an appreciation of how microelectronic, information-based, technology differs from electromechanical technology in terms of design, development and manufacture. This particular focus should have more general implications for the wider field of microelectronic innovation and DCs.

A detailed historical account of the technological and industrial integration of the MNC subsidiaries operating within Brazil's national boundaries is presented in Chapter 6. As with all the empirical chapters an attempt is made to 'measure' technological progress using a range of partial input and output indicators. These range from financial and human resource inputs to product, process and patent outputs. Local efforts by the MNCs to develop technology are assessed, both in the light of the government's specific technological objectives and in the wider context of microelectronic accumulation in a DC.

Finally, Chapter 7 examines the emergence of new firms of wholly Brazilian origin. Again, various indicators of industrial and technological output are employed to gain an appreciation of the success, or otherwise, of the government's post-1974 industrial policy. Given the conditions of severe and prolonged economic crisis during this period, particular attention is paid to the impact of the general industrial recession upon the new industry. This chapter also compares the prices of Brazilian-produced equipment with prices obtainable on the international market, and an assessment of the costs and benefits of Brazil's efforts in telecoms is made.

Throughout the discussion an effort is made to gain an understanding of whether or not 'leapfrogging' occurred, and in what sense the term is a useful one. At the same time it is hoped that the measurements taken together will generate a broad

Introduction

picture of Brazil's changing status in terms of shifting comparative advantage and the technological gap between Brazil and the advanced countries. As well as providing a measure of the investment costs to Brazil of establishing a base in digital telecoms, the book evaluates the role of government policy in managing the technology gap and effecting positive industrial transformation. To assist with the unavoidable technical expressions a glossary is provided (see Appendix 1).

Notes

1. See Hudson et al. (1981) for a review of the literature concerning telecoms and economic development.
2. The terms 'information technology', 'microelectronics' and 'semiconductor' are used interchangeably to describe the component inputs and technological basis of modern telecoms and computer technology. A glossary is provided to explain and define necessary technical terms. Barron and Curnow (1979) give an account of the role of telecoms as the infrastructure for IT activities.
3. Also sometimes called 'evolutionary' theories of technological change. The important unifying theme is the Schumpeterian origins of many of the expressed ideas.
4. For example, see Hoffman's (1985) study of the garments industry.
5. Although it is possible to think of some other products which have made this transition, such as electronic typewriters and calculators, these are minor in comparison.
6. China's investment plans are discussed in the Financial Times (4 March 1985); Malaysia's aims are reported in the Business Times Malaysia (17 May 1985).
7. Notably Kaplinsky (1982, 1984) and Rada (1982). The various arguments are examined in Chapter 3.

CHAPTER 1

'SCHUMPETERIAN LEARNING' - A NEW APPROACH TO TECHNOLOGY DIFFUSION AND THE DEVELOPING COUNTRIES

Introduction

The aim of this chapter is to provide some general theoretical guidelines to help explain Brazil's experience in telecoms, and to illustrate how the diffusion of IT has dramatically altered the structure of the international telecoms industry and, as a consequence, the opportunities and problems facing the DCs in acquiring telecoms technology. The new concept of 'Schumpeterian learning' is offered as a methodology to guide the empirical investigation, and as a means of arriving at a deeper analytical understanding of the nature of IT and its consequences for the international telecoms industry. The idea of Schumpeterian learning is to try and amalgamate two important, but separate, areas of technology theory - the 'learning' approach on one hand, and neo-Schumpeterian diffusion theory on the other.
It may be helpful to sketch briefly the background to exactly why this book introduces the notion of Schumpeterian learning, and why it is considered an appropriate means for examining the diffusion of a new technology within the context of a developing economy. In searching for a useful theory of technological development it becomes immediately clear that the dominant theory, neoclassical economics, fails to provide such a useful analytical approach. As many authors have shown, by disregarding the 'real world' economic issues of the sources, directions, costs and benefits of technological change, together with the role of government policy in promoting technological advance, neoclassical theory fails to come to grips with technology, although technology is widely recognised as one of the most important factors in economic progress.(1)

Schumpeterian Learning

Many economists in DCs, particularly Latin America, have adopted various forms of Dependency Theory (or <u>Dependencia</u>) to explain the problems industrialising nations face in transferring and assimilating technology from the developed economies. However, this area too has faced sustained and severe criticisms for internal inconsistency, for a failure to grapple with the intrinsic dynamics of technological change and for failing to explain properly why so many so-called dependent economies have exhibited prolonged and historically unprecedented economic growth in the post-war period.(2)

During the 1980s a promising new approach emerged - the learning approach to technological development in the developing economies. Within this school, various economists have provided tools to open up the 'black box' of technological accumulation at the level of the firm. The learning approach succeeded in providing a useful methodology for studying exactly how technology is acquired at the microeconomic level. It also provided important insights into the costs and benefits of technological acquisition, how technological learning occurs, and the important role of government policy in fostering technological acquisition.(3)

However, the learning approach has several limitations stemming mainly from its exclusive focus on technological learning at the level of the firm. Because the concept is not integrated within a broader analytical framework it is very difficult to generalise from the findings of the various studies. Important macroeconomic factors (national and international) tend to be ignored, as do the infrastructural requirements for technological change. This chapter attempts to broaden the narrow concept of learning to include learning at the level of the industry, sector, government and national economic levels. An effort is also made to overcome the theoretical isolation of learning by locating it squarely within the, technologically aware, economic framework of neo-Schumpeterian diffusion theory. There now exists a substantial body of theoretical and empirical study into the economics of technology. This is based on the original work of Schumpeter and extended by economists such as Nelson and Winter, Rosenberg and Freeman.(4) Although not yet comprehensively formalised, nor accepted as an alternative to neoclassical theory, the neo-Schumpeterian or neotechnology approach already offers a benchmark for studying a wide range of issues concerning technological progress. So far, the neotechnology approach has focused mainly on the developed rather than the developing countries. Also, as we show below, the neotechnology approach has not yet directly dealt with the issue of how technological capability is accumulated at the level of the firm. It seems appropriate therefore to link up the two approaches and to see how they can benefit from each other.

Section 1.1 begins by briefly introducing the main tenets of neotechnology theory. Sections 1.2 and 1.3 show how diffusion theory, within the neotechnology approach, can assist in our understanding of technology transfer across national boundaries. Finally, section 1.4 discusses the notion of Schumpeterian learning and argues that this notion of dynamic, active learning fills a gap in existing neotechnology theory and promises to provide a useful mechanism for the study of Brazil's experience in telecoms.

1.1 Ideas in Neotechnology Theory

As noted above, the nature, pace and origin of technological progress is a subject largely ignored by conventional economic theory. Since Schmookler (1966) introduced the well-known demand-pull thesis much advance has been made in understanding how economic opportunity and profit can motivate firms to invest in technological innovation. Early recognition of the forces exerted by science and technology upon the economic system led to alternative views stressing so-called technology-push factors. Authors including Nelson (1959) and Phillips (1966) showed how scientific and technological discoveries could establish an internal momentum of technological progress and a stream of subsequent innovations, leading to rising productivity and economic growth. Since these early classics much has been added to our understanding of the relationship between market forces and technological change.(5)

Theoretical advance has also been made in conceptualising the behaviour of firms with respect to technology, notably the evolutionary approach put forward by Nelson and Winter (1974, 1982). This has added to the broader understanding of the behaviour of firms within the economic system. Subsequent elaboration by Dosi (1984) attempts to overcome the indeterminate nature of Nelson and Winter's behavioural approach by locating firms' behaviour within the structural parameters of the macroeconomic system.

Borrowing from Kuhn, Dosi (1982) introduces the notion of 'technological paradigms' to describe the prevailing body of technological knowledge within the economy. Technological paradigms in a general sense

Schumpeterian Learning

act (a) to define the boundaries of technological enquiry by firms and institutions, (b) to provide methods of searching for technological solutions to problems, and (c) to define the meaning of 'success' and 'failure' outside the strictly economic system of commercial criteria. Within this body of knowledge and system of enquiry, the market acts to reward successfully innovating firms and penalises firms which fail to keep abreast of technological change. At the commercial level the market thereby acts as an economic environment, selecting certain innovations and rejecting others. While technological paradigms help to describe the origin of innovation, 'technological trajectories' attempt to describe the actual direction and pace of technological change within the economy. Technological trajectories illustrate the outcome of the natural internal momentum of specific technological forms and the manner in which the economic environment acts to shape the rhythm of technological advance with its system of rewards and penalties. A practical example of the usefulness of this approach is provided by Pavitt (1984) who attempts both to characterise and forecast the likely trajectory of the diffusion of microelectronic technology (within the semiconductor paradigm) for the UK.

More detailed study of the trajectories of technological progress is contained in the diffusion literature (discussed in detail below). Since the original work on the S-shaped logistic diffusion curve by Griliches (1957) and Mansfield (1961) efforts have been made to formalise theoretically the progress of diffusion both between firms (Davies, 1979) and within firms (Stoneman, 1981).(6) Extensions have also been made to try and explain observed patterns of diffusion at the macroeconomic level (Soete and Turner, 1984). Metcalfe (1981) illustrates, theoretically, why the macroeconomic environment is crucial to understanding the pace, pattern and profitability of innovation. At the international level patterns of diffusion can be explained through trade and direct foreign investment (Metcalfe and Soete, 1983). Although much has been achieved in modelling paths and patterns of diffusion at the microeconomic level, and to some extent the macroeconomic and international levels, very little study has focused on exactly how technology diffuses at the various levels. The notion of Schumpeterian learning, introduced later on, attempts to examine the relevance of diffusion theory for the DCs, and in particular to the role of learning as a mechanism of technology diffusion at the microeconomic, macroeconomic and international economic levels.

On the microeconomic level, neotechnology study has made considerable advance in illustrating the role of technological opportunity, appropriation, uncertainty and accumulation in the transformation of industrial structures and emergence of competing oligopolies (Sylos-Labini, 1969; Freeman, 1974; Nelson and Winter, 1977; Cooper and Hoffman, 1981). On the one hand, one sees the dynamic forces of technological opportunity and appropriation giving rise to asymmetry between firms in terms of profits, unequal costs, entry barriers and monopoly pricing. In this manner innovation and appropriation of technology lead to oligopoly and increasing market concentration.

On the other hand, opposing technological forces may lead to the competing away of monopoly profits and the emergence and entry of new firms. The main forces leading to competition are technological diffusion, imitation, capital mobility and in some cases the 'free good' nature of particular kinds of knowhow. New capital embodied process innovations can give cost advantages to emerging firms and competitive advantage over established firms using older vintage technologies (Dosi, 1984). These kinds of notions have given rise to a wealth of theory concerning the transformation of industrial structure, the emergence of oligopolies and the role of small firms in the production and diffusion of new innovations.

The concept of technological leads and lags has been employed to explain observed flows of trade and patterns of foreign investment. Economists such as Dosi (1984), Krugman (1983) and Metcalfe and Soete (1983) provide a critique of conventional models of comparative advantage in accounting for trade patterns, and point to the importance of technological innovation and diffusion in shaping international comparative advantage. Soete (1978), for example, gives a convincing critical reassessment of the factor proportions interpretation of trade, and emphasises the role of technological innovation in determining the relative international trade positions among the industrially advanced countries.

There remain significant areas of weakness and underdevelopment in this literature, particularly in the neglected area of the relationship between micro level activities, and macroeconomic growth and transformation. Exactly how the market acts through the price mechanism to allocate resources, yet at the same time provides the impulse for dynamic technological change, economic disequilibria and growth are still matters little understood. As Dosi and Orsenigo (1984) argue in their attempt to examine these relationships, this fundamental field of enquiry has been largely ignored throughout the history of economic thought from the classical to the neoclassical economists. The overwhelming concern of neoclassical economics with static general equilibrium analysis has drawn economics even further from these issues. So far, however, neotechnology study has not yet provided a convincing, technologically aware, account of the microeconomic foundations for macroeconomics nor of the role of institutional factors in determining rates and patterns of technological change.

Important advances have also been made in understanding the role of technology in long-term international patterns of economic growth and the reasons for international economic inequalities. The so-called Kondratieff long waves have stimulated interest and investigation into the role of technology in generating surges of economic growth and decline and the longer-term relationships between technology, economic growth, productivity and unemployment (Freeman et al., 1982; Freeman, 1984). Long-wave analysis has attempted to explain the changing historical economic ranking of different nations in terms of leads and lags in productivity, economic growth and changing patterns of comparative advantage. Despite strong disagreements from within and outside this area of study, long-wave theory has provided a benchmark for examining the 'broader sweeps' of economic history - a subject largely ignored by conventional neoclassical analysis.(7)

1.2 An Introduction to Diffusion Theory

Within the broader framework of neotechnology analysis, 'diffusion' theory tries to explain the determinants, pace and pattern of the adoption of technological innovations. Although most diffusion study is applied at the microeconomic level, some recent studies have attempted to extend diffusion theory to the macroeconomic level. This literature has also touched on the subject of how transitions to major new technological forms (or paradigms) may lead to historical changes in the economic ranking of whole nations. These considerations have a direct bearing on the international transformation of the telecoms industry and the position of DCs such as Brazil who are faced with meeting the challenges posed by new microelectronic innovations.

The basic argument of this section is that, within the broader neotechnology framework, diffusion theory offers a way to overcome the limitations of the learning approach to technological development, noted earlier. This particular area of 'technologically aware' economic theory provides a useful and consistent theoretical basis for the concept of learning. By locating the concept of learning within diffusion theory, the learning methodology can be developed and extended to include the mechanisms of technological development at the inter-firm, sectoral and macroeconomic levels, as well as the governmental level.

To date, diffusion theory is still a relatively unknown area of economic analysis and has not been applied to the DCs. It is helpful therefore to outline briefly the economic basis of diffusion theory.

To explain the nature, pattern and consequences of technological diffusion between firms, neotechnologists have 'borrowed' from various other disciplines concerned with diffusion. One of the major research findings in the study of diffusion in sociology, education, public health and many other areas of study is the S-shaped or logistic pattern of diffusion of new innovations (Rogers, 1976). In simple terms the sigmoid pattern indicates that, following an initial slow rate of adoption of a new innovation, a rapid acceleration occurs, only to be followed by a falling off in the speed of diffusion. This pattern holds too in the field of microeconomics where pioneering studies by Griliches (1957) and Mansfield (1961) led to more detailed investigations, both at the inter-firm level (Davies, 1979) and at the intra-firm level (Stoneman, 1981).

Unfortunately, the logistics curve, although an interesting empirical observation, has little theoretical or explanatory power, often presenting the diffusion process in a mechanistic, automatic way. Why should such a pattern of diffusion of new technologies be observed, and how does this relate to the diffusion of technology across national boundaries if at all? These questions have been the concern of several recent and illuminating studies which attempt to give stronger theoretical content to the S-shaped logistic curve and explain the crucial factors governing the diffusion of technology into the economic system.

In a perceptive and original contribution to the field Metcalfe (1981) places the supply and demand for technological innovations squarely at the centre of industrial growth and decline. Drawing from the work of Schumpeter, Kuznets and Hicks, Metcalfe explains why the S-shaped pattern is observed and how innovation will both condition, and be conditioned by, economic growth. This contribution marks a significant step forward in economic diffusion theory by (a) drawing attention to the importance of supply factors in the diffusion of innovations, (b) providing the beginnings of a macroeconomic framework within which technological innovation might be analysed and (c) analysing the cyclical causality and interdependence between the economic and technological systems.

We turn first to the demand for innovations and the sigmoid curve. Factors such as uncertainty, poor information, high cost and trial and error procedures act to 'retard' the immediate widespread adoption of a superior technology. Various case studies show that, after a period of slow adoption, the pace of diffusion accelerates after about 10 per cent and up to the 20 per cent to 25 per cent adoption level (Rogers, 1983). During this 'take-off' period learning proceeds rapidly, and technology-based profit opportunities spur on potential imitators; eventually a 'bandwagon' effect occurs. Acceleration usually continues to a maximum of around 50 per cent adoption, and then the rate of diffusion falls off as it becomes more and more difficult to find potential adopters. These diffusion factors, on the demand side, are well documented in the literature. The particular shape of the logistic or diffusion coefficient curve depends on many factors such as the specific characteristics of the technology, its cost and expected profitability, the receptiveness and size of the adopting firm, and the potential for incremental innovation to continue.

Astonishingly, as Metcalfe (1981) points out, the supply of innovations is almost entirely ignored in the literature. The supply environment is treated as exogenous, innovations are assumed to be perfectly elastic in supply, and the prices of technology inputs are normally assumed to be constant over time. This is clearly unsatisfactory as the pace and pattern of diffusion will also be determined by the many supply factors at work. These include the changing cost of the innovation to the user, output capacity and bottlenecks, supplier profit rates, and the potential for continuing incremental improvements on the part of the supplying firms. Metcalfe argues that supply factors will also play an important part in forming the S-shaped diffusion curve. As output increases, spurred on by profit opportunities, supply capacity is increased and new firms enter the industry. Eventually supply capacity is neared, supply bottlenecks come into play, and producer costs increase. Also the ability of producers to bring about incremental technological change reaches its limits, reducing the attractiveness of the innovation to potential users. As market saturation is approached, supplier profitability will fall off and the rate of increase in output will decline. By adding a supply side the model provides a useful way of showing how both demand and supply factors condition the path of diffusion. The adjustment path is mediated by the price of the innovation and the corresponding profit rates for both producers and users of innovations.

Within Metcalfe's model it is also possible to begin to locate the diffusion process within a macroeconomic framework. For instance, it is possible to show how an increase in economic demand will lead to an increase in the level of diffusion activity and alter the path of diffusion through time. Figure 1.1 (adapted from Metcalfe, 1981, pp.9-10) illustrates the 'equilibrium' demand curve (mm) and producers' supply curve (hh) for a specific new innovation. Beginning at price $P(0)$ and output z, both price and output will follow the diffusion adjustment path $DP(1)$ until the innovation's saturation level (c) is reached. The saturation level is defined as the point at which supply (hh) is equal to demand (mm). If an increase in demand occurs (represented here by a once and for all shift in the demand curve from mm to $mm(1)$) a new adjustment path $DP(2)$ is defined. Also a new, expanded, saturation level will occur at point $c(1)$ where hh intersects $mm(1)$. In Metcalfe's detailed model corresponding profit adjustment paths for producers and users are also described.

It is important to stress that there is no fixed adjustment path, nor equilibrium point. The interrelationship between diffusion and economic growth will constantly change the path of diffusion, and consequently the so-called diffusion gap z-c. Over time, both the diffusion paths and saturation levels will alter as a consequence of economic growth and decline. Nevertheless, Figure 1.1 illustrates how an increase (or decrease) in the level of demand will affect the patterns of supply and path of diffusion of innovations. By implication, one can envisage how Keynesian demand factors and other macroeconomic factors which act to contract or expand economic growth will spur on or retard diffusion. Equally though, the diffusion process itself will act as an impulse to economic growth and, eventually, decline.

There can be little doubt that Metcalfe makes a valuable contribution to the understanding of technology diffusion, both by adding a supply side to the traditional models and by introducing macroeconomic considerations. What Metcalfe (and other

Figure 1.1: The Diffusion Path of an Innovation Under Conditions of Increased Demand

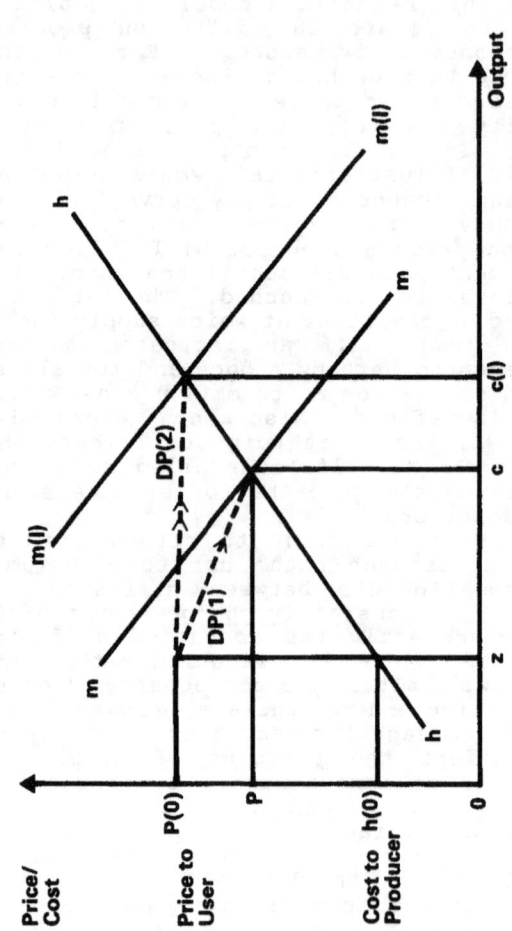

authors in this area) does not undertake is an analysis of the actual mechanisms by which technology diffuses at the firm level. Before outlining how the concept of learning could perform this task, it is necessary to examine how this branch of theory has been extended to the analysis of technology diffusion across national boundaries.

1.3 Diffusion Theory at the International Level

Soete (1983, 1985) extends diffusion analysis to show how technology may give rise to historical shifts in the relative economic positions of whole nations. By extending the analogy of innovating and imitating firms to whole nations, it is possible to illustrate how technological change may result in economic divergences and convergences at the international level. Like firms, leading nations will attempt to maintain economic advantage through the exploitation of technological opportunity. Technology-based, oligopolistic profits will be gained by continuous innovative effort on the part of technology leaders. Conversely, capital and technology flows from leading to lagging nations will erode economic advantage and reduce international technology gaps. By a process of imitation, backward nations may themselves gain the economic benefits from the use and development of new technologies and catch up with leading countries.

But why should the diffusion of major new technologies result in <u>international</u> economic convergences and divergences? As far as convergence, or 'catch-up' is concerned, as Soete (1985) argues, the very existence of a technology gap will act as a technology 'pump' from leading to lagging nations. Some elements of technological and scientific knowledge may be transferred as a free good across national boundaries. More commonly, technology will be transferred through importation, direct foreign investment and licensing agreements; migration may also play a role in the transfer of skills and knowhow from one country to another.

Freeman et al. (1982) suggest that during the maturation, or slow-down phase, of the diffusion cycle backward economies may well enjoy a period of convergence upon the leaders. As with diffusion at the level of the firm, the pace of productivity improvement and economic growth of leading countries will eventually slow owing to retarding factors. Factors such as capacity limitations, supply bottlenecks, existing widespread diffusion and the slow-down of the technology frontier itself will act to reduce the rate of technological and economic advance. At the same time factors retarding technological diffusion in the lagging economies may be overcome; technological opportunities will increasingly present themselves, and widespread imitation and adoption will occur. The slow-down phase of the logistic diffusion curve in the leading economies may therefore signal the opportunity for 'catch-up' growth on the basis of the same, perhaps incrementally improved, technologies.

Certainly, the evidence for the post-war period testifies to European and Japanese catch-up and convergence with the USA. As Soete (1981a) shows, the diffusion of technology from the USA to Europe and Japan generated an unprecedented cycle of economic expansion via technology imports, direct foreign investment and free flows of scientific and technological knowhow. Sustained investments, particularly in new vintage process technologies, gave rise to rapid economic growth during the 1950s and 1960s in several European economies.(8) Of course, governments too played a crucial role by providing the infrastructural and macroeconomic conditions for the technology-based expansion at this time.(9) During the post-war period Japan also experienced technology-based catch-up growth with the USA. In fact, Japan presents a model case of sustained economic growth based initially on technological imitation and later on adaptation and innovation. Consistent and heavy local investments in technology allowed Japan to shift from a mere imitator to a major international innovator with a strong autonomous technological capacity.(10)

While the evidence for technological catch-up growth is fairly well documented,(11) the reasons for international economic divergences are not so well established. Freeman et al. (1982) propose that divergences, like convergences, are associated with the cycle of diffusion of major new technologies or paradigms. It is helpful to explain this relationship by looking first at the latter part of the diffusion cycle of the previously dominant technology. As more and more newcomers exploit the technology and catch up with the leading economies, competition for markets will intensify, profit margins may well fall and, as Pavitt (1980) suggests, only those nations best equipped to meet changing economic and technological conditions will remain in leading economic positions. This period can be seen as a 'testing ground' for potentially new technological leaders, with the successful economies laying the foundations for a surge of economic growth.

As and when a recovery occurs based on a new technological paradigm, the country or countries best equipped to absorb and exploit the new technology will generate faster rates of productivity and economic growth and will diverge away from the lagging economies. The leaders will probably have already gained substantial experience with the new technology in the declining phase of the previous economic cycle. During the early phase of adoption, the leading economy or economies will be in a position to exploit their existing technological advantage and greater capacity to innovate. In this manner economic divergence will tend to coincide with the take-off phase of the diffusion cycle.

During the transition from one technological paradigm to another new technological leaders may emerge and a series of changes may occur in the relative international positions of several economies. Previously dominant nations may find difficulty in adapting to a radically new technological form for a variety of reasons. Commitment to previous technologies, at both the industrial and infrastructural levels, may act to retard diffusion. Vested interests in older technologies, combined with social and economic organisation centred around older vintage technologies, may give advantages to other nations less committed to the previous paradigm. This appears to be the case, for example, with the UK in the latter half of the nineteenth century when the USA and Germany overtook the UK as the most important centre for growth and innovation. There is no doubt too that since the Second World War Japan has moved to the forefront of technological innovation and world market leadership. Pavitt (1980) shows how Japan developed from being one of the weakest OECD countries in the early 1960s to a leading nation in many industrial sectors. At the same time the UK has progressively lost ground in several key sectors and faces decline relative to the technology leaders.

While these considerations are normally discussed in terms of whole economies, there is no reason why the analogies should not be extended to individual industries within countries in the process of catching up. It seems unlikely that the extraordinary industrial developments made by countries such as Japan and the Soviet Union this century will be repeated by other whole nations (of course this has to be pure speculation) in the short or medium term. However, it does seem probable that the DCs best equipped to assimilate new technologies will gain competitive advantages over the older, advanced countries incapable of such rapid and dynamic response to new technologies such as microelectronics. Rather than focusing on national catch-up, it might be more illuminating to search for new and changing patterns of specialisation along a common technological frontier.(12)

To sum up, the diffusion of major new technological paradigms can give rise to international economic convergences and divergences, can lead to changes in the economic ranking of whole economies or of specific industries within countries and can give rise to new technological leaders. The extension of diffusion theory provides a helpful way of understanding these changes. However, what the diffusion studies tend to overlook are the dynamic mechanisms by which particular economies catch up, accumulate technological capacity and overtake other countries. From this point of view diffusion theory remains, in part at least, mechanistic. If we examine international diffusion studies in more detail it is immediately clear that technological accumulation and catching up is by no means a passive, mechanistic process, but a painstaking, costly and deliberate effort on the part of successful firms, governments and nations.

1.4 'Schumpeterian Learning' and the Developing Countries

As noted in the introduction, the aim of this section is to attempt to place 'learning' within a broader Schumpeterian framework. In relation to diffusion theory, learning provides a valuable methodology for examining the mechanisms and processes of technological advance. Although diffusion studies hint at the importance of learning, the actual processes by which technology is accumulated at the firm, inter-firm and macroeconomic levels are rarely, if ever, explicitly examined. As far as the DC literature is concerned, learning becomes a far more useful and integrated concept when placed within a broader set of Schumpeterian considerations. Many of the limitations of the learning approach can be overcome by providing this set of theoretical underpinnings.

While this is only a first step in integrating these two separate approaches, the usefulness of this task is clear. For DC analysis, it is necessary to extend the notion of learning from the intra-firm level to inter-firm, government, sector and macroeconomic levels. By definition, DCs depend on the successful diffusion of foreign technology across national boundaries for technological and economic advance - an explicit analysis of how this may occur is therefore central to development economics, but cannot be confined to the firm level. The ability of

Schumpeterian Learning

learning to provide a systematic approach to the mechanisms, costs and benefits, and the role of government in the diffusion process may also add a further dimension to the neotechnology diffusion literature. This may overcome the mechanistic presentation of the diffusion process present in many of the diffusion studies.

1.4.1 Schumpeterian learning as a methodology

As Soete (1985) recognises, diffusion theory tends to treat the diffusion of technology as a mechanistic, passive and automatic process. This applies to the S-shaped diffusion curve and, to some extent, to the diffusion of technology across national boundaries. However, as many studies have shown, technological learning is neither passive nor automatic, and demands deliberate effort and resource allocation.(13) It is helpful to relate different possible learning mechanisms to the cycle of diffusion, both to illustrate the theoretical links between the two concepts and to show how learning can be used as a methodology for understanding the dynamics of diffusion.(14)

In the early, slow, adoption phase of the diffusion curve one might expect to see an emphasis on pre-investment learning, involving close co-operation between innovation users and suppliers. Firms will be learning by investigating new techniques, experimenting with innovations, assessing potential market needs and so on. Learning will be highly risk-intensive and information on capital investment costs, production costs, market prices and demand for final products will be sparse and unreliable. Learning will be particularly slow and painstaking, involving trial and error on the part of capital goods producers, users of process innovations and suppliers of final products to the market.(15) The uncertainty surrounding the potential market and the possible gains in cost reduction and profit will induce firms to learn by searching for information, by hiring specialists and by collaborating closely in R&D with innovation suppliers. Learning may well be of a radical nature, focusing on ways of developing entirely new innovations.

As an innovation enters the rapid adoption level, or 'take-off' phase, the emphasis will shift to setting up capital goods and expanding production capacity. Innovation users will learn by applying the innovation and setting up new plant and machinery. Users will learn by bargaining with capital goods suppliers and increasing their technical knowhow of

Schumpeterian Learning

the limitations and possibilities of the innovation. Information surrounding the technology and the market will increase, uncertainty will decline and the mechanisms of learning will become more stable and established. Capital goods producers themselves will learn by increasing investment in plant and machinery. There may be a shift away from the close collaboration between users and producers, as the suppliers of the innovation organise large-scale production to meet the growing demand from new customers. The experimental, painstaking nature of the learning procedures will give way to more predictable, production-oriented mechanisms. Suppliers will learn by making minor improvements to the innovation, which in turn will increase the attractiveness of the new technology to potential users. As learning proceeds the costs per unit of output will tend to decline, spurring on the diffusion bandwagon.

During this take-off stage a major feature of learning will be the learning which occurs between user firms. As information improves, costs fall and profits increase, potential users will learn by observing the technological activities of others. Learning by imitating will occur as firms gain confidence in the market potential of the new technology. Imitating firms may learn by reverse engineering and redesigning products to improve their market standing. These types of learning mechanisms are possible means by which technology is diffused during the formation of the industrial S-shaped logistic curve. Again, the process requires investment, effort and a conducive economic environment.

At the slow-down stage of the diffusion cycle the nature of learning will again shift, this time towards rationalising the production process. At this stage many new firms will have entered the market, and profits will be forced down. Leading firms will introduce labour and capital saving innovations to the production process in an effort to increase productivity and reduce costs. Firms will learn how to reduce capital expenditures for a given volume of output, and others will be forced to follow in order to remain competitive. It is not difficult to see how the mechanisms of learning and the capacity of firms to institute effective learning procedures will exert a powerful influence on the shape of the industrial diffusion curve. Both the rate and pattern of adoption of new technologies will be strongly influenced by the dynamics of learning.

Introducing the concept of learning to diffusion analysis in this way provides a methodology for examining the channels and nature of technological progress at the intra- and inter-firm levels. It also draws attention to the painstaking, cumulative nature of technological development and helps neo-Schumpeterian theory to unravel the complex and gradual nature of technological progress. In addition to this, it is possible to extend the notion of learning beyond the firm level to the sectoral, governmental and macroeconomic levels.

At the sectoral level, for example, learning will occur in trade associations and other organisations which provide information flows between firms as to new products, technological trends, employment opportunities, new markets and so on. At the government level learning will be crucial in deciding appropriate industrial and technological policies and effectively implementing them. Governments will (or should) learn, through experience, how to achieve the most effective balance between fiscal, monetary, trade, industrial and other policies. The 'correct' balance between these policies and strategies designed to encourage the diffusion of a new technology will depend on the particular stage of the diffusion cycle, the nature of the specific technology, ambitions towards foreign markets and so on. Successful learning will influence the ability of governments to formulate effective policies and create an economic environment conducive to technological advance. Failure or success in this area may be a deciding factor in economic and technological progress.

Most importantly for the study of the developing nations, the successful transfer and absorption of technology from the industrially advanced countries involves a gradual, costly and cumulative learning process. Learning, in this broadest sense, provides a methodology for examining diffusion at the macroeconomic level, and perhaps can help explain observed changes in the economic ranking of countries over time. Technology does not simply 'diffuse' effortlessly and mechanistically across national boundaries, but again will depend crucially on the allocation of resources, appropriate government policies and the capabilities of local firms and other actors involved in the technology transfer process.

Many different learning routes can be envisaged for DCs of different character and economic circumstances. Heavy reliance on direct foreign investment and joint ventures may be one route to technological accumulation. Relatively independent forms of learning by searching, learning by local R&D and learning by hiring in may prove an alternative route for other countries. Again the stages in the learning process may proceed from relatively simple tasks to methods of gaining full-blown R&D capabilities. As success is achieved and capabilities are accumulated, the actual stock of technology capital (or the overall absorptive capacity of the economy) will be augmented. Eventually, if successful, conditions will become ripe for catch-up growth at the sectoral level and perhaps at the macroeconomic level.

Soete (1985) highlights the importance of the absorptive capacity of the recipient country in successfully assimilating new technologies. The notion of absorptive capacity provides a way of distinguishing between DCs at different levels of income, economic and technological infrastructure, previous learning experiences and so on. Again, borrowing from the diffusion literature one can see how the size or critical income level of a nation will be a vital factor in acquiring a technology. Size, of course, is not equivalent to absorptive capacity but a proxy indicator for income, skills, management and technological and scientific infrastructure. Earlier, Strassman (1968, p. 272) made the same point, defining absorptive capacity as 'the ability of capital to manage and create technology'. It is the argument of this chapter that learning, in this dynamic, Schumpeterian sense, is the principal mechanism by which technology is absorbed and adapted, and by which the very absorptive capacity of an economy is augmented, at firm, sector and national level.

The usefulness of a Schumpeterian notion of learning lies not only in analysing how technology is accumulated; it may also provide a means for distinguishing systematically between technological forms. Depending on the intrinsic nature of the technology in question, the mechanisms of learning may well be different. With mechanical technology learning by undoing, or reverse engineering, has been identified as a major channel of technological acquisition. With electromechanical technology, reverse engineering will need to be supplemented with knowhow (or information-based skill) relevant to electrical engineering; electromechanical interfacing will also be crucial to effective accumulation. Other technological forms, for example chemical and pharmaceutical processes, will demand a different set of appropriate skills and knowledge. The mechanisms of learning for different technological forms will very probably differ right through from the development stages to volume production.

This aspect of learning – the ability to differentiate between technological forms – may provide a means for examining the diffusion of a new technological paradigm, when a whole new set of learning mechanisms may be required to absorb and utilise a technology effectively. The diffusion of microelectronic technology, based on advances in solid state physics, poses radically new technological challenges to DCs, not to mention the industrialised countries. Learning mechanisms relevant to previous technologies appear to be inappropriate to microelectronic technology. The following empirical chapters try to identify the types of skills and knowledge required in the design and production of one major sector of the microelectronics industry – telecoms. This industry is a particularly interesting case, as it appears to correspond to the early phase of the S curve, and there may still be time for DCs to formulate industrial strategies to take advantage of the current industrial and technological upheavals. An effort will therefore be made to map out the changing international technological and industrial conditions, and to provide a learning 'scheme' relevant to the acquisition of digital telecoms technology.

1.4.2 The implicit role of learning in diffusion theory

Throughout the diffusion literature the importance of learning is hinted at, and at some points accepted, but rarely if ever made an explicit subject for analysis. For example, at the level of the individual firm, Pavitt and Soete (1981, p. 117) confirm some of the findings of the DC learning studies.(16) Describing the innovative efforts of successfully expanding firms in the nineteenth century in the US and Sweden, Pavitt and Soete stress the difficulties involved during the accumulation of skills and knowledge. Leading firms in the US were able to diversify gradually from the production of textile machinery to machine tools, firearms, motorcycles and eventually automobiles. Swedish firms moved upstream and downstream from raw material processing into markets of greater technological sophistication, where greater profits presented themselves. However, the accumulation of the skills needed to diversify and allow movements upstream and downstream were neither 'easy nor automatic' (p. 117). Although not explicitly discussed, resources were clearly allocated to the process of learning in order to gain the monopoly profits associated with the early appropriation of the new technology.

Schumpeterian Learning

The role of learning can also be deduced from the study of technology diffusion between firms. As Soete (1985, p. 5) puts it: 'It is the learning from the experience of others which leads to imitative behaviour and the ensuing bandwagon effect, and which provides the underpinning of the S-shaped diffusion curve.' It could be added that the pace and pattern of learning will exert a powerful influence on the shape of the logistic curve. The learning channels and processes hinted at here closely relate to those identified in the DC studies. Rather than the passive, costless, learning-by-doing of the neoclassical school,(17) an active Schumpeterian learning process is occurring. Firms are deliberately investing in learning in order to imitate successfully other leading firms to gain the rewards of acquiring and adapting new innovations - and to avoid the penalties of failing to adopt new technologies.

If we turn to the macroeconomic level, one of the conditions for catch-up growth appears to be the capacity to learn from the achievements of other nations. Evidence from the case of Japan bears out this proposition. During the 1960s and 1970s, Japan rapidly achieved 'best practice' productivity levels in leading economic sectors such as motor vehicles, steel and electronics (Soete, 1985); it is well documented that this process was neither costless nor passive. Oshima (1984) provides evidence to show how local investments in Japanese technology (as proxied by R&D expenditures) were closely associated with expenditures on technology imports. The immense Japanese effort to master foreign technology is also noted by Soete (1981a) who illustrates the steady rise in technology imports from the 1950s through to the 1970s. Over this period Japan made the transition from a heavy and critical reliance on foreign technology to autonomous technological development. The Japanese success in establishing a strong independent technological base is without doubt one of the major reasons for Japan's rapid economic catch-up in the post-war era.

Various learning procedures are also evident in the Japanese case. Without suggesting any rigid linear progression, Japan learnt by adapting foreign technology to suit local conditions, by searching abroad for knowhow and by providing training programmes for local engineers and technicians at home and abroad. The types of learning activities undertaken almost certainly varied considerably from sector to sector. Nevertheless there was clearly a successful transition from elementary, to intermediate, to advanced forms of learning in most leading sectors.(18) A considerable degree of technological learning also occurred at the level of government. In the early stages of reconstruction the Official Reconstruction Bank was the largest source of liquid capital available for new firms. During the National Income Doubling Plan for the decade 1961-1971, the government provided almost 30 per cent of gross domestic capital formation (Allen, 1972). In the subsequent stages of extremely rapid economic growth the government played a leading role in encouraging and establishing a receptive economic and social environment for technological progress to occur. Oshima (1984) shows how the government's integrated industrial and technological policies were fundamental to Japan's technological and economic catch-up in the post-war period.

For the DCs, learning at the government, sectoral and macroeconomic levels is crucial to successful industrialisation. By definition, the DCs are removed - geographically, economically and socially - from the central poles of innovative activity. It follows that the main route to development for DCs is via the diffusion of technology originating in the industrialised countries and the main way this is achieved is through learning. The experiences of Japan and the so-called newly industrialised countries (NICs) demonstrate a variety of learning routes which may be followed to achieve catch-up growth across industries and countries. Japan's relatively independent route to technological progress can, for example, be contrasted with Korea's heavier reliance on direct foreign investment. Studies show that, contrary to common opinion, the governments of both Korea and Taiwan persistently intervened in the activities of foreign capital and played a major role in the successful technological progress of these countries. Wade (1984), for instance, illustrates the aggressive nature of government industrial policy in Taiwan. Similarly, Enos (1984) describes the persistent government direction of the activities of foreign capital in Korea. Luedde-Neurath (1984) also illustrates Korea's heavy reliance on foreign capital, combined with forceful policies governing the activities of the MNCs. There can be little doubt that successful technology diffusion at the macroeconomic level is intimately bound up with governments' ability to improve progressively their capacity to create and manage the environment for successful learning to occur.

Schumpeterian Learning

Conclusion

In order to provide a working framework for the present empirical study, this chapter has integrated the DC notion of learning squarely within neo-Schumpeterian diffusion theory. It was argued that learning belongs within the neo-Schumpeterian framework of analysis, and that the concept of learning can benefit greatly from the broader set of theoretical underpinnings provided by the neotechnology school. Also, the learning dimension itself provides a valuable contribution to diffusion theory by adding a new methodology for analysing the mechanisms and dynamics of technological accumulation at the level of the firm, industry and macroeconomy. This explicit attention to how technology is acquired helps to redress the tendency in the diffusion literature to treat technological progress as costless and automatic. According to the argument put forward, dynamic, Schumpeterian learning is the main channel by which technology diffuses to the DCs from the developed economies.

In the following chapters various elements of diffusion theory and learning, as developed here, will be drawn upon to examine the Brazilian experience in acquiring and assimilating modern telecoms technology. This is intended to illustrate how, and to what extent, Brazil succeeded in meeting its aim of assimilating microelectronic technology through heavy investment in telecoms.

However, before the Brazilian study is conducted it is necessary first to analyse the major structural, economic and technological trends in the global telecoms industry. The following two chapters therefore attempt to illustrate how the driving force of technological change has transformed the international market structure, the nature of telecoms products and their processes of manufacture and, as a consequence, the prospects facing the Third World in telecoms.

Notes

1. For examples of work in this well-trodden ground see for instance Nelson and Winter (1974, 1977, 1982), Pavitt (1984), Cooper and Hoffman (1981) and Dosi (1982, 1984).
2. Again this is well-trodden ground. Some devastating criticisms are provided by Warren (1980), Brewer (1980), Lall (1975), Schiffer (1981) and Soete (1981).
3. This area of work is less well known. For early discussions see Katz (1980), Bell (1982) and Lall (1982). For an applied example see Maxwell (1981) and Mlawa (1983).
4. Examples of these and other works are discussed below.
5. Mowery and Rosenberg (1979) provide a critical evaluation of demand-pull studies, while Rosenberg (1976) shows how 'technological imperatives' can lead to subsequent incremental innovations.
6. Griliches' original (1957) study maintained that 30 per cent of the variation in the rate of adoption of a new innovation (hybrid corn in the USA) was the result of profit opportunity and that economic factors determined the rate of adoption. Since Griliches, various studies have illustrated the role of other factors such as observability, imitation and compatibility (Rogers, 1983). Mansfield, another pioneer in diffusion study, explained the rate of adoption of a new innovation by (a) the number of firms who already had adopted, (b) the expected rate of profit and (c) the capital investment cost (a positive function of (a) and (b), and a negative function of (c)). Mansfield's study used data from firms in four industries, covering 12 important innovations to test his model. Davies (1979) extended the scope of diffusion analysis to account for the character of the innovation, the growth strategy of the firm and the nature of the specific industrial branch in question. Stoneman (1981) criticises earlier studies for concentrating on diffusion between firms, and offers a mathematical model to illustrate diffusion within firms on the basis of profit maximisation.
7. For a collection of views on long-wave theory, problems of measurement and so on, see Freeman (1984). Kondratieff's original paper (1978), written in 1936, is an excellent introduction to the scope, purpose, methodology and limitations of long-wave analysis. Schumpeter's disagreements with Kondratieff are outlined by Freeman et al. (1982) who also offer a neo-Schumpeterian interpretation. Rosenberg and Frischtak (1984) present a convincing critique of long-wave analysis, identifying major problems with the approach. The importance of social and institutional receptiveness to technological change is emphasised by Perez (1983, 1985).
8. Pavitt (1979) provides an analysis of the statistical evidence for catch-up growth, and the changing nature of investments in technology during the 1960s and 1970s.

9. The importance of the post-war Marshall Plan in the re-building of Europe, and the subsequent management of the international monetary system under the Bretton Woods agreement, are described by Spero (1977, Chapter 2). Magdoff and Sweezy (1977) document the crucial role of government in the US economy in generating aggregate demand. Leontief and Duchin (1983) provide evidence of the importance of the military industrial complex both in productive investment and as source of final demand in the post-war period.

10. Soete (1981a) documents Japan's local investments in R&D and shows how these complemented foreign technology imports.

11. See for example Pavitt (1979, 1980), Soete (1981a, 1985) and Freeman et al. (1982).

12. Nathan Rosenberg made this specific point during a seminar discussion in 1984 at the Federal University of Rio de Janeiro, Brazil.

13. A summary of the various DC learning investigations is provided by Bell (1982).

14. The following discussion is exploratory and does not try to be exhaustive. Although the learning mechanisms are presented in order of the technology cycle, no simple linearity is implied. The purpose of noting possible learning mechanisms is mainly to help guide the Brazilian case study.

15. The distinction between product and process innovations is often blurred in reality, as the product innovation of one firm may be the process innovation of another.

16. A full treatment and critique of the DC learning approach is contained in Hobday (1986) which also illustrates the distinctions between the neoclassical notion of learning and the DC approach.

17. See Arrow (1962) for the original neoclassical learning-by-doing model. This is not to be confused with the DC notion of learning which focuses explicitly on the costs, efforts and mechanisms involved in technological development, as well as the role of government.

18. This corresponds to Lall's (1982) learning scheme.

CHAPTER 2

THE IMPACT OF MICROELECTRONICS ON THE INTERNATIONAL
TELECOMMUNICATIONS INDUSTRY

Introduction

The world telecoms industry is currently undergoing a period of rapid technological change, market upheaval and uncertainty. There can be little doubt that the diffusion of microelectronics (the physical embodiment of the semiconductor paradigm) is the main driving force for change in the industry.(1) Microelectronic and, in particular, digital technology has given rise to a plethora of new products and services, far superior to electromechanical technology in terms of cost and performance, and has led to a rapid expansion of the international market despite economic recession. At the same time the convergence of several industries around microelectronic technology has progressively eroded traditional market boundaries. New entrants, particularly from the computer and office equipment markets, are challenging the traditional market leaders in several important product areas. In the face of increasing competition the major telecoms multinationals have invested massively in research and development in digital systems. This technology-based competition is aimed at protecting existing market shares and capturing shares in the new, rapidly growing, IT markets.

As far as the DCs are concerned, an understanding of these trends is vital. A modern telecoms network not only represents the infrastructure for IT activities, but is also crucial to the whole process of economic development.(2) Many developing nations are investing heavily in telecoms but there exists little appreciation of whether or not the shift to microelectronic technology will bring advantages in terms of use and local manufacture, or lead to a widening of the technology gap between the developed countries and DCs.

International Telecommunications Industry

The problems and opportunities facing the DCs are discussed in Chapter 3. This chapter examines the restructuring of the industry from the perspective of the diffusion of the new technological paradigm based on microelectronics. This analysis is essential to understanding the prospects for Brazil and other DCs in attempting to acquire and assimilate modern telecoms technology.

Section 2.1 briefly defines the parameters of the industry. Section 2.2 begins by analysing how microelectronic technology has altered the nature and performance of telecoms products and then examines the actual manufacturing process involved in the production of equipment. This section argues that it is precisely these changes at the level of product and process technology which underlie the transformation of the industry worldwide. Finally, Section 2.3 examines the current restructuring of the industry, focusing on market growth, MNC strategies and the newly emerging forms of competition.

2.1 Introduction to the Telecommunications Equipment Industry

Telecoms equipment can be defined as all the products and systems required to produce instantaneous, two-way communications across distance (Jequier, 1977). Conventional postal communications are excluded from this definition as they are neither instantaneous nor two-way. Television and other forms of broadcasting equipment are also excluded as they are not interactive, although telecoms facilities such as satellites and fibre optic transmission equipment are increasingly employed to carry broadcasting signals. The closely related informatics and telematics sectors are also excluded except where public telecoms equipment is employed for data transmission and switching. The telephone industry accounts for approximately 80 per cent of telecoms equipment sales, while telex, telegraph and data transmission form the large proportion of the balance (Arthur D. Little, 1983). According to the OECD (1983, p. 20) the telecoms industry accounts for roughly 30 per cent of output of electronics-based goods, and 10 per cent to 15 per cent of electrical engineering goods sales worldwide. Although the conventional public telecoms network accounts for the bulk of equipment demand, private applications are rapidly increasing in importance.

Table 2.1 presents estimates of equipment sales of the major telecoms product lines for 1980 and 1985. The telecoms products shown constitute a

International Telecommunications Industry

Table 2.1: Shares of Major Telecommunications Product Lines in World Sales 1980-1985 (estimated)

Equipment Category	Value of World Sales* ($b) 1980	1985	% of Total 1980	1985
1) Switching	12.6	18.4	31.9	31.7
2) Transmission	12.2	17.4	31.0	30.0
3) Peripheral:				
Terminals	5.8	8.0	14.7	13.8
Private Systems	4.3	6.4	10.9	11.0
Mobile Radio	3.8	4.9	9.6	8.5
Other	0.7	2.9	1.8	5.0
Totals	39.4	58.0	100.0	100.0

* Constant 1979 prices.
Source: Amended from OECD (1983, p. 20).

'family' of equipment necessary to provide telecoms services (via operating companies or carrier networks). The equipment market is normally sub-divided into three main segments according to function - switching, transmission and peripheral equipment. Switching or exchange equipment represents the technological 'heart' of the telecoms system performing the central operating function of connecting calls within and between networks. Large capacity public exchanges constitute the bulk of the market, but the private automatic branch exchange (PABX) market is growing very rapidly and becoming increasingly important.(3)

Transmission equipment is responsible for carrying the signals between exchanges and terminals and includes paired wires, coaxial cables for long distances, microwave radio, satellite systems and, more recently, fibre optics. Peripheral equipment includes all other components and equipment necessary for the functioning of the network. Peripheral equipment is responsible for sending and receiving signals, and includes a wide range of terminal devices from simple telephone handsets to sophisticated multifunction intelligent terminals. Other input/output devices are also included, such as modems and codec equipment, together with mobile radio and key systems.

International Telecommunications Industry

As Table 2.1 shows, in 1980 total product sales stood at just under $40b and were expected to reach $58b in 1985. Despite economic recession sales have continued to grow in recent years at an annual average rate of roughly 8.5 per cent, and in the latter half of the 1980s growth is expected to slow only slightly to 8 per cent per annum (Arthur D. Little, 1983). By the early 1990s the overall size of the equipment market is forecast to exceed $100b (in constant 1979 prices). Table 2.1 also gives a rough idea of the relative economic importance of the various market segments. Switching equipment accounts for approximately 32 per cent of total sales, transmission 30 per cent and all other products 38 per cent.

2.2 Technological Trends

2.2.1 Telecommunications products - microelectronics and technological convergence

Traditional analogue telecoms systems are based on a standard set of telephones connected by two pairs of copper wires, channelled through an electromechanical switching system. The two major exchange systems, still in widespread use in the developed countries, are Strowger (invented before the turn of the century) and Crossbar (patented in 1916). Strowger exchanges comprise large banks of rotary switches connected in series, and until very recently they were still being installed in some OECD countries, despite being technologically obsolete.(4) Crossbar, again obsolete, is used as an intermediate technology between Strowger and fully electronic exchanges. Analogue electrical signals are transmitted between the main exchanges through media such as coaxial underground and undersea cables and are then routed to subscribers through paired wires.

Today almost all current equipment production has shifted to digital, microelectronic technology. This is largely due to two main sets of reasons: (1) the greater speed, efficiency and capacity of digital systems, combined with steadily declining costs, and (2) the increasing demand for new IT services which depend on digital telecoms networks. It is helpful to examine the trends in product technology in terms of the three subsectors, exchange, transmission and peripheral equipment.

In exchange technology massive R&D investments during the 1970s succeeded in producing fully electronic, stored-programme-controlled (SPC) switching systems. Table 2.2 presents estimates of

Table 2.2: Estimates of Research and Development Costs of Digital Switching Systems (billions of dollars)

Company Name	Headquarters	System Name	Cost
ITT	USA	System 12	1.01
Ericsson	Sweden	AXE	0.50
CIT-Alcatel	France	E10 and E12	1.00
Northern Telecom	Canada	DMS	0.70
GEC/Plessey/BT	UK	System X	1.40
Western Electric	USA	ESS-5	0.75
Siemens	W Germany	EWS-D	0.70

Source: Dang Nguyen (1985, p. 108).

the R&D costs for digital exchanges incurred by the leading manufacturers. Although the costings are very approximate they indicate the enormous dimensions of these investments in technology. The costs to the individual manufacturers range from $0.5b for Ericsson of Sweden to $1.4b for the British System X.

The general acceptance of the superiority of digital over analogue, electromechanical exchanges is gradually leading to the replacement of Strowger and Crossbar systems in both developed and developing countries. Digital exchanges are solid state (no moving parts) which means they are less susceptible to breakdown and require less maintenance than previous technologies. Control by software allows continuous adaptation of the exchange to new traffic conditions without physically modifying the hardware. Advances in semiconductor technology have led to steadily declining real prices, and large capacity public exchanges are now cheaper than similar analogue units (Saunders et al., 1983, p. 35). Falling prices and other advantages of digital exchanges have also led to a surge in demand for PABXs from private users and it is estimated, for example, that over 50 per cent of major European companies will have PABXs installed by 1990 (see note 3).

A further major driving force for the adoption of digital exchanges is their key role in the provision of IT services. The expansion of many informatics and telematics services, and the objective of many countries to provide so-called ISDN (integrated services digital networks), depends crucially on the installation of digital switching. Modern exchanges are capable of simultaneously processing large volumes of voice, data, text and other forms of information in digital format at great speed and low cost. Public telecoms networks are increasingly being used to provide a wide range of IT services as telecoms and computer technologies converge.

Transmission systems have also benefited greatly from innovation with digital technology. The application of pulse code modulation techniques to traditional transmission methods such as coaxial and microwave systems has resulted in increased capacity and efficiency, and reduced costs. Terrestrial communications costs have fallen by approximately 11 per cent per annum in recent years, while satellite telecoms costs have fallen by roughly 40 per cent per speech/data channel per annum (Muller, 1982). Innovations centred on digital transmission, notably fibre optics and laser transmission, are also gaining wide acceptance. Fibre optics have far greater capacity than traditional wire cables and are not resistant to transmission signals (therefore fewer signal regenerators or 'boosters' are needed). Installation costs are far lower than with conventional cable (e.g. the costs of laying submarine cables have been cut by 75 per cent). The rapidly falling costs of fibre optics mean that they are likely to become cost effective in an increasing number of applications. Digital transmission is capable of simultaneously handling various types of data in digital format without cross interference, and is therefore a vital component of modern informatics and telematics services.

Peripheral equipment is also at the forefront of the convergence of computer and telecoms technology. With the rise in private applications and the integration of telecoms with other IT activities, the range of intelligent terminals, key systems, mobile radios, modems and other office equipment has expanded considerably. With developments in word processing, multifunction microcomputers, electronic messaging and various other types of workstations, there is also an increasing demand to link up these office systems with services. Many peripheral products are needed both to provide an interface with the public telecoms network and to integrate electronic systems within firms and other private organisations. In fact, broadly defined, the share of peripheral equipment in total telecoms sales exceeds both switching and transmission technology as Table 2.1 showed.

In short, advances in semiconductor technology, and in particular the introduction of digital techniques to telecoms, have greatly expanded the range of products available and led to sustained improvements in cost/performance ratios. Convergence with computer technology has also produced many new applications and products. These factors, together with the pressures to provide a wide range of new IT services, largely explain the increasing demand for telecoms equipment and services throughout the advanced economies.

2.2.2 Telecommunications production processes – new techniques of manufacture

To understand how microelectronic-based telecoms equipment is produced, it is helpful to contrast the mechanisms of manufacture and technological development of electromechanical products with those related to microelectronic products. Indeed, the telecoms equipment industry provides a rare opportunity to make this contrast as it is the only major industrial sector which has undergone an almost complete transition from one technology to the other. Other industries are either (a) in a relatively early stage of the adoption of the technology (e.g. the automobile industry) or (b) generated from the new technology itself (e.g. computers and informatics) and have no previous counterpart of sufficient similarity to make such a comparison.

In general the production of electromechanical systems is a highly complex and closely integrated task. A large number of specialised component inputs, such as relays, screws and connectors, require exact interfacing both mechanically and electrically. In contrast with microelectronic technology there are a large number of moving parts which must be engineered precisely to ensure the long-term durability and reliability of the system.

Not surprisingly, the production process demands a heavy concentration of engineering and technical skills to ensure the quality of the fine engineering and electromechanical interfacing involved. A thoroughgoing engineering capacity is required not only in the design and development stages but also in virtually all stages of component production, equipment assembly, testing, installation and maintenance. One of the prerequisites for market entry in electromechanical telecoms is a sufficient supply of telecoms-specific engineering and technical skills. The very specialised nature of the skills and knowhow required to produce and install telecoms equipment may have assisted in preventing entry by non-telecoms manufacturers in the past. (The important role of government policy in preventing entry is discussed below.) Certainly, within the industry there exists a recognition of the specialised and complex nature of the technology.

International Telecommunications Industry

The complex and highly integrated nature of the production process was reflected in the vertically integrated market structure which prevailed in the industry for several decades. Virtually all major telecoms firms integrated backwards into the production of intermediate products (OECD, 1983, p. 42). The many specialised component inputs were either manufactured in-house or purchased from firms dedicated to supplying telecoms parts. According to the Belgian Ministry of Industry, material input costs to the switching industry amounted to around 20 per cent of the value of output in 1965; at this time production was predominantly Crossbar and Strowger electromechanical technology. By 1978, with the gradual shift to microelectronic exchanges, total material input costs, primarily semiconductor components, represented 70 per cent of the value of the industry's output (OECD, 1983, p. 57). As semiconductor technology continues to advance, and increasing numbers of switching functions are integrated onto single chips, the value of components purchased in is expected to continue rising.

In direct contrast with the manufacture of electromechanical products, the production of microelectronic equipment is characterised by modularity of design and divisibility in manufacture. Also the engineering effort is heavily concentrated in the design and development stages, rather than spread throughout the production process overall. It is necessary to explain these points in more detail.

Digital telecoms are intrinsically modular or divisible in nature. A telecoms network is built up from a range of independent units (or 'building blocks') which together form an expandable system. This modularity holds true at the level of design as well. When a new product is being designed, increasingly complex software programs are gradually built up from a range of standardised modules. This means that it is possible to design a small exchange, for instance, and gradually expand its capacity using similar hardware and software. The modular nature of the technology also means that systems are 'evolutionary' and can be improved and expanded continuously. The development of modular software techniques occurred partly because of the incredible complexity of the tasks demanded of large-scale exchange systems, and partly because of the inherent nature of the technology. Modularity facilitates the management and execution of more and more complex designs.

At the level of manufacture microelectronic telecoms can be viewed as 'divisible'. Modern systems do not demand the high degree of electromechanical interfacing and fine engineering of previous technologies. The main functions are built into the system logic. Consequently the emphasis on engineering and technical effort in the manufacturing process is substantially reduced, and there is a shift in technological emphasis to the software task of program design. Semiconductor components represent the 'building blocks' of the products and with technological advance increasingly take on the functional characteristics of the final product. Following the highly complex design and development stages the microchips are assembled in a fairly simple assembly-style operation. The scale of the integration of circuits used in manufacture is constantly increasing and standardised devices can be purchased 'off the shelf' from outside semiconductor manufacturers (or manufactured in-house). The components are then mounted onto printed circuit boards (PCBs) and tested. Some engineering supervision is required but in general the operation is an unskilled task. Once assembled the PCBs constitute the functioning units of the various systems. Almost all functions are solid state and consequently there is relatively little need for trained engineers and technicians in the actual manufacturing or, more precisely, assembly stage.

With microelectronic technology, engineering effort is concentrated mainly in the research, design and development stages of manufacture. A small range of information-based design skills are required, rather than the broad range of mechanical and electromechanical skills demanded throughout the production of Strowger and Crossbar systems. Indeed, the most formidable technological barrier to entry in digital telecoms lies in mastering the software involved in the design and development stages. For example, public switching software must be capable of interconnecting, storing and transmitting many thousands of messages simultaneously, and at the same time controlling hardware operations, recording subscriber traffic, billing and so on. The complexity of exchange software has proved to be the greatest challenge to leading manufacturers, and has absorbed a large share of the development costs described above. Partly as a result of the complexity of the software and the huge R&D thresholds, so far the traditional telecoms manufacturers have maintained their dominance of this particularly important market segment. In other areas such as PABXs new competitors are seriously challenging the 'traditional' telecoms producers.(5)

2.2.3 Technological convergence and microelectronics

As a consequence of the convergence in product and process technologies between telecoms and other areas of IT, the leading telecoms manufacturers are now competing directly with firms from traditionally separate industries, including office equipment, computer, aerospace and microchip component manufacturers (discussed below). Although other factors, particularly government policy, are also important to a full understanding of industrial change within the sector, the root of the present industrial upheaval can be traced directly to the convergence of several industries around digital microelectronic technology. In the IT industry, technological convergence not only applies to finished products and manufacturing processes, but also to the actual raw materials of the industry - microelectronic components. Although these devices are employed in many different industrial sectors and applications (spanning consumer goods, military equipment, computers, industrial process controls, communications etc.) they are all made in basically the same way.(6)

The emergence and diffusion of semiconductor technology has acted in several ways to break down the traditional market structure of the telecoms industry and allow the entry of new competitors. Before the adoption of microelectronics, the slow-changing oligopoly of the leading manufacturers was supported by the vertically integrated market structure and the control this permitted over input supplies. Close, collusive links between local manufacturers and government buyers and the heavy capital investment requirements of the industry also acted to prevent competition. In addition, the highly complex and specialised nature of the engineering skills required in the manufacturing process mitigated against entry from other industries. The breakdown of the vertically integrated market structure under electromechanical technology entailed a loss of control over input supplies, and indeed a transfer of value added to microelectronic component manufacturers (OECD, 1983).

The information-based software design skills which now characterise the telecoms industry are common to several other industries in the area of IT. The divisible nature of digital technology means that it is increasingly possible for firms outside the telecoms sector to select a specific product area and to accumulate gradually the technological knowhow and skills needed to move up the scale of technological complexity. It is not surprising that the ability of telecoms firms to appropriate technological knowhow has steadily declined in many product areas. Furthermore, the demand for new products and services has led several OECD governments to relax their monopoly control over the supply of telecoms services and to permit greater competition in the equipment supply sector. The following section attempts to examine in detail the present restructuring of the telecoms industry and, in particular, the response of leading manufacturers to technological change.

2.3 Industrial Trends - Competition and Industrial Convergence

Technological change has undoubtedly led to a transformation of the telecoms industry, altering market boundaries and giving rise to competition from other industries. The outcome of these changes has yet to be fully realised and will depend on many economic, institutional and political factors as well as technological change. Although a great deal of uncertainty surrounds the future of the industry, it is possible here to outline some of the main trends occurring within telecoms, and between telecoms and the wider area of IT. This section identifies some of the competitive strategies currently being adopted in response to technological change, and illustrates the important role of government policy in defending domestic telecoms firms and facilitating technological change.

2.3.1 Telecommunications market size, growth and geographical distribution

The telecoms sector overall is one of the largest and fastest growing of the major sectors in the world economy. According to Arthur D. Little (1983) total telecoms turnover (comprising 1/3 equipment sales and 2/3 service sector revenues) for the EEC, Japan and the USA amounts to an equivalent of roughly 3 per cent of world GDP. (Arthur D. Little's figures do not refer to the actual share of telecoms in GDP, but to telecoms turnover in relation to GDP. The share of telecoms in GDP is the value added of purchased-in components, material, products and services from other sectors - a far smaller figure.) This ranks telecoms alongside the largest industries worldwide including motor vehicle manufacturing, electricity production, aerospace and petrochemicals. In recent years annual growth worldwide averaged 8 per cent per annum (roughly 10 per cent for the DCs) despite economic recession. By 1990 telecoms activities will reach an equivalent of 4.4 per cent of GDP, second only to the motor vehicle industry. By the year 2000, if this very rapid growth continues, telecoms will have surpassed all other major sectors with turnover around 7 per cent of GDP. Furthermore, the closely related telematics sector, which includes data processing and communications, is expected to reach similar proportions by the early 1990s. (Although one must be sceptical of consultancy forecasts, Arthur D. Little's is probably the most widely respected and comprehensive study of the worldwide telecoms industry available.)

Turning to the equipment supply industry, Table 2.3 shows estimates of telecoms equipment sales by region for the period 1982-1992. In 1982 shipments were in the region of $47b. This is expected to more than double by 1992. Over the total period average annual growth is forecast to be 8.1 per cent. The OECD countries account for approximately 80 per cent of total equipment sales, which reflects the very unequal distribution of telecoms infrastructure between the developed and developing countries. The North American market represents over 40 per cent of world sales and Europe 25 per cent. Japan accounts for around 45 per cent of the total Asian market.(7)

The DCs together account for only 11 per cent of world sales. However, this market is more important

Table 2.3: Estimated Regional Markets for Telecommunications Equipment (shipments in billions of dollars - 1979 prices)

ITU World Zone	1982	1987	1992	Growth Rate (%/year)
North America	19.9	29.1	41.9	7.8
Europe	12.5	17.2	23.7	6.7
Asia	11.8	19.1	31.7	10.1
Latin America	1.4	2.0	2.9	7.7
Oceania	0.9	1.2	1.5	6.6
Africa	0.4	0.7	1.0	8.2
Totals	46.9	69.3	102.7	8.1

Source: Arthur D. Little (1983).

than the low percentage would suggest. As potential export markets they are a source of intense competition among the multinational suppliers because, unlike the developed countries, they are to a large extent open, uncommitted markets. Also, aggregated figures can be misleading; the Latin American market, for example, amounts to less than 3 per cent of the world total, but in terms of digital public switching Latin America accounts for 16.3 per cent of total sales - this compares with 27.3 per cent for the USA and 28 per cent for Europe. Africa represents only 1 per cent of the world market yet accounts for approximately 4.5 per cent of digital switching sales. The ITU (1984) puts total Third World investment in telecoms at approximately $8b in 1983, and estimates that this figure will need to be increased to around $12b per annum to meet infrastructural needs.(8) Given that the DCs are currently installing and expanding their basic telecoms infrastructure, there is enormous potential for future growth and the suppliers are keen to 'lock in' these markets to their particular systems.

2.3.2 Competitive strategies and industrial convergence

Table 2.4 presents sales of the largest ten manufacturers of telecoms equipment for 1982 and 1983. The industry is highly oligopolistic with the ten leading corporations accounting for approximately 70 per cent of total world sales for both years. The largest firm, AT&T, built up its sales lead through a long-term monopoly of the large US market, and until very recently was prohibited from competing in international markets. All other firms are multinational to various degrees with L.M. Ericsson and ITT almost wholly multinational as judged by equipment sales. The majority of the remaining companies rely on their monopoly of domestic markets for the bulk of their sales. Outside the protected OECD markets the dominant corporations for many years were L.M. Ericsson, ITT and Siemens. More recently NEC of Japan has made substantial inroads into the relatively unprotected markets, particularly in the Third World.

In 1982 new US legislation was introduced to allow AT&T, then the world's largest company, to compete for overseas orders and to enter other areas of IT, which earlier anti-trust legislation had prohibited. At the same time IBM, the world's largest computer manufacturer, was allowed to enter telecoms markets. The purpose of the new US

Table 2.4: Sales of Major Telecommunications Equipment Manufacturers, 1982 and 1983 (current prices)

Rank	Company/Headquarters		Sales 1982 ($b)	Company	Sales 1983 ($b)
1	AT&T/Western Electric	USA	12.49	AT&T Technologies*	11.16
2	ITT	USA	4.87	ITT	4.86
3	Siemens	W Germany	4.49	Siemens	4.49
4	L M Ericsson	Sweden	2.72	L M Ericsson	3.16
5	GTE	USA	2.72	Alcatel-Thomson (F)	2.74
6	Northern Telecom	Canada	2.72	Northern Telecom	2.66
7	NEC	Japan	2.17	NEC	2.41
8	GEC	UK	2.17	GTE (US)	2.38
9	Thomson	France	1.63	Motorola (US)	2.31
10	Philips	Holland	1.09	IBM (US)	1.73

*New name following reorganisation.

Sources: Arthur D. Little, cited in International Business Week (24 October 1983) (1982 sales) and Financial Times (12 July 1985) (1983 sales).

legislation was widely seen (a) as an effort to stimulate oligopolistic competition in the face of successful Japanese competition both at home and in Europe (although this applied mainly to the computer industry, there was also the perceived capability of Japanese firms (NEC, Hitachi, Oki and Fujitsu) to gain larger telecoms market shares in the future) and (b) to encourage the introduction of new digital information services in the private and public sectors within the USA.

Governments throughout the OECD play an extremely important role in framing the competitive environment within which telecoms equipment companies operate. Government purchasing accounts for between 60 per cent and 85 per cent of all telecoms sales (OECD, 1983) and the service carriers are either owned or strictly controlled by governments through postal and telecoms administrations. Partly because of the perceived importance of a strong national supply industry, and partly to ensure economies of scale in development and production, government orders were (and still are to a large extent) allocated to local telecoms companies. This government purchasing support to local manufacturers led to very high concentration ratios within countries where major producers were based. For instance, in a study conducted in the late 1970s covering a sample of seven OECD countries, it was found that the four largest domestic firms supplied an average of 87 per cent of equipment sales (within those countries sampled) (OECD, 1983, p. 34). Before the diffusion of microelectronic technology government policy was therefore a key factor in supporting the relatively static, cartelised and oligopolistic structure of the electromechanical industry.

Until recently there were few changes in the ranking of the top ten to fifteen major telecoms companies. Data for 1973 (cited by Dang Nguyen, 1985, p. 93) show almost exactly the same ranking for the major manufacturers as for 1982. However, as Table 2.4 shows, by 1983 Motorola (a leading semiconductor manufacturer) and IBM had entered the ranking in positions nine and ten respectively. These two new competitors from outside industries are indicative of deeper industrial readjustments currently occurring both within telecoms and between telecoms and other fields of IT. Two interrelated factors are responsible for the entry of these and other companies into the telecoms sector: first, government deregulation of the telecoms sector in the USA enabled IBM to compete in telecoms markets, and also allowed AT&T to move into the computer industry and into markets outside the USA (the government response to technological change in other OECD countries is discussed below); second, technological convergence around semiconductor technology has permitted other IT companies to gain a firmer grasp of telecoms technology.

To help identify the emerging trends within the industry, Table 2.5 presents a selection of major, recent joint ventures and acquisitions by leading manufacturers and service providers. The listing is not exhaustive and does not include a growing number of joint ventures in the Third World. Also, the IT product areas identified do not necessarily refer to the principal product range of the manufacturer, but rather to the central purpose of the joint venture. Among the large number of acquisitions, mergers and joint ventures, a wide variety of competitive strategies are developing (most of the above occurred in 1984 and 1985) which testify to the increasing risk, competition, internationalisation and industrial convergence throughout the telecoms and IT industries.

Soaring research and development costs, coupled with the need to achieve economies of scale, have led many telecoms firms into joint ventures with other equipment makers and increasingly, as Table 2.5 shows, with the providers of telecoms services (or carriers). Successive 'waves' of Japanese firms have gained significant shares of the international IT markets and intensified the degree of competition.(9) As yet, Japanese firms have not established a stronghold in the main public switching markets, but in other areas such as PABX, transmission and peripherals Japanese corporations are steadily gaining market shares. In the deregulated PABX market, for example, NEC had already gained a 5 per cent market share by 1985 (Dang Nguyen, 1985).

US and European firms see greater export orientation as a means of gaining greater market shares and, in the process, increasing their own international competitiveness. European companies have entered into a wide range of commercial and technological joint ventures, both to improve technological cooperation within Europe and to gain entry into the large US market. In addition, the European companies hope to protect themselves against competition from AT&T and IBM. In their turn, US multinationals are engaging in joint ventures with European firms to gain access to the growing European markets. Some Japanese companies are also beginning to engage in joint ventures both to sell superior technology to European companies (mainly in semi-conductors and other areas of IT rather than in telecoms) and to link up with US firms attempting to

International Telecommunications Industry

increase market shares in Japan.

The US government's response to technological change and the internal pressures to 'open up' the new value added networks to competition was the deregulation of the local market. Under pressure from the US and Europe, Japan also has agreed recently to open its telecoms market (the second largest in the world) to foreign competition.(10) In Europe, Britain has taken the lead in market deregulation with the privatisation of British Telecom and the approval of outside competition from the Swedish firm L.M. Ericsson for the public switching systems. There are signs that several other European countries will also follow suit. The West German government has appointed a commission to review the national telecoms strategy and, in particular, the role of the Bundespost (post office). In Italy the government-owned telecoms company sold 30 per cent of its shares to private investors in 1985. The French right-wing opposition parties indicated that they would press for deregulation if they won the 1986 national elections. In the Netherlands the government is in the final stages of legislating for a reduction in the power of the state telecoms monopoly and also allowing for some private ownership to take place. In Ireland, too, the government has changed the status of the telecoms administration from a government department to a state-owned company.(11) In the USA and Europe these moves have one thing in common - to ensure that the monopolies become more commercially oriented and to accelerate the introduction of new IT services.

Recognition of the generally weak position of European equipment manufacturers in relation to US and Japanese corporations (in the area of IT in general rather than telecoms specifically) has led to major government support programmes for local industry and technology. Among others, these include Esprit (the European Strategic Programme for Research and Development in Information Technologies), the UK Alvey programme engaged in R&D in fifth generation technology (involving cooperation between firms, universities and government) and more recently Eureka (the European Technology Cooperation Programme). These programmes are all in the general area of IT and hope to galvanise domestic firms into successful competition with Japanese and US companies.

Turning to the nature of firms' competitive strategies, some major telecoms service providers are integrating backwards into the actual production of equipment. Following deregulation of the US market AT&T has taken the lead in this area. AT&T has already reached agreement with Philips, ICL, Olivetti

Table 2.5: Recent Major Joint Ventures and Acquisitions Involving Leading Telecommunications Companies by Firm and Product Area

Telecoms Company*	Telecoms Equipment Manufacture	Telecoms Service Provision	IT Product Area Computers/ Data Processing	Semiconductor Manufacture	PABX, Office Automation and Other
AT&T* (US)	Philips (H)	BT* (UK)	ICI (UK)	-	Convergent (US) Olivetti (I) Ricoh (J)
BT* (UK)	-	IBM (US)	-	-	Mitel (C)
Cable and Wireless* (UK)	-	TDX Systems Inc.* (US)	-	-	-
CIT-Alcatel (F)	Thomson (F)	-	-	Italtel (I) Siemens (WG) Plessey (UK)	-
L.M. Ericsson (S)	-	BT* (UK)	IBM (US)	-	Honeywell (US) Thorn/EMI (UK)
GTE (US)	Italtel (I)	-	-	SEMI (US)	-
MCI* (US)	-	Western Union* (US)	IBM (US)	-	-

Philips (H)	Thomson-Brandt (F) CIT-Alcatel (F)	-	Signetics (US)	-	-
Plessey (UK)	Stromberg-Carlson (US) Kyocera (J) GEC, STC, BT* (UK)	-	-	-	-
Rolm (US)	-	-	-	IBM (US)	-
Siemens (WG)	GTE (US)	-	AMD (US) Litronic (US) Toshiba (J) Philips (H)	Xerox (US)	-
STC (UK)	-	ICL (UK)	-	-	-

C - Canada J - Japan
F - France S - Sweden
H - Holland WG - West Germany
I - Italy

*Primarily telecoms service provider.

Sources: Financial Times (various issues); Roobeek (1984).

and Ricoh (a major Japanese group) to market their telecoms products abroad. AT&T's lack of experience in international markets means that joint ventures are one means of forging instant marketing channels into Europe and other countries. In the UK, British Telecom has become the leading supplier of PABX systems, and is attempting to gain a controlling share in the Canadian PABX manufacturer Mitel to extend its in-house production capacity and possibly to gain inroads into the North American market. Several telecoms administrations (PTTs) in DCs including Telemex (Mexico), Telebras (Brazil) and NPTIC (China) are currently engaged in various forms of joint venture with MNCs. Most major service companies have supported and participated in the development of digital systems. Market deregulation may permit more PTTs to exploit their technological base and gain additional equipment markets as well as service revenues.

As far as telecoms equipment makers are concerned there is an increasing degree of diversification by most major companies into the production of other areas of IT such as computers, office automation, semiconductors and data processing equipment. This reflects the technological convergence of telecoms with IT and the desire for telecoms manufacturers to recover large development costs and capture new markets. In addition, diversification via joint venture presents itself as a means of meeting competition. As Table 2.5 shows, several leading corporations, including L.M. Ericsson, AT&T, MCI and STC, have entered into joint ventures in the computer and data processing markets. Telecoms makers are also entering joint ventures in semiconductor component production. With the breaking down of the vertical market structure which prevailed under electromechanical technology, value added has been steadily transferred to outside semiconductor manufacturers (OECD, 1983). At the same time the large electrical and telecoms companies have accumulated considerable experience in semiconductor development and production. Several major telecoms manufacturers are therefore attempting to gain or increase shares in the microcomponent market. Siemens, Italtel, CIT-Alcatel and Plessey are engaged in a joint European venture to develop very large-scale integration (VLSI) chips. Siemens is also cooperating with Philips on VLSI development, and recently began negotiations with Toshiba to acquire the knowhow to produce 1 and 4 megabit chips. These joint ventures in semiconductor production can probably best be viewed as straightforward diversification into other fields of IT, rather than

International Telecommunications Industry

increasing vertical integration. This is because the components in question are not telecoms-specific but are intended for general purpose IT applications.

Other joint ventures also reflect the effort by telecoms firms to gain a broader base in IT. AT&T, L.M. Ericsson, Plessey, STC and Siemens have all entered into joint ventures, or are competing independently for shares in the rapidly growing office automation and business equipment markets. In microcomputers AT&T are marketing a whole range of personal computers and, as Roobeek (1984) notes, will almost certainly compete head on with the computer giant IBM. To gain an international marketing network AT&T has joined up with Philips who have well-developed multinational distribution facilities. Even in fibre optic technology the traditional market leader, Corning Glass, is being increasingly challenged by ITT, AT&T, NEC, Northern Telecom and Philips. The leading Japanese telecoms manufacturer, Nippon Electric (NEC), now provides a model of horizontal integration across the whole spectrum of IT products, and the large electrical and telecoms companies may be following suit for fear of falling further behind in the technology race.

One general trend illustrated by Table 2.5 is a diversification by IT firms into the traditional telecoms markets. In several areas the previously secure positions of the 'traditional' telecoms firms are being challenged, for the reasons discussed earlier. So far, the public switching market has remained with the major telecoms suppliers owing to extremely high R&D thresholds, technological complexity and market saturation.(12) However, many computer and office equipment manufacturers including IBM, ICL and Olivetti have entered the growing PABX market. This pattern is reflected in other areas of IT where manufacturers of office equipment, computers and semiconductors are increasingly competing in telecoms markets for shares in transmission, peripheral and private applications equipment. These diversifications can be seen as aggressive market responses to new market opportunities afforded by technological convergence, rather than the defensive strategies adopted by the traditional telecoms makers to resist competition.

A final trend illustrated by Table 2.5 is the growing network of technological cooperation and marketing joint ventures, and the intensification of international competition. This is clearly leading to a growing internationalisation of the industry. As already noted, several European manufacturers are pooling their technological resources to meet competition from Japan and the USA. At the same time

Japanese firms have had considerable success in gradually increasing their market share in both Europe and the USA. Other European-led marketing ventures and acquisitions reflect the effort by firms to increase sales abroad. For instance, Plessey (UK) has recently acquired Stromberg Carlson to sell switching technology to the USA. Siemens has a proposed joint venture with GTE for the same reason. L.M. Ericsson has also entered an agreement with Honeywell to market PABXs in the USA. Conversely, to gain entry to the European market AT&T has linked up with ICL, Olivetti and Philips. With the recent 'opening up' of the Japanese home market, North American manufacturers including AT&T, Canada's Northern Telecom, GTE and IBM's new telecoms acquisition Rolm are all in the process of establishing marketing links in Japan (Taylor, 1985). Although it is quite possible that several of the joint ventures will not be successful, they demonstrate the increasing concentration and fierce technology-based competition currently being waged.

To sum up, technological competition, convergence and market deregulation have led to a wide variety of new alliances and new forms of competition. Within the complexity of the current upheavals the main trends occurring at present appear to be as follows: (a) backward integration by telecoms service providers into equipment production; (b) increasing diversification by telecoms firms into other areas of IT such as computers, peripherals and semiconductors; (c) aggressive moves by non-telecoms companies into traditional telecoms markets; (d) an increasing internationalisation of the industry through new forms of joint ventures; (e) increasing competition throughout the telecoms and IT industries; (f) the emergence of new market niches with lower economic and technological barriers to entry; (g) a steady increase in market shares for Japanese firms; (h) a progressive erosion of the traditional market boundaries and the emergence of multiproduct IT corporations. Until the pace of technological change slows it is impossible to predict if and when new, stable, less transient organisational forms will take the place of the current uncertainty and industrial transformation.

Conclusion

The emergence of the semiconductor paradigm has irrevocably transformed the telecoms industry. New patterns of competition are emerging, traditional industrial boundaries are changing, and new technology leaders are beginning to challenge the traditional market leaders. There can be little doubt that the once stable, cartelised, electromechanical oligopoly is currently breaking down as competitors from the computer, aerospace, office equipment and semiconductor component industries enter the telecoms market - and telecoms makers, in their turn, attempt to capture new IT markets. Technological change and convergence at the level of product and process lie at the root of these widely observed industrial upheavals.

In terms of products, microelectronic technology has brought about sustained reductions in cost, improved performance and greatly enhanced operating flexibility in a wide range of new applications. The clear technological and economic superiority of digital over analogue equipment has led to sustained rapid increases in demand despite economic recession, and has resulted in an almost complete industrial transition from electromechanical to microelectronic technology. However, one must look beyond the telecoms industry to understand fully the market restructuring and increasing demand for new products. Telecoms play a leading role in providing the infrastructure for a wide range of new IT activities, and this 'leading edge' property of telecoms has further stimulated the diffusion of microelectronic products in the public and private sectors.

At the level of process technology, the diffusion of microelectronics has radically altered the nature of the manufacturing process from the design stage to assembly. Instead of the wide range of mechanical and electromechanical skills needed with earlier technologies, modern telecoms require a relatively small range of information-intensive design skills. With semiconductor-based technology there is also a sharp reduction in the importance of manufacture which is reduced to a simple assembly operation. In the Brazilian case study, an effort is made both to substantiate these arguments further and to elucidate the means and mechanisms of the accumulation process with microelectronic technology. Many of the skills and technical knowhow demanded in the development and manufacture of digital telecoms are now common to other information-intensive industries. With the convergence of these industries around digital IT, an increasing number of previously unrelated products and industrial sectors are becoming closely related on a manufacturing technology basis. As a result, new competitors from other sectors have found it possible and profitable to enter the telecoms market.

During the 1970s leading telecoms and IT manufacturers attempted to gain technological leads over competitors by investing heavily in semiconductor-based technology. The new technology has rapidly been adopted by almost all major firms, either as an offensive strategy to gain the rewards from technological leads or as a defensive strategy to avoid the penalties of failing to keep abreast of microelectronic technology. US and Japanese firms have forged technological leads over many of their European counterparts. In response, European firms appear to be attempting to catch up through various form of technological cooperation, joint ventures and acquisitions.

For their part US and Japanese firms are establishing links with European firms to gain greater shares of the rapidly growing telecoms and IT markets. Other forms of joint venture have been spurred on by microelectronic technology. Risk and uncertainty is clearly a motivating force in several companies' sharing of R&D expenditures and resources. Other joint ventures are the result of technological opportunities as telecoms makers find themselves in a position to diversify into IT - and vice versa.

As microelectronic technology diffuses widely throughout these major world industries, OECD governments are retreating from their historical role of protecting home markets and giving support to the static, cartelised telecoms industries. Increasingly, government legislation and intervention is being brought to bear on privatising local industry, opening up markets to foreign competition and providing technological support to local firms in an effort to speed up the diffusion of new IT services and force domestic manufacturers to become more competitive. While the nature of these policies differs from country to country, they have one aim in common - to ensure the international position of local industry as the diffusion of IT continues.

Notes

1. The term 'semiconductor paradigm' was coined by Dosi (1982). 'Semiconductor' refers to the special material used in the production of most microelectronic circuitry. The terms 'semiconductor' and 'microelectronic' are used interchangeably here - both describing the inputs to, and the technological basis of, modern telecoms and computer technology. 'Digital' is also used to describe the latest generation of telecoms equipment. For a full discussion of the 'semiconductor paradigm' and the microelectronics industry see Dosi (1984). A glossary is provided to explain and define necessary technical terms.

2. The role of telecoms as IT infrastructure is discussed below. Also see Barron and Curnow (1979). Hudson et al. (1981) illustrate the crucial role of telecoms in the economic development process.

3. Financial Times (17 June 1985). Muller (1982) gives full details of the economic and technological superiority of digital exchange technology.

4. In the UK, for example, Strowger was, until the mid 1980s, the most commonly used exchange. The most recent, and last, installation took place in April 1985.

5. International Business Week (1983) provides a graphic account of the dynamism and competition of the PABX market.

6. For a detailed analysis of the semiconductor manufacturing process, see CSE Microelectronics Group (1980).

7. Unless otherwise stated, these data are from the World Telecommunications Programme conducted by Arthur D. Little (1983).

8. It is not clear, however, how this investment is to be financed.

9. Wilmot (1985) describes how Japanese IT firms have successfully 'targeted' US and European markets, each with the objective of achieving a given percentage of the world market. Once NEC, Fujitsu, Hitachi and Toshiba had each gained 5 per cent of the world market in their respective fields, a new 'wave' of firms surfaced - Matsushita, Mitsubishi, Sharp and Oki now being followed by a third wave - Ricoh, Sony and NMB.

10. Japan agreed to open its telecoms market to foreign competition in July 1985 Financial Times (31 July 1985). It is not clear whether other, unofficial barriers to entry will remain.

11. Information on deregulation is from the Financial Times (31 July 1985).

12. Evidence of market saturation is provided by Muller (1982).

CHAPTER 3

DEVELOPING COUNTRIES: THE POTENTIAL FOR TECHNOLOGICAL LEAPFROGGING

Introduction

In the present conditions of market uncertainty and rapid technological change, the prospects facing Third World countries in telecoms are both extremely complex and difficult to assess. Indeed, in the wider literature concerning the diffusion of microelectronics and DCs there is little agreement as to the medium- or long-term outcome of these changes. Most economic observers are highly pessimistic about the prospects for DCs to acquire and use this new technological form to their advantage. Authors such as Kaplinsky (1984) argue that the likely outcome will be a shift in comparative advantage against the Third World and a widening of the technology gap. Others, such as Soete (1985), maintain that there is a possibility of 'leapfrogging' earlier technological forms and advantageously exploiting the intense international competition for Third World markets. In its turn, this view is criticised for failing to account for the 'cumulative' and complex nature of technological advance (Pavitt, 1984). Still others stress the need for more careful empirical research to unravel the complexities of technological change across sectors, countries and technological applications (Hoffman, 1985).

Certainly, this debate will not be resolved in this study. However, as a major world industry which has already substantially experienced the diffusion of microelectronics, the telecoms industry is an especially important and interesting case in point and should throw some light on the arguments. This chapter therefore examines the various arguments and existing empirical material to try and assess the opportunities and problems facing DCs in terms of building up local capabilities, developing domestic industry and actually installing modern telecoms systems.

Section 3.1 begins by analysing the concerns of research in other areas of microelectronic diffusion and the DCs. The arguments for 'technological leapfrogging' are weighed against the fears of deepening technological dependence and shifting comparative advantage. Astonishingly, research to date has almost entirely ignored the telecoms and IT industries, which are already substantially into the take-off stage of the diffusion cycle. Instead, as Section 3.2 shows, empirical work has focused on more traditional industries where the adoption of semiconductor technology appears to be at a far earlier stage, and future prospects remain extremely uncertain. From this perspective too, the telecoms industry is a timely test case of the opposing arguments.

Section 3.3 considers the telecoms sector within the wider context of microelectronic diffusion and points to the important role of communications technology in economic development, and especially as infrastructure for IT. Finally, Section 3.4 tries to substantiate the preceding arguments in the context of the Latin American market. The transition to microelectronic telecoms in the region is assessed, alongside the possibilities for import substitution and local technological development. Within the region Brazil has the greatest scope for assimilating microelectronic-based telecoms, in view of the country's large domestic market and relatively well-developed technological infrastructure.

3.1 The Diffusion of Microelectronic Technology and the Third World - the Current Debate

Most observers stress the negative implications and the obstacles facing DCs in acquiring and applying semiconductor-based technology to their advantage. There are probably three main concerns in the field: first, that the shift towards microelectronic technology, and especially the adoption of automation and semi-automation techniques, will erode the comparative advantage of DCs whose recent growth has been based upon cheap labour. Authors such as Kaplinsky (1982, 1982a, 1984), Rada (1982) and Boon (1982) argue that as it becomes technologically feasible, and theoretically more profitable, to relocate production facilities back from the DCs to the developed countries, a 'northward drift' will occur. MNCs will take advantage of microelectronic technology to automate production facilities and locate industry near to the markets they serve.

The second worry is that the heavy concentration

of microelectronic developments in the industrially advanced countries, and especially within the leading MNCs, may lead the DCs into a new and economically detrimental phase of technological dependence - just at the point where several industrialising countries have mastered previous forms of mechanical and electromechanical technology.(1) As the international information technology industry becomes increasingly competitive and concentrated, the possibilities for market entry by new firms will be correspondingly reduced. The appropriation of the new technological form will therefore place the DCs in a weaker bargaining position to acquire and employ microelectronics to their advantage.

Third, the highly sophisticated, labour-saving nature of microelectronic technology is seen as 'inappropriate' and unsuited to the needs, skills and factor endowments of DCs. On the one hand, the complexity of the technology will mitigate against assimilation into existing industrial structure. Skill constraints and the lack of R&D capabilities will, it is argued, prevent firms in the DCs from developing microelectronics-based industries. On the other hand, given the abundance of unemployed labour in most Third World countries, the technology is inherently inappropriate to existing economic and social needs.

Given these sets of difficulties some writers even forecast a 'reopening' of the technology gap, with the bulk of the Third World relegated to pre-microelectronic technology, while the advanced economies proceed to push the technology frontier further and further away from the grasp of the DCs.(2)

In stark contrast with these views, other economists, notably Soete (1983, 1985), are far more optimistic. Soete (1985), for example, maintains that given an adequate 'absorptive capacity' the NICs are in a position to leapfrog older, less efficient technologies and go directly to microelectronic technology. In historical terms the NICs are less committed to previous vintages of technology in terms of productive and social organisation, existing infrastructure and industrial investment (Perez, 1985). In terms of diffusion these countries may be better equipped for, and better prepared to adjust to, the new technological paradigm based on semiconductor technology.

In fact, most of the pessimistic arguments noted above can be countered without too much difficulty. To begin with, the diffusion of microelectronic technology has 'destabilised' the traditional electromechanical oligopolies, increased the degree of competition and begun a process of market restructuring. Old-established economic relations of dependence and exploitation may therefore also be disrupted. The intense competition suggests that there is a 'buyer's market', not only for microelectronic-based products, but also for the training needed to acquire and adapt the technology.

In terms of skill constraints, it may well be possible to utilise existing resources in universities and other institutions. The information and science-based skills needed to develop and apply microelectronic technology are often abundant, especially in the larger DCs. The transition to microelectronic technology may actually assist in overcoming skill bottlenecks in electromechanical engineering and allow the employment of people currently engaged in information activities outside the industrial sphere. In fact, a number of the larger DCs including Brazil and India have already established fairly sophisticated capabilities in such areas as software development, and in the application of computer-aided design (CAD).

Moreover, as Soete and Dosi (1983) show, microelectronic technology is not only labour saving but capital saving, and this could prove an advantage to DCs facing capital shortages. The employment issue certainly cannot be considered within a crude technological or microeconomic framework. If the move to microelectronic technology facilitates increased production and the development of local industry, then the overall employment-creating effect may well outweigh any tendency towards labour displacement. In addition, capital/labour ratios cannot be considered 'fixed' in relation to microelectronic technology. Within production based on the new technology there may well be flexibility in relation to capital/labour ratios and a tendency for increased employment in non-manufacturing service-related activities such as marketing and distribution. Certainly, it is not possible to deduce one way or the other the net employment effect without careful empirical research.

3.2 The Need for More Relevant Empirical Research

The preceding generalised, hypothetical, arguments are probably not very helpful for understanding the likely outcome of microelectronic change for individual DCs. The prospects and opportunities facing specific countries will vary considerably according to the economy in question, and the specific microelectronic sector, or application, being considered. So far most of the literature has failed to take sufficient account of the major differences between the DCs. Clearly, it is vital to differentiate systematically between the least developed economies with poorly developed technological and economic infrastructure, and at the other end of the scale the NICs and other larger DCs with well-developed indigenous capabilities - and all those groups in between. Equally important is the specific sector under examination. To date, there has been little attempt to account systematically for the unequal patterns and rates of diffusion across the various sectors experiencing microelectronic innovation.

If we turn to the actual empirical evidence the complexity of the changes occurring becomes immediately clear. There are two main areas of research which have a direct bearing on the position of individual DCs: first, studies of the patterns of diffusion in the advanced economies, and second, the impact of these changes on the developing nations.

The evidence shows that in the developed countries the rate of diffusion of microelectronic technology in manufacturing industry (upon which most of the pessimistic forecasts are based) has proceeded at a far slower rate than originally anticipated. Fully automated manufacturing systems (known as computer-integrated manufacturing - CIM), and even the adoption of robotics and CAD/CAM in the advanced countries, has gone ahead in a piecemeal and uneven manner. A growing number of empirical studies illustrate that for a range of processes and sectors the impact of semiconductor technology has yet to be fully realised.(3) Resistance to technological change, economic recession and constraints in terms of demand and capital have acted to slow down the potential rate of diffusion. These studies would suggest that, for the major industrial sectors, semiconductor diffusion is still probably in the slow pre-take-off phase and retarding factors are acting to restrain the widespread adoption of the technology.

Institutional and social barriers, as well as shortages of skilled personnel, are also acting to restrict the potential rate of diffusion of automation technology into manufacturing industry. As Freeman (1980) argues, the diffusion of radically new innovations is not simply a technological matter. There are many other crucial economic, social and political factors involved. In fact, a massive reallocation of production facilities to the north has not proceeded as expected (Leppan, 1983) and there may well be a 'breathing space' for DCs to formulate industrial policies to respond strategically to prevent any widening of the technology gap (Bessant, 1983; Perez, 1985).

The limited number of empirical studies directly concerned with the DCs also demonstrates the uneven patterns and rates of diffusion across sectors. The emerging evidence on the semiconductor component industry, the garment sector, the microcomputer industry, CAD and the capital goods and industrial machinery sectors(4) illustrates the wide range of different economic and technological effects, and testifies to the dangers of generalising.

As far as leapfrogging is concerned, the empirical evidence also cautions against generalisations and naive suggestions as to the possibilities of whole economies by-passing generations of technology. Pavitt (1984a), on the basis of data covering over 2000 UK firms, shows clearly that the diffusion of semiconductor technology is a complex, gradual process with the new technology building on the old. Pavitt presents the accumulation of microelectronic technology as a process of 'creative accumulation' which builds upon existing strengths in terms of organisation and skills. Casual observation of Japanese electronics firms also indicates that the successful corporations require a mastery of electromechanical technology to compete in the advanced IT markets. This does not necessarily mean that the successful firms will be drawn exclusively from those based on the previous technology, but that any new entrants will require at least a strategic base in the old technology as well as the new.

Pavitt's view also corroborates our earlier interpretation of the complex set of learning mechanisms involved in the diffusion process. The mechanisms and processes of learning are inherently cumulative, complex and, in most cases, costly. Rather than leapfrogging to a radical new technology, firms, industries, organisations, governments and ultimately whole countries tend to learn their way along the diffusion curve gradually. This interpretation, however, does not dismiss the notion of leapfrogging as completely unhelpful. In fact, as Section 3.3 below argues, the leapfrogging of technological <u>infrastructure</u> may well be possible. In addition, new firms may emerge, capable of acquiring strategically the necessary electromechanical support technologies to enable them to be competitive in the information-intensive technology markets. In this sense, new firms may leapfrog some of the stages of accumulation gone through by the older-established firms, and avoid many of the organisational and technological problems involved in the transition from electromechanical to microelectronic technology. What does not seem to be possible is a complete by-passing of the development of crucial supportive and complementary technologies rooted in various, 'established' technological paradigms.

A final but extremely important point to be made regarding the studies of microelectronic change and the Third World is the almost complete omission of any investigation of the actual IT and telecoms industries themselves. This is a most serious oversight. It is precisely in these industries where the widest and most rapid diffusion of microelectronic technology has already occurred - yet there exists almost no research from the point of view of DCs.(5) As the previous chapter showed, virtually all current production of telecoms equipment is now semiconductor based, and almost all computer and data processing technology has evolved directly from digital, microelectronic technology. In terms of the diffusion cycle, the IT industries are probably already substantially into the take-off stage. The evidence of rapid industrial growth and industrial dynamism shows that, in spite of economic recession, the advantages of microelectronic technology have overcome potential retarding factors and led to imitation and bandwagon effects throughout the industry.

With the general adoption of automated data-processing systems and digital telecoms in the advanced economies, IT is becoming crucial to more and more economic and social activities, ranging from manufacturing to government administration, communications, transport and commerce. For several years now, many DCs have been confronting decisions on the installation and use of digital computing facilities, and many DCs are now adopting microelectronic-based telecoms in the expansion of their networks. Nevertheless, research in the field of microelectronic change and the DCs has largely ignored the economic impact of the adoption of these technologies and focused instead on traditional industries where diffusion is at a much earlier stage. Consequently, a great deal of uncertainty surrounds the capacity of DCs to use the technology to their advantage and the potential for DCs to develop local technological and industrial capabilities to supply the growing home demand for these products and services. Given the paucity of research it is useful to look briefly at the role telecoms play as infrastructure for IT, and then to outline the general prospects for DCs wishing to use and manufacture modern telecoms equipment.

3.3 Telecommunications in the Transition to Microelectronic Technology

3.3.1 Telecommunications as a 'carrier' for information technology

In the advanced countries telecoms occupy a strategic position in the IT industries and in the overall accumulation of national capabilities in microelectronic technology. Without an efficient digital telecoms network many informatics and telematics activities simply cannot be considered. As Barron and Curnow (1979) argue, inadequate telecoms facilities represent the major obstacle to the transition to the so-called information society. In their assessment of the UK position they say:

> The major obstacle to the development of the information society will be the provision of adequate telecommunications capability....From a national point of view the greatest leverage might be obtained by an active programme of investment in advanced telecommunications systems. This would provide the infrastructure for an information society and would generate a positive market for the information technology industry in the UK (pp. 18, 20).

The aim of many countries to install ISDN, which effectively utilise public telecoms facilities to provide a wide range of digital switching and data transmission services, is critically dependent on a modern telecoms infrastructure. While it is possible to utilise traditional electromechanical facilities for transmitting information in digital form, there is little doubt that this places severe constraints on the capacity of networks to process, store and distribute information to users efficiently. From an economic perspective electromechanical systems are relatively costly to install, operate and maintain. From a technological perspective fully electronic systems have clear advantages in switching speed, reliability, transmission capacity and flexibility - especially when it comes to expanding, modifying and introducing new services.

In addition, as Chapter 2 showed, the telecoms equipment supply industry is increasingly becoming recognised as a 'leading edge' in the accumulation of broader IT capabilities. Successful telecoms companies are now developing and manufacturing other IT products such as semiconductor components, data processing and office automation equipment. As the range of technologies centred on IT continues to converge, several OECD governments are supporting their domestic supply industries in their efforts to diversify their production, design more advanced systems and compete in the rapidly growing international markets. Policy makers recognise the national long-term importance of maintaining a strong independent development and manufacturing base in telecoms technology.

For DCs, too, telecoms potentially represents a means of acquiring IT capabilities and keeping abreast of development in microelectronics. As noted earlier, DCs are currently embarking on large-scale investment programmes in telecoms infrastructure, amounting to an overall total of approximately $10b per annum. The MNCs are well aware of the massive market potential in the DCs. Many DCs are planning to install microelectronic systems in the future upgrading of their networks and, as in case of the Latin American region (discussed below), there does appear to be some potential to use these heavy sustained investments in infrastructure as an opportunity for selective import substitution and as a cutting edge in acquiring microelectronic technology. The exploitation of these opportunities will depend crucially on the absorptive capacity of the economy in question. Equally important, practical policy measures will be needed to organise investments in such a way as to ensure that local capabilities are developed and that developing nations do not simply become buyers and users of the technology.

Together with these concerns with IT, in a much more fundamental sense an efficient modern telecoms infrastructure represents a necessary condition for economic development. As Parker puts it:

> The communications technology of a society determines who can speak to whom, over what distances, and with what time delays, and with what possibilities for feedback or return communications. This is the heart of what is meant by social organisation.(6)

In historical terms telecoms can be viewed as the latest, most modern form of heavy economic infrastructure. Like other forms of transportation infrastructure, such as road, rail, sea and air travel, and energy infrastructure (electricity, nuclear power, water, oil and gas), telecoms are vital to economic growth, organisation and efficiency.

Among the economic functions telecoms perform is to reduce dramatically the cost of transmitting information by removing the need to physically transport information and often goods and people too. Also, as Leff (1980) points out, modern communications technology reduces the risk and uncertainty involved in production, investment, distribution and other economic activities; at the same time telecoms increase the amount and quality of market information, or signals, in the economy.

There now exists a huge body of literature on the subject of telecoms and economic development. Despite problems of measurement these studies convincingly demonstrate that telecoms are a necessary condition for modern economic development (although of course not a sufficient one).(7) Without a modern telecoms infrastructure, the kinds of economic organisation taken for granted in the developed countries, at the level of the firm, the market and government, simply would not be possible.

The historical significance of the shift to microelectronic-based technology is a dramatic improvement in the capacity, efficiency, speed and flexibility of communications infrastructure. Combined with lower equipment and operating system costs, this implies significant capital savings over the previous technological paradigm. In fact, the benefits of today's modern communications may prove to be similar to those recognised by Marx in the mid-nineteenth century. Describing advances in communications and transportation shortly after the invention of the telegraph, he wrote:

> The chief means of reducing the time of circulation [i.e. of capital] is improved communications. The last 50 years have brought about a revolution in this field comparable only with the industrial revolution of the latter half of the 18th century.... The period of turnover of total world commerce has been reduced to the same extent [i.e. 70 per cent to 90 per cent] and the efficacy of capital in it has been more than doubled or trebled. It goes without saying that this has not been without effect on the rate of profit. (Bracketed comments added.)(8)

It is for these reasons that DCs should identify and acquire the appropriate levels of industrial and technological capabilities to install, operate and expand their telecoms networks as efficiently as possible. If there are possibilities for local import substitution geared towards supplying the growing domestic demand for equipment and services, then this may prove to be one means of adding to local technological capabilities and helping to ensure that a new technology gap does not arise as a result of the diffusion of microelectronics.

3.3.2 Prospects for technological leapfrogging in telecommunications

Infrastructure
Most DCs are currently installing and expanding their basic telecoms infrastructure and this opens up the very real possibility of by-passing or leapfrogging previous vintages of technology. In fact, the generally accepted superiority of digital telecoms over analogue electromechanical systems means that countries currently installing and expanding their domestic networks have little choice but to leapfrog earlier vintages of technology. Certainly, there can be little argument for installing what is now considered to be an obsolete form of communications infrastructure.

The advantages of infrastructural leapfrogging in telecoms are clear. Fully digital systems are, in general, less costly, more efficient and more flexible than electromechanical systems. In the tropical and inhospitable climates and terrains facing many DCs, solid state technology is far more efficient and robust and requires much less maintenance than Crossbar and Strowger systems. The older electromechanical technologies have many moving parts, wires and physical connections, and need a high degree of insulation from the outside environment (called 'tropicalisation' in tropical countries). Tropicalisation can be very expensive and requires ongoing attention, rather like the painting of ships and suspension bridges. Microelectronic technology, on the other hand, requires little maintenance as there are no moving parts; modern telecoms are usually self-diagnostic, which means that if a breakdown occurs the problem is identified within the computer-controlled system and the repair usually involves the simple replacement of a circuit board.

Progress in semiconductor technology has led to a continued fall in real prices across the board in telecoms, and sustained improvements in overall cost/performance ratios. For example, where comparable, digital exchanges are now cheaper than electromechanical analogue exchanges (Saunders et al., 1983, p. 35). As Muller (1982) shows in detail, cost/performance ratios for digital products are continuously improving.(9) The intense international competition, particularly for Third World markets, has placed the DCs in a strong bargaining position, and they are probably able to buy the latest equipment at lower prices than telecoms administrations in the developed countries.(10) As discussed earlier, several of the leading corporations are justifying heavy R&D investments on the basis of uncommitted DC export markets. In digital exchange systems, for example, there are currently 16 major systems, developed at a cost of over $6b, competing for relatively small open export markets. The OECD (1982) suggests that, owing to the degree of competition and market saturation, it is probable that several of these systems will not yield a positive return on investment. These conditions mean that, in terms of cost/performance and price, DCs stand to make considerable capital savings as a result of the new technology.

To give some idea as to the extent of overall cost savings, Jequier (1977) estimated that DCs installing, say, one million telephone lines, typically pay three to five times less than the developed countries did 30 to 40 years ago. Since 1977, prices have continued to fall in real terms and the advantages of the 'economics of lateness', as Jequier calls it, have continued to improve.

The advantages of technological leapfrogging are not only restricted to capital savings. In fact, in the long-term transition to IT the DCs may have an advantage over the now industrialised economies. The developed countries are heavily committed in terms of investment to previous technologies, mainly Strowger and Crossbar. In the UK for example, until recently, the most widely used exchange technology was Strowger, the most recent exchange of this type having been installed in 1985 (bearing in mind Strowger was invented in 1889!). While it is technically possible to transmit digital information through electromechanical systems, it places severe limitations on the quality, flexibility and capacity of the network, as well as imposing far higher operating costs. To make the transition to fully digital IT infrastructure, the advanced economies are faced with a serious economics of scrapping problem or with finding piecemeal ways of patching in new digital services as and when demand is perceived to be sufficiently high. The opportunity for leapfrogging inferior and obsolete technologies, and moving directly to IT infrastructure, therefore presents itself to the DCs but not generally to the developed countries.

Thus, as far as the purchasing of telecoms equipment is concerned, and the installation of an efficient communications infrastructure, microelectronic technology offers substantial, if potential, advantages. However, in terms of local manufacture and local technological accumulation, the position is far less clear.

Industrial and technological leapfrogging
As argued above, the possibilities of whole economies leapfrogging vintages of technology are remote, to say the least. Nevertheless, because of the present competitive environment in this particular sector, and because of the divisibility of microelectronic technology, the shift to digital systems may have opened up new opportunities for both local manufacture and domestic technological accumulation.(11) However, this issue is certainly not straightforward and there remains considerable doubt as to the feasibility of, especially smaller, DCs entering production. As a prelude to the Brazilian investigation, it is useful here to present briefly the main economic and technological barriers to entry and counterpose these barriers against new opportunities for market entry in telecoms. Regardless of the impact of technological change, an overriding factor will be the absorptive capacity of the specific economy in question, and this issue is also briefly discussed below.

The most significant barrier to entry in modern telecoms lies in the exchange sub-sector. The massive R&D investment cost required to develop new systems can exceed $1b for large public exchanges.(12) In public exchange technology the huge R&D thresholds have so far acted to prevent entry from other closely related IT industries, and there appears little prospect of even the largest computer manufacturers entering the market in the near future (Roobeek, 1984). Coupled with these financial barriers there exist very substantial technological barriers to entry. The enormously complex telecoms-specific software involved in the design of exchange technology has proved a major difficulty even for experienced telecoms manufacturers.

At first sight, these daunting entry barriers would indicate poor prospects for DCs wishing to manufacture and develop systems. However, this may not necessarily be the case for three main reasons. First, the intensifying international competition, and the desire of the MNCs to gain Third World markets, has already placed some DCs in a strong bargaining position in relation to the corporations. When sales are linked to setting up manufacturing and technological facilities in the recipient country, the bidding for orders is even more intense than with straightforward equipment sales, as the stakes are that much higher. The competition for a recent major Indian contract testifies to this. Ten major suppliers competed for the contract, and eventually the well-established French system won the order. In order to win the order the French government was obliged to step in and offer an 'aid for trade', cheap loan arrangement, together with full technological training by French scientists. A similar situation appears to be emerging with the Chinese plans to upgrade and expand the telecoms network of the industrial Yangtze Delta region. In Malaysia, too, the major MNCs are showing willingness to transfer technology, engage in joint ventures and produce locally in order to remain in the competition for the local market.(13) At present, at least, there appears to be a buyer's market for digital exchange technology, which is leading the MNCs to compete with each other by transferring manufacturing facilities and cooperating in domestic development plans.

A second reason for optimism relates to the divisibility of modern telecoms systems. Among the effects of this greater degree of technological divisibility over electromechanical systems is a trend towards smaller-scale private exchanges (PABXs), and the opportunity for smaller-scale public exchanges suitable for low density urban and rural use. In recent years the PABX market has witnessed extremely rapid growth. In this area the software is far less complex and many new firms have entered the market. For example, in the USA in 1961 there were only four PABX manufacturers; by 1980 there were more than 30, and in terms of sophisticated terminal equipment overall there were over 1000 approved local manufacturers (OECD, 1983). The growth of small-scale private systems may have opened up an opportunity for market entry not present under electromechanical technology. This trend potentially applies to public exchanges, too. In the DCs there is growing demand for smaller-scale public exchanges suitable for rural use and for use in smaller townships. Although complex, the design of these types of systems is a far less daunting task than attempting to design central public exchanges.

A third potential benefit from the move to semiconductor technology is the modular nature of the design process. The modularity of software design in digital telecoms means that it is now possible to develop capabilities in exchange technology gradually. The shift away from centralised design prevalent in electromechanical and early electronic exchanges allows for the possibility of developing a small-scale exchange suitable, say, for rural use, and then building upon the same system, gradually increasing its capacity and slowly moving up the scale of technological complexity towards larger systems. The central importance of switching technology means that in spite of the technological barriers to entry, for DCs with large internal markets, it is desirable to attempt to gain capabilities. Most systems are designed in the developed countries for use in the developed countries. Consequently, these systems have to be modified to suit the telephone traffic conditions of DCs. In order to install and operate a telecoms network efficiently a certain level of knowhow is demanded. One possible route to acquiring this knowhow, and indeed to designing systems better suited to local conditions, is to engage in the development of small exchanges for rural use. The design modularity enables the continuous evolution and improvement of a small exchange and the graduation towards more complex, larger-scale exchanges. This is, in fact, the Brazilian strategy. Brazil has produced a small-scale rural exchange of 1000 lines, and intends soon to follow this with a 4000-line system (see Chapter 5).

Of course, this is not to suggest competing with the MNCs in state-of-the-art technology, but rather to engage in a long-term strategy of selective R&D investment which complements the current importation of foreign technology and equipment. This type of strategic investment may have the advantage of gaining a foothold in digital telecoms and facilitate the adaptation of foreign technology to suit local conditions. An improved local understanding of the technology can assist in bargaining with the MNCs for greater levels of technology transfer and help in unpacking the imported technology. In addition, this type of pragmatic approach to foreign (and local) technology may help avoid any delays and setbacks in the important task of expanding the local telecoms infrastructure.

Despite the substantial barriers to entry in exchange technology, there may well be 'points of entry' as a result of the diffusion of semiconductor technology. Potential for exploitation of any technological opportunities will depend very much on the size of the domestic market and the level of scientific and technological infrastructure, as well as coordinated policy towards foreign and domestic technology.

While discussions of telecoms tend to focus on exchange technology, the non-exchange sector now constitutes around 68 per cent of the total market for telecoms (see Chapter 2, Table 2.1). In most areas of transmission and peripheral technology the barriers to entry are far less formidable than in the exchange market. In the transmission sub-sector the familiar pattern of increased competition within the industry has developed as a direct result of semiconductor technology. However, the much lower degree of technological complexity and lower financial barriers to entry have given rise to many new entrants, principally from the technologically convergent areas of radio and aerospace manufacturing. The traditional dominance of the coaxial cable manufacturers has given way to microwave system producers, and new microelectronic-based satellite and fibre optic systems are increasingly being adopted.

In the peripheral sub-sector the barriers to entry are generally the lowest in digital telecoms. Semiconductor technology has led to a far larger market and in spite of economic recession new products are registering record sales. In the industrial countries many new firms have entered this sector as a result of industrial convergence based on microelectronic technology. Consequently, it is in the peripheral area where the greatest technological opportunities present themselves to the DCs.

In terms of manufacture, the relatively low barriers to entry indicate that there may well be opportunities for DCs, especially the larger economies, to develop transmission and peripheral products locally. For example, in the areas of pulse code modulation (PCM) and time division multiplexing (TDM) transmission, fibre optics and satellite ground stations, there may be points of entry for the larger DCs. In peripheral equipment there may be opportunities for local entry in many important areas such as intelligent terminals, mobile radio, key systems, visual display units, modems, codec equipment and so on. Ultimately though, the opportunities will depend very much on the domestic DC context.

To sum up, in the absence of detailed empirical research it is only possible to hypothesise over the general prospects for DCs to leapfrog industrially and technologically to digital telecoms. The limited evidence examined here does suggest at least a potential for industrial leapfrogging to occur. The transition to microelectronics has 'destabilised' the traditional economic relations between the developed and developing countries. DCs appear to be in a stronger bargaining position in relation to the MNCs as a direct result of the increasing competition. This factor is already encouraging some of the larger DCs to insist that manufacturing and technological facilities are transferred to their own economies. Furthermore, the modular, divisible nature of the technology may have opened up new opportunities for entry by domestic firms. In all three telecoms sub-sectors – exchange, transmission, and peripheral equipment – there does appear to be more scope for local manufacture and gradual technological accumulation. Before examining these hypotheses in the context of Brazil, it is necessary to draw attention to the importance of the absorptive capacity of the economy in question.

The absorptive capacity of the specific developing country

Any assessment of opportunities for market entry in telecoms must take into account the prevailing economic and technological conditions of the DC in question. The size and technological infrastructure of the particular economy will to a large extent determine the bargaining position of the DC in relation to the multinational suppliers. Again, the evidence related to this question is very sparse. Nevertheless, it is useful to review the evidence which does exist as a background to the Brazilian study.

Whether or not a DC should install manufacturing (as distinct from technological) facilities depends largely on domestic market size. On this issue Jequier (1977) provides a 'rule of thumb' for choosing between local manufacture and importation.(14) Defining telecoms demand in terms of lines, which includes all the equipment associated with each line, and assuming an annual average growth rate of 8 per cent over the next 10 to 15 years – then for a DC with less than 100,000 installed lines at present, it is probably not economically viable to establish any local production facilities at all. The very small annual average demand of approximately 10,000 new lines means that the most cost-effective solution is to import all the equipment needed. Investment in local production would push the cost per line far above international market prices. Pursuing this logic, a DC with around 200,000 lines could justify some domestic production of peripheral and perhaps transmission equipment. All DCs with relatively large internal markets such as China, Brazil, India and Mexico have sufficient annual demand to warrant a complete manufacturing facility to service the indigenous market.

Unfortunately, this procedure gives little indication as to the appropriate degree of <u>technological</u> capacity needed to guarantee successful and <u>dynamic</u> industrial growth. However, the learning studies mentioned earlier strongly suggest that for DCs with large local markets there are sound economic reasons to develop their own capabilities to manufacture, install, operate and modify technology in telecoms as in other areas. Whether or not a country has the absorptive capacity to achieve this depends on the prevailing level of scientific and technological infrastructure, and the availability of local skills and knowhow. This is often, but not always, related to the size of the market. It is therefore necessary to distinguish between countries with well-developed technological infrastructure and experience in acquiring and assimilating new technologies, and those with relatively underdeveloped capabilities. As we see below, Brazil is an example of a large DC with a well-developed technological infrastructure and therefore has a large absorptive capacity.

Other smaller countries probably require some level of technological capacity, even though they may not justify any manufacturing capacity. This is because some strategic minimum technological capability is needed simply to identify, choose, purchase and operate a network efficiently. Regardless of economic size, DCs could benefit from at least the minimum management and software skills and knowhow to maintain and expand their local infrastructure, both to gain the benefits of efficient communications and to avoid the costs of excessive technological reliance on foreign suppliers. These costs potentially involve foreign exchange payments, delays, and mistakes in planning, purchasing, operation and so on. If we turn to Latin America the wide diversity between the individual countries of the region immediately becomes clear.

3.4 The Latin American Telecommunications Market - Current Demand and Possibilities for Local Industrial Development

Potentially, the shift to semiconductor technology has introduced new opportunities for import substitution and local technological progress. Three features of the Latin American market tend to support this view: first, the large overall size of the market; second, the general trend towards fully digital technology; third, the centralisation of telecoms purchasing and planning under direct government control. From the evidence discussed below there appears to be considerable potential for leapfrogging earlier forms of communications infrastructure and moving directly to microelectronic-based technology. Within the region, Brazil is a particularly interesting case to study. Brazil's extremely large internal market and relatively well-developed economic and technological infrastructure suggests that there exists sufficient absorptive capacity to exploit fully any technological opportunities presented by the diffusion of microelectronics in telecoms.

3.4.1 Dimensions and growth of the Latin American market

Table 3.1 presents selected telecoms and economic data for the major countries of the Latin American region. As can be seen, country variations in terms of population and economic size are reflected in existing levels of infrastructure. Although these data are now somewhat out of date, they clearly illustrate the wide variety in installed infrastructure across countries. Brazil, Mexico and Argentina are the top end of the scale with several millions of telephone lines, and countries such as Bolivia and Ecuador are at the lower end with installations in the hundreds of thousands.

Gross national product (GNP) per capita broadly corresponds to telephone density, reflecting the well-established correlation between telecoms and economic development indicators (Saunders et al., 1983, Chapter 4). Countries with relatively high per capita incomes such as Venezuela, Argentina and Costa Rica also register high telephone densities. Conversely, poorer countries such as Bolivia, Peru and Ecuador register both low incomes per capita and low telephone densities.

As a result of the poor overall condition of much of the existing infrastructure in many of the countries of Latin America, systems are often subject to overloading at peak periods, and there is a general problem of unreliability and technical incompatibility across countries. Furthermore, in most countries there is a large unmet demand for telephones. These problems have led most of the countries of the region to establish government control over the operating companies which supply the services. By centralising the telecoms administration under one government entity it is possible to plan a coordinated expansion of existing networks, and to introduce new technology systematically.

Table 3.1: Selected Telecommunications and Economic Indicators - Latin America circa 1980

Country	Total Telephone Lines (thousands)	Total Telex Subscribers	Telephone Density Per 100 Population	Total Population (millions)	GNP per Capita Income ($1979)
Argentina	1850	5000	10.3	27.0	2210
Bolivia	127	330	2.6	5.0	550
Brazil	4000	28000	6.3	115.0	1770
Chile	380	2000	5.0	11.0	1890
Colombia	1250	3400	6.0	30.0	1060
Costa Rica	112	800	10.4	2.3	1630
Dominican Rep	110	900	n/a	6.0	n/a
Ecuador	220	1500	3.2	8.3	1110
Mexico	2520	8700	7.5	70.0	1880
Peru	232	2000	2.8	17.7	850
Venezuela	750	8000	8.6	14.1	3440
Sub-totals	11550	60600			
Other (17 countries)	1280	8200			
Totals	12830	68800			

Sources: Arthur D. Little (1983), Saunders et al. (1983).

Technological Leapfrogging

Indeed, this centralised feature of telecoms administration is a peculiar feature of telecoms and does not apply to other areas of IT, where purchasing is distributed across industry, government and mass market sectors. In most DCs, as with developed countries, telecoms purchasing is centralised under government-owned or government-controlled administrations. This places a centralised monopsony purchasing power in the hands of government in all except for the very smallest markets. Already this feature of telecoms has enabled the larger Latin American countries such as Brazil, Mexico and Argentina to bargain effectively with the MNCs for some degree of local manufacture and technology transfer.(15)

To understand the scope for local production overall it is helpful to examine the current and forecast equipment markets by value across the region. As in the case of the international market data, the most widely accepted and authoritative telecoms estimates for the Latin American region are from Arthur D. Little (1983). As Table 3.2 demonstrates, total telecoms demand is estimated to have grown from $1.2b in 1980 to $1.8b in 1985; by 1990 total telecoms demand is expected to reach $2.4b. This represents a doubling of the market over the 1980s. It should be noted that Arthur D. Little's estimates are based on domestic plans for telecoms expansion, and these may well be affected by balance of payments constraints, accelerating inflation and other economic difficulties. Nevertheless, the data provide a useful means for understanding Brazil's position in relation to the other countries of the region.

Overall, the current market size represents around 3 per cent of the total world market. Although 3 per cent appears very small, in some respects Latin America represents an extremely important share of the world market. In terms of digital public switching, for example, as Chapter 5 noted, Latin America accounts for 16.3 per cent of sales worldwide; this compares with, say, 27.3 per cent for Europe and 28 per cent for the USA. Third World markets are extremely important to the major MNC suppliers and Latin America represents a major and increasing share of these sales. Equipment sales for the region are more than three times the total for Africa, and one and a half times that for Oceania, and far larger than that for less-developed Asia. Regional plans for installing digital technology increase the importance of the Latin American market, and corporate competition within the region is expected to be very intense throughout the 1980s.

Table 3.2: Telecommunications Equipment Markets in the Latin American Region (millions of dollars)*

	1980	1985	1990	Annual Average Growth (%) 1980-85	1986-90
A) Total Market					
Argentina	116.0	162.3	226.1	6.9	7.0
Bolivia	11.0	15.5	22.2	7.7	7.0
Brazil	474.6	713.3	868.3	8.5	4.0
Chile	25.9	42.1	61.4	10.2	8.0
Colombia	68.4	105.2	147.5	9.0	7.0
Costa Rica	18.2	24.1	29.4	5.8	4.0
Dominican Rep	6.5	9.3	13.7	7.4	8.0
Ecuador	11.2	17.4	24.5	9.2	7.0
Mexico	175.6	285.5	430.9	10.2	9.0
Peru	21.5	41.0	81.5	13.8	15.0
Venezuela	97.1	188.1	248.3	14.1	6.0
Other Countries	146.7	200.5	236.9	6.5	3.0
Grand Total	1172.7	1804.3	2390.7	9.0	6.0
B) System Market					
Telephone	978.0	1524.1	2010.4	9.3	6.0
Telex, Telegraph and Data	104.9	144.3	186.4	6.6	5.0
Satellite Comms.	14.2	14.6	34.0	0.6	18.0
Mobile Radio	70.4	111.9	145.3	9.7	5.0
Radio Paging	3.5	6.8	10.6	14.2	9.0
Cable TV	1.7	2.6	4.0	8.9	9.0
Grand Total	1172.7	1804.3	2390.7	9.0	6.0

* Constant 1979 dollars.

Source: Arthur D. Little (1983).

The rapid growth of 9 per cent per annum over the period 1980-1985 is expected to fall off to around 6 per cent per annum in the period 1985-1990. The estimated fall off in growth is due partly to assumptions regarding the Brazilian market, which represents around 40 per cent of the overall total, and partly to the fact that the starting base is that much higher. The five largest markets - Brazil, Mexico, Argentina, Colombia and Venezuela - represent around 80 per cent of total sales. The top eleven countries listed in the tables constitute about 90 per cent of the region's installed infrastructure.

Technological Leapfrogging

Part B of Table 3.2 gives a breakdown of equipment sales within the telecoms sector. As in other regions the telephone market overwhelmingly dominates, accounting for roughly 83 per cent of total demand. Within the telephone market the shares between switching, transmission and peripheral equipment are not significantly different from international shares as described earlier. In keeping with international trends the PABX market is expected to continue to grow rapidly. The balance of the market is largely accounted for by telegraph, telex, data transmission, mobile radio and radio telephone equipment.

3.4.2 Technological trends within the region

Although the pace of technological change is very uneven between countries, there is a general move towards fully digital, semiconductor-based switching technology. Recognition of the clear superiority of microelectronic over previous systems has led most countries to establish plans to expand networks using the latest technology. Brazil, Mexico, Argentina, Colombia and Peru, for example, have all begun the process of planning and contracting for digital systems.(16) Some of the smaller countries of the region (in terms of telecoms market size), including Ecuador and Bolivia, are proceeding much more slowly towards microelectronic exchanges.

As far as transmission equipment is concerned, there are general plans for the upgrading of old paper-insulated underground cables and the diffusion of digital PCM and TDM systems. In terms of microwave transmission there is a slow move towards digitally modulated systems, and more digital satellite transmission will be adopted throughout the 1980s and 1990s. In the PABX and peripheral markets new demand is generally for microelectronic technology because of its economic and technological superiority, and there is a growing demand for new applications including mobile radio, key systems and modems. Most of the larger economies are also expanding digital data transmission and telex facilities.

Brazil in many respects is very much a special case in Latin America. The relatively large size of the Brazilian economy and well-developed technological infrastructure is reflected in the demand for telecoms equipment. As Table 3.2 shows, Brazil's total equipment market rose from roughly $474m in 1980 to $713m in 1985, and is forecast to rise to over $850m by 1990. Brazil's domestic market is therefore greater than 2.5 times the size of its nearest rival (Mexico), and many times larger than the other nations of the region. Over the period 1981-1983 total investments in Brazil's telecoms network averaged more than $1b per annum, which means that the Brazilian investments constitute around 12.5 per cent of total DC investments in telecoms.(17) The Brazilian market is therefore very large by any international standards, and the well-developed technological base would suggest that, potentially at least, there exists a prime opportunity for acquisition of microelectronic technology in telecoms. Brazil's expressed wish to develop an independent local base in digital technology makes the country's experience especially relevant to other large DCs such as India and China, who have expressed similar desires to establish local capabilities in telecoms.

3.4.3 Multinational corporation competition in the Latin American market

In Latin America, as indeed throughout the Third World, four major telecoms corporations have traditionally shared the international markets. The four MNCs - ITT, L.M. Ericsson of Sweden, Siemens of West Germany and, since the 1960s, NEC of Japan - either export products directly, or service local markets through manufacturing subsidiaries. Table 3.3 provides details of the major suppliers, by country, in rough order of importance for the switching equipment market. With the shift to microelectronic technology, Japanese firms such as NEC are challenging the dominant position of the other MNCs. The established US and European suppliers are also facing serious competition from Japan in the transmission and peripheral equipment markets. Increasing competition is also being encouraged by the governments of the larger countries of the region. The centralised telecoms administrations are using their monopsony power to insist on certain rules regarding the location of production and technological facilities within national boundaries. The intensity of competition for local markets means that in some cases the suppliers are obliged to comply with government ruling in order to gain new orders and remain in the market. This is most clear in the cases of Mexico and Brazil, but there may also be scope for some of the smaller countries of the region to bargain with the MNCs for a greater transfer of technological and manufacturing facilities.(18)

Table 3.3: Multinational Corporation Suppliers of Telephone Exchange Equipment in Latin America

Country	Principal Suppliers in Approximate Order of Importance
Brazil*	Ericsson, NEC, Seimens, ITT
Mexico	ITT, Ericsson
Argentina	ITT, Siemens, Ericsson, NEC
Colombia	Ericsson, ITT, Siemens
Venezuela	Ericsson, ITT, Hitachi
Chile	ITT, NEC
Peru	ITT, Philips
Ecuador	Ericsson
Bolivia	Oki, Ericsson
Costa Rica	Ericsson, ITT, GTE
Dominican Rep	GTE

*Information amended.

Source: Arthur D. Little (1983).

Conclusion

Potentially there are important new opportunities for DCs as a result of the diffusion of microelectronics in telecoms. Contrary to most current research in the area of microelectronics and the Third World, there appears to be good reason for optimism at the level of infrastructure and, more controversially, at the level of manufacturing and technological development. At least four factors indicate that indigenous technological progress might not be so daunting a task as authors in the field have suggested. First, with the shift to microelectronics, the degree of international competition has increased substantially, and there now exists a 'buyer's market' for equipment and technology. Second, the centralisation of purchasing under telecoms administrations places a monopsony power in the hands of government, especially in the larger countries, and this may facilitate more effective bargaining with the MNCs, both for technology transfer and for general cooperation with local aims towards technological progress. Third, the greater divisibility of microelectronic (over electromechanical) technology has introduced new 'niche' markets with relatively low barriers to entry. Fourth, the modularity of design in modern digital systems allows a gradual process of capability accumulation, beginning with small systems and gradually moving up the scale of technological complexity.

Considered together, these factors suggest that there may be new technological opportunities opening up as a result of the transition to microelectronics. While the possibilities of widespread leapfrogging appear remote, on the basis of the limited empirical evidence available there appears to be scope for (a) infrastructural leapfrogging and (b) gradual and selective entry into the manufacture and technological development of modern microelectronic systems. The advantages to be gained from by-passing electromechanical technology include substantial capital savings and the acquisition of a communications infrastructure which has proven advantages over the previous technology in terms of speed, flexibility, and efficiency and durability. Given purposive government policies and a sufficiently large absorptive capacity, DCs may well benefit considerably from the shift to microelectronic technology.

Evidence from Latin America suggested that there is scope for local manufacturing and technological development in telecoms. However, it was only possible to examine superficially the Latin American region and clearly each country must be examined on its own merits, taking into account the local market size and absorptive capacity of each economy. Within the region, Brazil stood out as a prime subject for detailed research, boasting a very large internal market and a relatively well-developed technological and economic infrastructure. What follows is a detailed account of Brazil's historical efforts to build a modern telecoms infrastructure and to establish a strong local industrial base in digital telecoms.

Notes

1. The views of Rada and Kaplinsky are mirrored by writers in the field of communications and the DCs such as Cruise O'Brien and Helleiner (1980).

2. Notably Kaplinsky (1982, 1984), but also see, in the communications literature, Mitchell (1978, 1978a) and Clippinger (1977, 1977a).

3. See, for example, Bessant (1983), Hoffman and Rush (1985), Edquist and Jacobsson (1984), Jacobsson and Ljung (1983) and Rempp (1981). Perez and Freeman (1986) give a valuable guide to the varied rates and patterns of diffusion across sectors.

4. See Braun (1982), Hoffman and Rush (1985), Tigre (1982), Kaplinsky (1982) and UNCTAD (1982) respectively.
5. For a rare exception see O'Connor (1985).
6. Quoted by Hardy (1980, p. 280).
7. For a review see Hudson et al. (1981). Wellenius (1977) provides a useful summary article on the subject.
8. From Capital, Vol. 3, cited by Rosenberg (1982, p. 46).
9. Chapter 2 drew attention to some of the more remarkable cost reductions in digital transmission and fibre optic technology.
10. Although it is extremely difficult to support this argument with empirical evidence, it is well known that service providers (PTTs) in the developed countries are frequently obliged, contractually, to support domestic equipment suppliers financially in terms of R&D and also to guarantee output prices to domestic producers.
11. The reasons why a country might wish to maximise local manufacturing and technological development are not dealt with here in detail, but follow logically from the discussion on the benefits of learning and technological advance analysed earlier. These benefits include increasing local value added through domestic production, and increasing domestic revenues and profits for local firms. Important external benefits include increased employment, rising numbers of local firms and contributions to balance of payments. In addition, the telecoms sector might represent a means for gaining a 'foothold' in this important area of IT and could play a role in establishing linkages between the telecoms and other important areas of IT. The specific reasons why a DC might wish to engage in local manufacture of telecoms equipment are discussed in International Telecommunications Union (1984). The general importance of Third World participation in manufacturing and technology is discussed fully in Fransman and King (1984).
12. See Chapter 2, Table 2.2, for details of R&D expenditures by the leading MNCs on the various exchange systems.
13. For a report on the Malaysian efforts to bargain with the MNCs, see Business Times Malaysia (17 May 1985). India's position is described in Electronics Times (20 May 1982), and the Chinese investment programme is reported in the Financial Times (4 March 1985).
14. Although the criteria used by Jequier are somewhat out of date and are very sensitive to assumptions regarding growth rates and costs per line, they nevertheless illustrate the principle involved.
15. The evidence used here is from Arthur D. Little (1983) unless otherwise stated.
16. See, for instance, Tigre (1983), and below for the Brazilian case.

17. Brazil's investments are presented in detail below. The Brazilian percentage of total DC investment is based upon the International Telecommunication Union's (1984) estimate of total DC investment for 1983 of $8b.

18. For evidence of Mexico's efforts to develop and manufacture telecoms equipment, see Galli (1982) and Tigre (1983). A review of the evidence for the individual countries of the Latin American region and the prospects for import substitution is provided by Hobday (1985).

CHAPTER 4

THE EXPANSION OF BRAZIL'S NEW COMMUNICATIONS INFRASTRUCTURE

Introduction

The purpose of this chapter is twofold. First, it gives a brief historical account of the progress of Brazil's telecoms industry before the diffusion of microelectronic technology and before the concerted policy initiative of the mid-1970s. This is necessary to provide a benchmark from which subsequent technological and industrial developments can be judged. Second, it provides an assessment of Brazil's success in leapfrogging earlier forms of technology and moving directly to a digital IT infrastructure.

Section 4.1 looks at the origins of the industry and describes the state of the telecoms network up to the so-called 'economic miracle' period of 1967-1973. Section 4.2 discusses the following period of rapid industrial development on the basis of direct foreign investment by the major MNCs operating within Brazil. Finally, Sections 4.3-4.5 evaluate Brazil's infrastructural developments in telecoms over the decade 1974-1984. In the course of the analysis, Brazil's failure to distribute the benefits of the new investments is also recognised and highlighted.

4.1 The Origins of Brazil's Telecommunications Industry

During the 1920s, before Brazil had any telecoms manufacturing facilities, the main supplier of equipment and services was the Companhia Telephonia Brasileira (CTB), a wholly Canadian-owned subsidiary of Canadian Traction Light and Power Company.(1) CTB imported the equipment needed to supply the network, mainly Crossbar exchanges and associated transmission and peripheral equipment, under government licence. The MNC suppliers of this equipment at this time were

Chicago Electric, Standard Electric (an ITT subsidiary) and L.M. Ericsson, the major Swedish telecoms corporation.

The first real attempt to establish a manufacturing capacity began in 1952 when the Vargas government decided to reduce expenditure on foreign telecoms imports and persuade the MNCs to locate manufacturing facilities in Brazil. The government restricted CTB's import quotas and insisted on local manufacture of equipment and the use of local inputs wherever feasible. To comply with the new government regulations L.M. Ericsson immediately set up a manufacturing subsidiary to produce the simplest of telecoms technology - telephone handsets. By this time the German electrical corporation, Siemens, had entered the market and L.M. Ericsson was keen to ensure that market shares were not lost either to Siemens or the other main competitor, ITT. L.M. Ericsson invested roughly $1m in a manufacturing plant in São Paulo with a capacity of 300,000 handsets per annum. ITT's subsidiary, Standard Electric, also set up a factory in Rio de Janeiro with a capacity of approximately 100,000 units per year.

Even in these early stages the government employed its monopsony purchasing power to ensure that manufacturing facilities were located within national boundaries and to encourage competition among the MNCs. By 1957 L.M. Ericsson had begun to manufacture more complex equipment including Crossbar switching systems. In the early 1960s L.M. Ericsson expanded and modernised its plant in São Paulo to supply the growing market for equipment and to stave off competition from ITT and Siemens. However, it is important to point out that core elements of the technology remained squarely in the hands of the MNC headquarters abroad. The local factories were mainly concerned with assembling equipment and had little autonomous technological capacity. At this stage the government was simply attempting to regulate imports and played no active role in ensuring any transfer of technology.

As far as telecoms infrastructure was concerned, Brazil entered the 1960s with a wholly inadequate, poorly organised and fragmented network. The Canadian company CTB privately operated approximately 68 per cent of installed telephones, and no less than 800 small private firms were responsible for the balance. No overall authority was responsible for providing inter-state transmission networks, and most of the small firms were severely lacking in technical, managerial and financial resources. Consequently, investments were unplanned and sporadic, and tariffs differed widely for similar service in different regions (SSI, 1982).

The disorganised state of the telecoms service companies was reflected in the inefficiency and inadequacy of the network coverage. For example, in 1962 there were less than 1.3 million telephones servicing a total population of 74 million - i.e. less than two telephones per 100 population. Also there were less than 1000 telex terminals covering the whole of Brazil's industrial and domestic needs. This poor telecoms coverage was compounded by an inadequate local transmission network, which only efficiently connected up four of the major cities - Rio de Janeiro, São Paulo, Bela Horizonte and Brasilia. When other cities were interconnected they depended on low-capacity, inefficient systems. Similarly, international linkages were wholly inadequate and based on a small number of submarine coaxial cables and some short-wave radio facilities. Given this state of affairs it is hardly surprising that the network was unable to cope with peak period demand because of congestion and frequent system failures.

4.2 Post-1964 Reorganisation and Rapid Industrial Development

4.2.1 Service sector administration and finance

Following the coup of 1964 the new military government made it clear that it looked favourably on direct foreign investment. The government accelerated the reorganisation of the telecoms network and introduced new legislation to coordinate the upgrading and expansion of the infrastructure. The planned expansion of the network and the open-door policy towards foreign capital encouraged an unregulated expansion of MNC activities, especially during the economic boom period 1967-1973. Before examining the activities of the MNCs it is helpful to show how the telecoms administration evolved to cope with the new telecoms objectives.

In September 1965 a new authority, EMBRATEL, was established with responsibility for planning and operating all domestic and international long-distance communications. Soon afterwards (1967) the existing telecoms council, CONTEL, was replaced with a more powerful Ministry of Communications (MINICOM) with jurisdiction over all telecoms planning and development. One of the first acts of the ministry was to nationalise CTB by acquiring all their equity.(2) MINICOM's mandate was to prepare for a rapid and thoroughgoing expansion of Brazil's telecoms network to meet the demands of the growing economy. Figure 4.1 presents a recent organisation chart of MINICOM, and illustrates the range of responsibilities now carried out. A major new holding company, Telecomunicacoes Brasileira S.A. (TELEBRAS), was established with responsibility for coordinating all Brazilian telecoms. Following the nationalisation of CTB, TELEBRAS set up 25 regional telecoms companies, one for each state, to establish comprehensive and interconnected telecoms services throughout Brazil. TELEBRAS was also given responsibility for all long-distance communications under EMBRATEL. As Figure 4.1 shows, MINICOM also has ministerial control of the Brazilian postal and radio services.

In order to finance the growth of telecoms services MINICOM set up a novel self-capitalising scheme whereby potential customers were obliged to 'subscribe' to the telephone company (Pelton, 1981, p. 218). At the start of the programme in 1964 the number of subscribers far exceeded the network capacity; this proved to be an asset, not only for raising capital but for registering actual demand for planning purposes. A second major source of finance was from EMBRATEL who transferred approximately 80 per cent of their international telecoms profits to a central fund (the Brazilian National Telecoms Fund). TELEBRAS also received funds from surtax on domestic services, and it was from these internal sources that investments in the network began.

4.2.2 Multinational corporation investments in manufacturing

In contrast with developments in the service sector, the telecoms equipment sector showed no such signs of planning, coordination and control. On the contrary, manufacturing expansion followed the overall industrial pattern of rapid, unchecked growth over the 'boom' period 1967-1973. After an initial period of slow growth from 1964 to 1966, a phase of rapid expansion based on MNC investment took place. The subsidiary of L.M. Ericsson, Ericsson do Brasil (EDB), and the other MNCs began to expand their manufacturing capacity rapidly to meet the increased demand for telecoms equipment.

Evidence of the MNC operations for this period is sparse. However, the case of the leading manufacturer EDB illustrates some of the important corporate activities of the period.(3) To supply the demand for telecoms equipment EDB expanded both horizontally and vertically. The capacity of their main plant in São Paulo was doubled by 1968 and two

Brazil's New Communications Infrastructure

Figure 4.1: Organisational Chart of the Brazilian Ministry of Communications, 1982

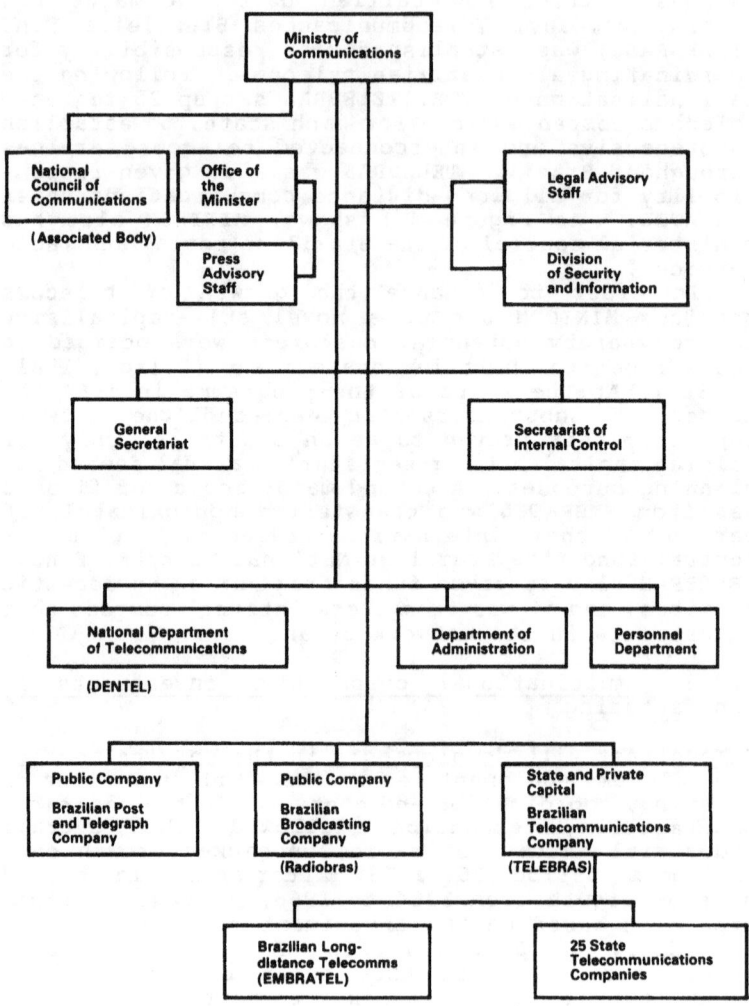

Source: SSI (1982)

further assembly plants were built in the states of Minas Gerais and Rio Grande do Sul. As in the previous period the main technology produced was electromechanical Crossbar equipment. Vertical expansion also took place to ensure local supplies of inputs and network installation capabilities. A components fabrication plant, Telecomponentes S.A., wholly owned by EDB, was set up near the existing São Paulo factory. Two further plants were developed, the first a transmission cable manufacturer, Ficap, and the second a network installation company, Sielte. These new companies were either wholly or partly owned by EDB and did not include any Brazilian capital participation.

By the mid-1970s EDB had gained a series of major orders and the company's employment rose sharply from 3676 in 1971 to 10,853 in 1975. Company sales also grew rapidly from $54.4 million to $254 million over the same period. To put EDB's role in perspective, throughout this period they maintained an overall market share of roughly 40 per cent of the public exchange market. Slightly later, in 1977, the relative share of the MNCs stood at EDB 43 per cent, ITT/Standard Electric 38 per cent, Siemens 14 per cent and NEC 5 per cent. In terms of manufacturing of exchange equipment the entire supply sector was owned and controlled by a small number of MNCs with no domestic capital participation. In the transmission and peripheral markets MNC subsidiaries also overwhelmingly dominated the market.(4)

4.2.3 Technology transfer after 1964

Given the structure of ownership and control in the industry it is hardly surprising that technology was transferred according to the overall dictates of the MNCs - rather than according to government policy objectives or any demands of local subsidiaries. An examination of the L.M. Ericsson/EDB technology transfer arrangement illustrates the passive role this major subsidiary played in technology transfer, and the limited, peripheral nature of the technology transferred.(5)

The main technology transfer agreement in force before the 1970s was a ten-year technical assistance contract, signed in 1957, between the parent L.M. Ericsson and the subsidiary EDB. This contract enabled manual and automatic exchange equipment to be manufactured in Brazil, in return for agreed payments and restrictions on exports to prevent any competition in other markets. With the large rise in production capacity after 1968 the need arose to transfer more technology to support local manufacture; this was met by a further technology contract, signed in 1970, which allowed the transfer of some disembodied knowhow, such as construction and tool drawings, together with a limited amount of embodied technology in the form of staff training in Brazil and Sweden.

At this stage, EDB was manufacturing public and private Crossbar exchanges, some transmission equipment, and other peripheral items such as telephone handsets. Although some peripheral technology was transferred to support local manufacture, trade marks and licence rights were not granted, and neither were any central elements of technology such as R&D capacity or product and process modification capabilities. Like the earlier contract, this agreement contained substantial restrictive clauses and financial payments. Product sales to other markets were prohibited along with the transfer of any technology to other parties. On the other hand, the parent company had all rights to any technology generated by the subsidiary in Brazil.

If we examine the royalty payments it is tempting to conclude from the range and extent of payments made - in contrast with the minimal amount of technology transferred - that the agreement was primarily a means of transferring revenue to the parent company. Royalty payments included (a) a fixed commission of 5 per cent on the selling price of all telecoms equipment and 5 per cent on all installation charges, (b) travel and living expenses for all EDB visits to L.M. Ericsson in Sweden and all Swedish visits to Brazil, (c) a fixed price of 60 Swedish crowns for every technical document supplied by L.M. Ericsson,(6) and (d) substantial consultancy fees and other costs amounting to about 2 per cent of all EDB's investments in buildings, machinery, tools, testing and other factory equipment. It is worth emphasising that the nature of the technology transferred under this agreement remained very much manufacturing support technology rather than design or development capacity. No design capabilities were transferred nor any capacity to modify plant, processes or products. No ability to adapt or to add to the stock of technological capacity was transferred, and the dynamic innovative capabilities needed to create new products and processes remained exclusively in the hands of the parent company in Sweden.

Table 4.1 shows the steady rise in remittances from EDB to the parent company under the technology agreement. The total recorded royalties for the period 1972-1977 amount to 93 million crowns, roughly $18m. According to Brundenius and Goransson (1982)

Table 4.1: Royalties on Technology Remitted from Ericsson do Brasil to L.M. Ericsson, 1972-1977 (Swedish crowns)

Year	Amount
1972	2,206,893
1973	9,146,840
1974	12,183,287
1975	11,881,967
1976	26,068,796
1977	31,608,480
Total	93,095,903

Source: Ericsson do Brasil, published by Brundenius and Goransson (1982, p. 29).

total technology payments over this period were much higher, in the region of $52m, with other estimates suggesting that even this figure was an understatement. Evidence of a later technology contract (discussed below), involving a substantially greater degree of technology at a far lower cost, suggests that much of these remittances may well have been a means of transfer payment, rather than a genuine remuneration for the cost of technology. If total technology payments were indeed $52m then they far exceeded EDB's total profits for the six-year period which only amounted to $37.2m (Table 4.1).

4.3 The Industrial, Technological and Infrastructural Position of the Early 1970s

By the end of the boom period, following the general pattern of uncontrolled expansion, the telecoms industry faced severe problems of overcapacity, falling internal demand and growing financial debt. Again concentrating on the EDB case, the company's debts had risen remarkably by 1975. Imports of equipment and technology, mainly from L.M. Ericsson, forced EDB's debt ratio (i.e. debts over liquid assets) from under 2 per cent in the early 1970s to over 10 per cent in 1976. As Table 4.2 shows, large losses were being sustained by 1975-1976 in spite of rapidly growing gross profits, partly as a result of large payments to the parent company. In response to these problems the older manufacturing plant in São Paulo was shut down, and the local managing director and 3000 other employees were made redundant, reducing total employment by EDB from 10,836 to 7835 over the period 1976-1977. As a result of general

Brazil's New Communications Infrastructure

Table 4.2: Employment, Sales and Profits of Ericsson do Brasil, 1971-1980*

	Employ-ment	Gross Sales (million $US)	Gross Profits (million $US)	Net Profits (million $US)
1971	3,676	54.4	26.4	6.5
1972	4,535	71.5	32.3	12.3
1973	5,813	104.5	37.9	10.0
1974	8,108	173.1	49.9	3.1
1975	10,853	254.5	57.6	-21.4
1976	10,836	329.9	108.5	-11.4
1977	7,875	335.8	121.0	44.6
1978	6,344	236.9	102.8	31.5
1979	5,877	191.7	74.8	21.6
1980	6,244	128.8	67.3	21.5

*Sales and profits converted to $US from cruzeiros, using official currency rates.

Source: Brundenius and Goransson (1982, p. 22), (original data from Relatorio anual do Ericsson do Brasil, 1971-1980).

overcapacity in the supply sector two other minor competitors, Plessey and Philips, were forced out of the market entirely. The other two major competitors, Siemens and ITT/Standard Electric, faced similar problems of overcapacity, falling profits and enforced redundancies.

To sum up, despite efforts to reorganise and expand telecoms services, Brazil entered the 1970s with a badly organised and wholly inadequate communications infrastructure. Over the five-year period 1968-1973 telephone coverage increased by only 700,000 - from 1.7 million in 1968 to 2.4 million in 1973. Telephone density remained very low at approximately 2.4 per 100 population and the economy still lacked an efficient and accessible telex network. Tariffs still varied irrationally between regions and many towns and cities lacked dependable communications facilities. At the time, it was generally considered that the communications infrastructure of the country was failing to meet the domestic and industrial demands of the rapidly growing economy.

The equipment supply sector was almost completely owned and controlled by the MNCs operating within the country. There was no Brazilian capital participation in these subsidiaries, and there were no major Brazilian firms supplying equipment or developing technology. The subsidiaries themselves played only a passive role in technology transfer, itself designed to support local assembly and manufacture rather than adapt and develop equipment to suit local needs. The Brazilian government played no significant role in directing the technological and industrial activities of the MNCs, nor in developing its own R&D capabilities - a role frequently played by governments in developed and developing countries. Except for a few poorly financed and disorganised research activities, mainly in the various universities, the country was devoid of any organised and focused local scientific and technological capacity. In short, Brazil entered the 1970s with an inadequate telecoms infrastructure, virtually no local Brazilian industry, no R&D capacity and no significant technological base.

4.4 The Development of Brazil's Telecommunications Network - Evidence of Infrastructural Leapfrogging

Following the establishment of TELEBRAS (the overall Brazilian telecoms service provider) in 1973, Brazil's telecoms network improved dramatically in terms of both coverage and quality. Chapter 3 argued that given an appropriate government policy and absorptive capacity, the possibility exists for DCs to leapfrog earlier forms of infrastructure and move directly to one based on digital information technology. It is therefore important to investigate not only the expansion of conventional telecoms (telephones, telegraph etc.), but also the extent to which the technology employed was capable of storing, processing and distributing data in digital form. One indicator of this is the introduction of new digital IT services, and this is also explored below. In order to understand properly Brazil's progress in modernising and expanding the telecoms network it is necessary to examine the policy aims and strategies of the government.

4.4.1 Post-1973 government policy objectives

Although the reorganisation of the telecoms administration began in 1967 with the establishment of MINICOM, it was not until the government changeover of 1974 that the most dramatic changes in telecoms policy took effect. The incoming Geisel government was sensitive to criticisms of dependence on foreign capital and technology, and adopted a strongly interventionist approach to telecoms based on a well-defined industrial and technological strategy.

Through MINICOM the government committed itself to three main objectives: (a) to accelerate the expansion of a dependable and comprehensive telecoms infrastructure; (b) to gain ownership and control of the MNC subsidiaries operating within the country; (c) to build up a government R&D centre in microelectronic telecoms, capable of reducing dependence on foreign technology and fostering the development of local industry.

The main infrastructural objective of the new government was to accelerate the installation of a dependable and modern telecoms infrastructure across the length and breadth of the country. Although some improvements had been carried out to the network under the previous administration, the main services were generally recognised as being inadequate in terms of coverage and quality. As part of the planned rationalisation of telecoms, TELEBRAS assumed overall financial control over EMBRATEL and the state operating companies. Investments were coordinated across the regions, and tariffs were restructured so that differences in service prices were eliminated. Furthermore, as early as 1976, policies were introduced to ensure that new investments were based on the latest technology. In retrospect TELEBRAS intended to capture the potential benefits of leapfrogging intermediate, electromechanical forms of technology. However, policy statements at this time were not couched in these terms.(7) Aware of the international trend towards microelectronic technology, the main concern of TELEBRAS was to ensure that Brazil did not make the mistake of installing obsolete forms of technology. In fact, this concern was part of the reason why TELEBRAS started up its own R&D centre for telecoms.(8)

4.4.2 Indicators of infrastructural progress

The historical growth of telephone coverage from 1948 onwards is detailed in Table 4.3. Following the stagnation in coverage up until the early 1970s, Brazil experienced a remarkable acceleration in absolute quantities and densities of telephones. From only 2.4 million telephones in 1972 the overall quantity increased to nearly 11 million in 1984. This raised the density per 100 population from only 2.42 in 1972 to 8.5 in 1984. Annual average growth for the period 1975-1980 was roughly 17.3 per cent, and over the period 1980-1984 approximately 10 per cent. Brazil's telephone density now compares well with that of most other DCs, and is well above the average for Latin America, Africa and Asia.(9) By 1984 the domestic network covered 3641 (88 per

Brazil's New Communications Infrastructure

Table 4.3: Quantities and Densities of Telephones in Brazil - Selected Years 1948-1984

	Quantity of Telephones (thousands)	Density of Telephones (per 100 population)
1948	484	1.30
1964	1283	1.55
1968	1660	1.88
1970	1980	2.15
1972	2380	2.42
1974	2917	2.70
1976	4036	3.50
1978	5552	4.90
1980	7535	6.30
1981	8085	6.80
1982	9309	7.80
1983	10135	8.10
1984	10992	8.50

Sources: Compiled/calculated from Maculan (1981), SSI (1982), Mattos (1983), Telebrasil (Nov/Dec 1981) and Telebrasil, Suplemento Tecnico: 6 (1984).

cent) of Brazil's municipalities, including all major towns and cities. By the end of the decade Brazil intends to increase coverage further to around 20 million (Pelton, 1981, p. 222).

Telex coverage witnessed a similarly rapid expansion. By the end of 1980 Brazil had installed a fully automatic public network, servicing 535 localities with 53 domestic exchanges. The number of telex terminals increased from the low level of around 1000 in the late 1960s to over 43,000 in 1982, and stood at roughly 56,000 in 1984 (SSI, 1982; Wajnberg, 1984).

This extremely rapid growth in telephone and telex coverage facilitated a large increase in the communications capacity of the country, as indicated by the volume of national and international telecoms traffic. The volume of international telephone calls rose from only 4 million in 1969 to over 340 million in 1980, with an average annual growth of over 20 per cent during the period 1975-1980. In addition, Brazil now has direct dialling access to 56 other nations.

To support the expansion of telecoms services it was necessary for Brazil to invest heavily in the network. Table 4.4 shows the magnitude of total investments by the overall operating company TELEBRAS

Table 4.4: Investments in the TELEBRAS System, 1976-1983 (current US dollars)

Year	Value
1976	1790
1977	1540
1978	1340
1979	1280
1980	890
1981	950
1982	1090
1983	1210

Sources: 1976-1981, SSI (1982, p. 52), exchange rate of December 1981, $1 = Cr127.8; 1982-1983, Telebrasil (1983), exchange rate of $1 = Cr242 as per MINICOM.

over the period 1976-1983. Although these figures are extremely sensitive to exchange rate conversions,(10) they show clearly the large dimensions of total investments - amounting to approximately $10b over the eight-year period. As Chapter 7 shows, these large investments did not represent a resource drain to the economy but were largely financed through internal operating revenues.

Much of the investment described in Table 4.4 was directed to developing a modern transmission infrastructure. Updating of the technologically backward and fragmented transmission system was needed not only to integrate the country within a single telecoms network but also to lay the foundations for Brazil to 'digitalise' the whole telecoms network and so meet current and forthcoming informatics and telematics demands.(11) Again, these objectives towards IT were by no means crystal clear in the early 1970s but emerged during the organisational development of TELEBRAS towards the latter part of the 1970s.

The predominant form of domestic transmission installed was microwave line-of-sight relays, which today integrate all the states and most cities. High-capacity microwave links were also used to connect Brazil directly with Argentina and Paraguay. Where Brazil's environmental conditions did not permit access by land, other modern means of transmission were employed. Satellite channels (transponders) were leased from INTELSAT to cover the massive Central East Amazon region, and troposcatter systems were set up to cover the remote north/north

Brazil's New Communications Infrastructure

east regions. In addition, satellite and short-wave radio systems were established to provide full coastal telecoms services.(12)

After microwave relays, satellites are now the second largest means for transmitting telecoms signals. Brazil is now one of the largest Third World leasers of transponders from INTELSAT. Owing to the cost and inflexibility of these facilities, the first Brazilian satellite, Brasilsat 1, was launched in 1985, and a second was due in 1986. Both of these satellites are capable of providing telephone, data communications, telex and TV transmission in digital format.

Satellite transmission has played an increasingly important role in integrating Brazilian telecoms both nationally and internationally in recent years. Satellites now provide domestic telecoms linkages to Boa Vista, Macaro, Manaus, Porto Velho, Rio Branco and Tangua (near Rio de Janeiro). This coverage is to be expanded substantially throughout the 1980s. International satellite links are centred around two main earth stations at Tangua which connect Brazil directly with over 40 other countries. The present capacity of around 700 international circuits is to be increased to 3500 by 1993.

Underwater international coaxial networks were also developed extensively after 1974. During the past 10 years or so Brazil has installed two major underwater systems. The first, 'Bracan 1', was developed jointly with the International Telephone Company of Spain and provides 160 telephone voice circuits to Europe. The second, 'Brus', with 1640 circuits, began operating in 1980 to provide transmission to the USA. Brus was developed together with a group of corporations led by AT&T. A further high-capacity coaxial system called Atlantis began operating in 1982 to expand Brazil's telephone and telex links with the continents of Africa and Europe. Atlantis has two major submarine cable sections, the first with a capacity of 1380 voice circuits and the second with 2580 circuits. In general, the overall expansion of the network proceeded as planned and in addition, as Chapter 7 shows, the telecoms service sector has proved both profitable and largely self-financing.

4.4.3 The role of telecommunications as information technology infrastructure for Brazil

If we examine the nature of telecoms technology investment it becomes clear that Brazil has made significant steps towards establishing a network capable of providing major IT services. Virtually all transmission is based on digital techniques and recent exchange installations employ digital technology. Digital exchanges are supplied by two of the major MNC manufacturers, Ericsson and NEC. Where exchanges are not based on the latest digital switching technology (time division switching) the policy is to upgrade the equipment with the use of codec and modem equipment, which converts analogue signals into digital for transmission and back again for reception. The average vintage of technology is, not surprisingly, fairly advanced as more than 70 per cent of existing telephones were installed after 1974. This probably puts Brazil in a more advanced position in terms of technology vintage than, say, most of developed Europe, where many networks still rely on older systems.

To illustrate the advantages of establishing a telecoms infrastructure from scratch it is helpful to look briefly at the problems of moving to a digital telecoms infrastructure in a currently developed economy. Britain, for example, until very recently, was a classic case of an economy dependent on an almost obsolete telecoms infrastructure.(13) Despite a policy of introducing digital exchanges and digital IT services by 1986 Britain had failed to make the transition to digital technology, relying almost exclusively on an electromechanical analogue infrastructure. In 1984 the predominant form of exchange technology was the ancient Strowger system. Out of a total of 6292 local exchanges, 3708 (59 per cent) were Strowger, 571 (9 per cent) were Crossbar, and the bulk of the remainder, 1965 (31 per cent), were TXE exchanges. (TXE are semi-electronic employing electromechanical relay switches to make the switching.) Only 48 (1 per cent) of British local exchanges were digital in 1984 despite the publicised commitment to 'going digital'. The position with trunk exchanges was similar. Out of the total of 459 trunk exchanges in operation in 1984, 331 (72 per cent) were Strowger and a further 126 (28 per cent) were Crossbar (Dang Nguyen, 1985, p. 103). Only two trunk exchanges were digital.

The British public telecoms service provider, British Telecom, planned to replace the analogue trunk network by installing new digital exchanges at very substantial overall costs.(14) This transition had been discussed for many years by British Telecom but problems of software development and the commitment to previous forms of technology, both by management and unions, blocked the move until very recently. To give some idea of the painfulness of the move to digital technology, the installation plans for the trunk network at that time would have

Brazil's New Communications Infrastructure

meant an estimated loss of 4000 jobs, or 80 per cent of the maintenance workforce. Yet the trunk network is really the 'tip of the iceberg' - the most significant transition problem is installing digital local exchanges upon which the subscriber network is dependent. Although it is difficult to obtain exact data on installation patterns, it appeared that in 1983 the main purchasing by British Telecom was still the obsolete TXE exchanges, and in 1985 observers were fairly sure that this type of old-fashioned technology would continue to be installed for some time to come.(15)

The barriers to diffusion facing the UK in digital technology are variously described as organisational commitment to existing practices and technology, technical difficulties in the local development of a digital exchange, poor management, and general resistance to change by management and workers alike. Although the new digital services to a large extent depend on the installation of digital subscriber exchanges, British Telecom, by December 1985, had not yet announced a schedule for the full digitalisation of the network (<u>Electronics and Power</u>, Nov/Dec 1985, p. 201).

If we contrast the UK with Brazil, the ease of the transition to digital technology and the leapfrogging of various intermediate forms of telecoms technology is striking. In 1976, when the decision in Brazil to 'go digital' was taken, there had been a deliberate effort to install a range of informatics and telematics services. Some of the major information systems introduced under MINICOM are listed in Table 4.5. Apart from Transdata all these facilities use the national telephone or telex network for switching and transmission. Renpac is to replace Transdata by providing a 'packet switched' communications system via the national telecoms network. Almost all large Brazilian companies and institutions have access to data banks and data communications facilities, and approximately 80 major computers are interlinked through the national telex network. It should be noted that Table 4.5 is not comprehensive and does not include several other telematics services currently being provided by the telecoms authority, nor does it include systems in experimental use. These include an electronic mail system, a maritime information service, an international banking network (Findata) and a pilot videotext project which permits access to a central computer through a subscriber's telephone. Excluding broadcasting and telephone services, the telecoms operating companies provide a total of 19 IT services.

103

Table 4.5: Selected Brazilian Informatics and Telematics Services

Name of Service and Date of Introduction	Description	Technology Employed	Coverage
Transdata 1980	Data communications network for firms, individuals and institutions	Digital TDS multiplex	Independent of national telecoms network, 4000 terminal points
Renpac 1984	New public data communications network	Packet-switched technology using existing telecoms and telex switching centres	Capacity to cover all regions with existing telecoms facilities
Sicram 1978	Computerised telegraph system for national and international messages	Digital switching (TDS) via telex network	All towns served by national telex network
Interdata 1982	International data network providing access to foreign data banks	Digital TDS switching	Access to over 300 data banks via Renpac or telex network

Public Telex Network*	National telex network Can be used for data communications	Digital switching (TDS)	Appx. 60 telex exchanges and 56,000 terminals nationwide All major towns covered
Airdata 1981	Communications link with SITA, the international airline organisation	Digital switching (TDS)	Access to most international airline traffic information

*Rapid expansion after 1980.

Compiled from various sources.

4.5 Policy Failures - the Low Priority Accorded to Rural Telecommunications

Whilst recognising the successes achieved during Brazil's infrastructural development, it would be wrong to suggest there were no failings. In the course of the research severe problems were identified in relation to telecoms developments in the rural areas. The original telecoms planning called for extensive investments in poor, especially rural, areas to bridge the gross inequality in infrastructure as between the major towns and cities and the neglected rural areas. However, as a result of the deepening economic crisis, in 1975 restrictions were placed upon the MINICOM investment plan by the overall government planning authority (SEPLAN), and substantial financial resources were diverted from the telecoms sector to other sectors of the economy.(16) This led to a restructuring of investment priorities to one based almost entirely on profitability. Areas of social investment with low return on capital, notably regional and rural telecoms, fell to the lowest level of priority after international, inter-state, inter-urban and urban investment. As a consequence, the growth of rural telecoms proceeded at a far slower rate than that of the major cities and urban areas.

According to the census of 1980 the total number of terminals in the rural sector amounted to only 75,000. In 1983 this figure stood at little more than 90,000 or, put another way, only 1 per cent of rural households in Brazil possessed a telephone.(17) This extremely poor level of telephone coverage reflects, on the one hand, the investment restrictions imposed by the government and, on the other, the much deeper poverty of the rural areas in relation to the main industrial centres.

Despite the absence of any thorough and detailed research in Brazil into this problem, it is possible to illustrate the effects of the investment cutbacks using information gathered from the various regional operating companies.(18) On the whole these data show that throughout the poorer regions of Brazil the economic crisis and the investment cuts resulted in frozen investment projects, low telecoms growth and unsatisfied demand. For example, evidence from Telepar, responsible for providing telecoms services to Parana in the south of Brazil, shows that as a consequence of investment restrictions the growth of telephone coverage is insufficient to meet local demand. At the same time, plant utilisation has not reached its target level and is operating at lower than optimum capacity.

Brazil's New Communications Infrastructure

In the poor regions of the north-east severe problems, intensified by the recession, are reported by most of the regional operating companies. In Pernambuco several major rural projects have been frozen since the mid-1970s because of investment restrictions. As a consequence, telephone coverage still only amounted to 2.6 per 100 population in 1984 and the inadequate transmission facilities often result in inter-urban congestion. A similar situation exists in Rio Grande de Norte, where investment cuts have prevented the full communications integration of the state. Also, in the north-east, Telebahia of Bahia report a continued inability to meet current demand for telecoms services owing to lack of investment resources.

Serious problems are also evident in the northern region of the Amazon, where Teleamazon are unable to provide further infrastructural expansion to many of the interior regions because of investment cuts. Despite the progress made in extending satellite communications to many parts of the Amazon, the coverage of this area is still very poor. Restrictions on operating expenditures also mean that the maintenance of the system (often requiring boats and planes) has become a very severe problem for the operating company.

In the central eastern region of Goias, Telegoias reports increasing debt, again especially due to the maintenance of existing equipment. In addition the company is unable to expand infrastructure to meet the currently unsatisfied demand in the region owing to the low priority accorded to regional projects.

Other regional service companies report similar problems to lesser or greater degrees. Overall it is clear that as a result of the economic crisis and the subsequent investment restrictions, rural and regional telecoms have not progressed to anywhere near the same level of coverage or quality as the major industrial centres or the capital Brasilia. Research by the Banco National Credito Cooperativo (the National Bank for Credit for Cooperatives) shows that, from a sample of 100 of Brazil's rural cooperatives, there exists an unattended demand of 26,000 terminals. This study suggests that in each of Brazil's 2140 rural production and electrification cooperatives there exists a similar unsatisfied demand. In spite of this large demand the service companies are forced to restrain their investment programmes because of government-imposed investment cuts. In the longer term this low priority may prove a very grave problem given the vital need for social overhead investments in the poorer areas, and the threat to agricultural efficiency posed by a weak and sparse telecoms network.(19)

The failure to address telecoms coverage in rural areas is part of the wider problem of underdevelopment and inequality in Brazil. Although this subject is not the main concern of the present study it should be remembered that, although Brazil's basic telecoms network experienced nearly a fourfold expansion since 1974, the overall coverage still remains very limited. Despite the huge investments in the network by 1984 only 8.5 people in every 100 possessed a telephone compared with, say, 51.7 in the UK, 78.8 in the USA, and 85.6 in Sweden.(20) These problems of inequality in telecoms coverage are a separate and major subject of concern and investigation.(21) Suffice it to say that the disparity in telecoms coverage within Brazil is a reminder of the poverty of the country and the severe income inequalities both within and between regions.

Conclusion

Infrastructural leapfrogging and the developing countries

Since the policy initiative of 1974, Brazil has successfully leapfrogged various vintages of electromechanical telecoms technology and moved directly to an IT infrastructure. Seventy per cent of Brazil's telephones were installed after 1974 providing the country with both conventional telecoms and various new forms of digital IT services. Unlike the developed countries with existing infrastructure based on electromechanical technology, Brazil faced few barriers to the diffusion of the new technology. Brazil's experience bears out the hypotheses put forward in Chapter 3 that infrastructural leapfrogging may well be possible for DCs currently installing and expanding their basic telecoms network. An indisputable feature of the Brazilian success in this area was the government's recognition of the importance of exploiting the new investment to the full, and the strong policy intervention of the period. Most other DCs also recognise the need for central coordination of telecoms investment and have established government departments to carry out national telecoms policy.(22) This suggests that Brazil's success in leapfrogging is relevant to other DCs, and that other countries might be able to follow suit.

In Brazil, the barriers to the diffusion of the new technology were clearly low. Since 1974 the telecoms network has expanded dramatically and most

Brazil's New Communications Infrastructure

Brazilian towns, and all cities, are now part of the integrated national communications network. The development of the telecoms infrastructure greatly increased the overall communications capacity of the economy, in terms of both conventional telecoms and the new IT services. Many of these informatics and telematics services are now functioning to provide data access and transmission facilities to government departments, firms, banks, universities and other institutions. Unlike the advanced countries with existing electromechanical networks, there was little commitment to the old technology, and no need to begin scrapping large sunk investments in analogue technology.

The benefits of infrastructural leapfrogging are quite considerable, if difficult to measure. Brazil was able to install a less costly, more flexible, more robust and more efficient technology than that which faced the currently developed economies during their telecoms expansion. By avoiding the stages of electromechanical technology the rapid expansion of digital IT services has already begun. Furthermore, the market for digital products created by the network expansion has impacted on employment, industrial development and technological accumulation. The following chapters attempt to chart Brazil's progress in these areas.

Notes

1. This section draws heavily on evidence from Brundenius and Goransson (1982) and SSI (1982). However, this does not imply any endorsement by these authors of the interpretation of the evidence as presented here.
2. Unless otherwise stated the following information is from SSI (1982).
3. Most of the historical evidence of the activities of EDB is from Brundenius and Gorannson (1982). Over the period 1967-1973 EDB accounted for just over 40 per cent of telecoms sales and as market leader 'set the pace' of the activities of the other major MNCs.
4. Details of the minor MNCs involved are outlined in Chapter 6. This chapter also examines the progress of local firms in capturing the peripheral and transmission markets.
5. Again, details are from Brundenius and Goransson (1982). More updated information on the MNC technological developments is presented in Chapter 6.
6. At this time the exchange rate was roughly 5 crowns to the US dollar.
7. For details of early policy statements see Earp (1982) and Albuquerque and Waldman (1980).

8. As Chapter 5 shows, the other main reasons for starting up the R&D centre were to develop technology locally and help in guiding the activities of the MNCs.

9. The average DC telephone density is barely 1 per 100 population (Pelton, 1981, p. 208); for detailed international comparisons see SSI (1982, p. 39).

10. The official dollar/cruzeiro exchange rate rose from 130 in January 1982 to 979 in December 1983, over which time the cruzeiro was devalued 93 times!

11. See Appendix 1 for explanations of technical terms.

12. SSI (1982) provides full details of Brazil's transmission network.

13. Britain is perhaps an extreme case in that the general level of telecoms network technology is probably behind that of most other European countries, and certainly lags well behind the USA. However, this type of data is sensitive and difficult to obtain across countries. Also, the contrast with Britain does adequately serve to illustrate the issues involved.

14. Details of British Telecom's plans were reported in Electronics and Power (Nov/Dec 1985, p. 201).

15. Evidence from Electronics Times (1983, 13 March).

16. The financial transfers from the telecoms sector are detailed in Chapter 7 below. It is outside the scope of the present study to describe the severe economic problems facing Brazil after the 'economic miracle' period and the oil price rises of 1973. Essentially these problems centred around the balance of payments deficit, rising unemployment, accelerating inflation and a significant slow-down in the rate of economic growth. For two contrasting accounts see Wells (1979) and Balassa (1979).

17. Source: Minister of Agriculture (Telebrasil, 1983, July/August). Although these figures refer to the strictest definition of 'rural' this is an extremely low figure, especially when one considers that 7.8 per cent of the overall population possessed a telephone in 1983.

18. Sources: interviews with MINICOM, and various issues of Telebrasil and Revista Telebras.

19. Ample evidence as to the role of efficient communications in agricultural development is provided by Hudson et al. (1981) and Saunders et al. (1983) in their assessments of the literature.

20. Full details of telephone coverage by county are provided by International Telecommunications Union (1984), pp. 103-105.

21. The high level International Telecommunications Union (1984) report addresses these issues in detail.

22. Arthur D. Little (1983) confirms this point on a country by country basis. Spero (1982) also notes that many DCs have set up departments to deal with long-term planning issues in telecoms.

CHAPTER 5

TECHNOLOGY DIFFUSION THROUGH BRAZILIAN RESEARCH AND DEVELOPMENT IN DIGITAL TELECOMMUNICATIONS

Introduction

During the early 1970s the Brazilian government decided to establish their own centre for R&D in advanced digital telecoms. The Centre for Research and Development of TELEBRAS, CPqD, was viewed as crucial to the long-term policy of establishing a strong national base in digital technology. In fact, as CPqD grew and developed it became, probably, the principal institutional means by which the technology policy of TELEBRAS was carried out. As a central focus of national technological expertise, CPqD became more and more involved in developing microelectronic systems suited to Brazilian conditions, bargaining with the multinationals for greater transfers of technology and fostering the development of local industry. CPqD actually represented the first centre for the accumulation and diffusion of digital IT within Brazil. This experience presents a unique opportunity to study a developing country's attempt to acquire telecoms technology, and to illustrate the learning mechanisms by which digital technology was assimilated and diffused into the wider economy.

In order to illustrate how CPqD was conceived, Section 5.1 discusses Brazil's policy aims towards industry and technology during the early 1970s. This section will also serve as a statement of TELEBRAS's policy towards the MNCs and local industry - the subject of the following chapters. Section 5.2 shows how the R&D centre was established during the period 1972-1976, and outlines the responsibilities of CPqD in organising, choosing and developing Brazil's technological resources. The financial resources allocated to CPqD are also analysed to establish the cost to Brazil of attempting to build an indigenous base in digital telecoms.

Brazilian R&D in Digital Telecommunications

In Section 5.3 an assessment is made of the performance of the centre in assimilating and developing microelectronic-based telecoms. The achievements of the main programmes in terms of product output are discussed. Other indicators of technological output are also considered, including human resources, patents, technological developments and technology transfer to industry. The success of local industry in absorbing and commercially producing CPqD's technology is followed up in Chapter 7.

Section 5.4 tries to identify the learning paths and mechanisms followed by CPqD in its efforts to identify and develop digital systems suited to Brazilian needs. Presumably this technology was not 'reinvented' by CPqD, so during the interviews an effort was made to identify the international sources of technology, and how local expertise was organised in such a way as to assimilate and adapt what, in many ways, was a very new and foreign technological form. During this case study the opportunity is taken to compare the mechanisms of learning with microelectronic technology with those associated with electromechanical technology. As most of the engineers engaged in CPqD had direct experience with both they were able to help characterise the nature of the accumulation process.

In concluding, the chapter returns to the earlier propositions of the book. We ask what light, if any, CPqD's experience throws on the nature of technological accumulation with digital IT. Does CPqD's experience have any bearing on the wider prospects and opportunities facing DCs in digital telecoms? More specifically, can the potential advantages of microelectronic divisibility and modularity be exploited by DCs in such a way as to overcome the financial and technological barriers to entry in modern telecoms? As a country attempting to gain a base in digital telecoms with virtually no existing industrial experience in microelectronics, Brazil may well hold insights and lessons for other countries wishing to follow a similar path.

5.1 Post-1974 Industrial Policy Objectives

As Chapter 4 showed, Brazil entered the 1970s with severe industrial problems in the area of telecoms. As a result of the laissez faire approach towards telecoms, Brazil could claim little in the way of an indigenous industrial and technological base in this sector. Furthermore, the acute dependence on the MNCs for equipment and technology was proving costly and inefficient, and increasingly coming under criticism from members of government, industry and, in particular, the telecoms service companies TELEBRAS and EMBRATEL.

With the establishment of the Geisel government in 1974 the previous policy of reliance on MNCs for industrial and technological development was radically changed. The new government committed itself to reversing the trend of foreign ownership of industry and decided to increase local industrial and technological capabilities in several key capital goods and infrastructural industries including telecoms.(1) If we examine the legislation introduced after 1974 it is possible to identify a clear set of objectives towards (a) the MNC subsidiaries operating within Brazil's national boundaries, (b) the development of a national base in digital technology and (c) the encouragement of new wholly Brazilian firms to enter the industry.

During the post-1974 period a large number of decrees and regulations were established to govern the direction of the telecoms industry.(2) Within this extensive legislation it is possible to identify three main laws which illustrate Brazil's overall policy. First, law 102 of January 1975 defined the aims of TELEBRAS towards reducing dependence on foreign sources of technology and increasing local capabilities. MINICOM was given the authority to identify and deploy the existing technological resources of the universities and other government institutes. In the areas of telecoms materials, components and equipment, this legislation defined Brazil's overall policy aims in terms of reducing dependence and increasing local technological participation.

In August of the same year the second law, 661, was passed to define how the Brazilian take-over of the market was to proceed. This involved outlining the responsibilities of CPqD and establishing how the MNC subsidiaries were to be subordinated to Brazil's national telecoms policy. Under the law TELEBRAS could use its newly granted monopsony power to gain a measure of control over equipment production and technology. By concentrating the previously decentralised purchasing power under one administration, TELEBRAS was able to insist, first, that the MNCs transferred majority ownership to Brazilian capital, and second, that they begin developing technology for the Brazilian market, within Brazil, wherever feasible. As discussed below, this was by no means an easy task and depended to some extent on the capacity of TELEBRAS to marshall and deploy existing Brazilian expertise to bargain effectively with the corporations.

According to law 661 the MNCs were only permitted to continue manufacturing electromechanical systems in the short term, and were instructed to begin the manufacture of digital programmable exchanges immediately - that is, if they wished to remain in the market. TELEBRAS was also given the power to issue specifications for the type of exchanges to be built, to ensure the systems produced by the MNCs and, eventually, CPqD were all compatible. Law 661 also gave TELEBRAS the mandate to set up CPqD and begin the development of Brazil's own family of switching systems. Initially, 40 per cent of the local market was to bo reserved for technology produced by CPqD; later on a further law, 215, increased this share to 50 per cent. These measures were deliberately aimed at strengthening TELEBRAS's economic and technological bargaining power in relation to the MNCs.

The third major law, 622 of June 1978, completed and updated the first two laws. Law 622 reaffirmed the rules regarding the reduction of telecoms equipment imports. It also allowed the government to introduce rules specifying the minimum local value of inputs to goods produced by the MNCs within Brazil - the so-called nationalisation indices of final equipment. The inter-ministerial group for telecoms components and materials, GEICOM, created in 1975, was empowered to coordinate the reduction of telecoms imports and to ensure that goods produced locally used Brazilian inputs wherever possible.(3) Law 622 also contained more specific measures to assist local capital towards technological self-sufficiency and provided facilities for developing human capital resources.

To summarise Brazil's telecoms policy aims at this time, one can identify a 'three-pronged' approach to building up the technological and industrial base of the country: first, the setting up of a major new government-owned centre in digital technology; second, to 'persuade' the MNCs to transfer ownership to Brazilian capital and to increase the level of manufacturing and technological facilities within the country; third, to sponsor the development of new Brazilian companies to manufacture equipment and develop technology. In terms of strategy, MINICOM planned to use its monopsony purchasing power and new legislation as a means of persuasion and direction. In addition, the new R&D centre was to play a key role in carrying out all three aspects of telecoms policy.

5.2 Aims and Strategies of CPqD - Technology 'Catch-up' in Digital Telecommunications

The main purpose of state investment in R&D was to establish an indigenous base in microelectronic telecoms in order to assist TELEBRAS in specifying the local network, to develop systems locally and to help in the 'Brazilianisation' of the industrial sector. CPqD was to act for TELEBRAS to identify and deploy Brazil's existing technology resources at the outset. Although Brazil had several universities and other institutions engaged in electronics-related research, these activities lacked direction, organisation and finance. In the planning stage, during the period 1972-1976, TELEBRAS therefore conducted a series of meetings and developed formal agreements with the universities and other bodies involved in telecoms and electronics-related research.(4) The aim was not only to define existing research activities being carried out, but also to officially set up and fund various research projects and begin planning for the human capital resources needed to master the technology. In 1976 CPqD took over this coordinating role, and also the central responsibility for developing the new digital systems, from basic research to design and development, and ultimately the transfer of the technology to industry.

Table 5.1 describes the distribution of R&D activities as originally planned by CPqD and

Table 5.1: The Distribution of Research and Development Activities in Telecommunications According to the CPqD/TELEBRAS Plan

R&D Activity	Groups Responsible
Basic Research	Universities and centres of research
Applied Research	Universities, CPqD and other centres of R&D
Prototype Development	CPqD and other centres of R&D
Product Development	Industry (eventually CPqD and other research centres)
Adaptive Development	CPqD, other research centres and industry

Source: Albuquerque and Waldman (1980, p. 3).

TELEBRAS. Essentially, basic research was to continue within the universities but under the coordination and financial umbrella of TELEBRAS. Applied research and prototype development was to be conducted by CPqD, with the option of contracting out work to other institutions if necessary. In terms of executing government policy, CPqD was given considerable power. Under the new authority of TELEBRAS, CPqD could also choose which firms were to collaborate in the design and eventual manufacture of the products, and in effect were able to allocate final market shares to the firms of their own choice. Even at the initial establishment of CPqD, this was an extremely important task as, by legislation, 50 per cent of the future market could be allocated by law to systems developed by CPqD.

Figure 5.1 reproduces one of TELEBRAS's own internal documents showing both the ambitious aim towards technology and the time scales involved in the transition from human resource development through to state-of-the-art contributions. Although this document contains an element of post hoc rationalisation, it demonstrates the recent objectives of TELEBRAS, which to some extent followed on from the original plans for CPqD. The early 1972-1976 period of programme conception and development was followed by the building up of industrial and R&D infrastructure over the decade 1976-1986. This involved a steady progression up the scale of product complexity and ultimately into high risk R&D (analysed below). In the post-1986 period CPqD intended to enter experimental high risk R&D.

The early philosophy of CPqD demonstrates the crucial role of the government sector. Under TELEBRAS CPqD was the means by which local technological activities were to be identified, organised, financed and expanded. By integrating CPqD into the industrial structure of the economy, TELEBRAS could begin exercising control over the equipment supply sector and fulfil its mandate of supporting the growth of local firms. At the same time CPqD could react to the needs of the network in terms of new products and technological support, as expressed by the state operating companies under TELEBRAS. By subjecting the universities and R&D institutes to CPqD's overall technology planning, Brazil could begin taking over the important 'choice of technology' decision, previously under the sole direction of the MNCs.

In the early stages CPqD's choice of technology was determined by the government's aim of achieving self-sufficiency in telecoms technology and avoiding the costs of choosing obsolete electromechanical

Figure 5.1: Research and Development at TELEBRAS

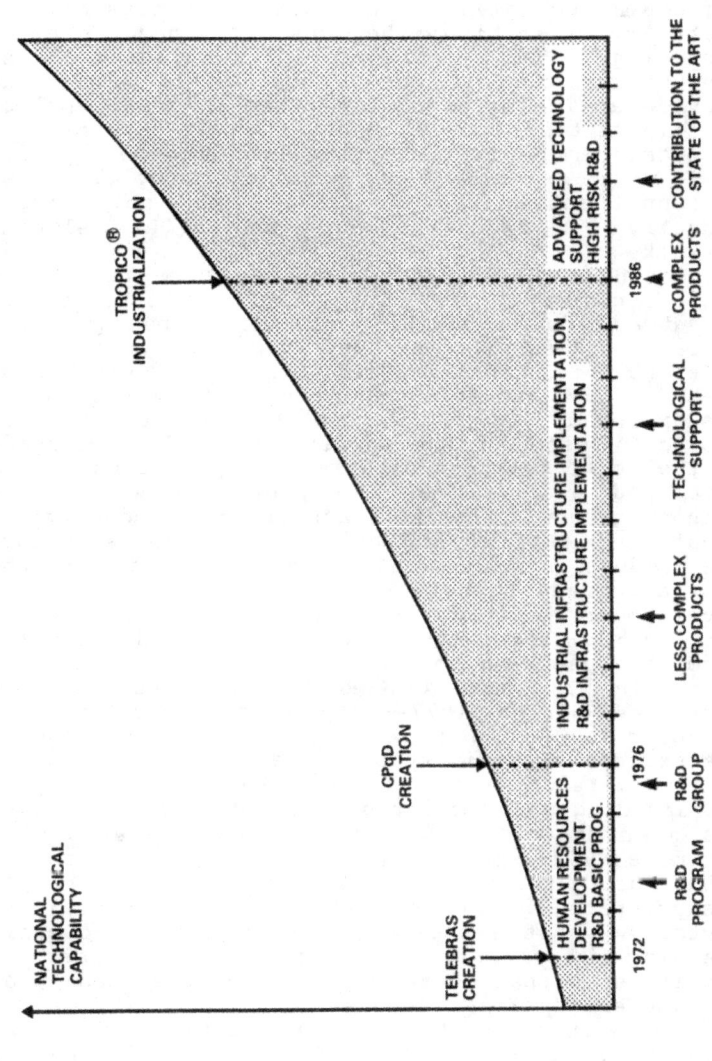

Source: TELEBRAS (1984)

technologies. By 1976 the advantages of fully electronic systems were becoming clear to those involved in telecoms development both internationally and in Brazil, and the conscious decision was taken to develop a range of digital, microelectronic systems. This required mastering technology in the three main areas of switching, transmission and peripheral equipment. The idea later crystallised that, by absorbing the most advanced digital technology, Brazil could prevent a widening of the 'technology gap' in the broader field of IT and provide an IT infrastructure. Again, early policy statements tended to be couched in more conventional telecoms terms. By the early 1980s, however, policy aims were expressed in terms of supplying the personnel and knowhow needed for developing local industry and 'digitalising' the entire telecoms network.

Besides these strategic long-term plans for mastering digital technology, CPqD was to respond to the day-to-day requests from the state operating companies. Requests for special product development were to be channelled to CPqD for development in-house, or contracted out, provided the technology was approved. In this way the R&D centre was to be geared to respond to the specific technological needs of the local telecoms network. After a product was developed and reached the prototype stage, the technology would then be transferred to industry for manufacture. Firms would generally be chosen before the production stage as it would be necessary for the chosen company to be actively engaged in the early development. Patents belonging to TELEBRAS would then be registered and royalties received, normally from the operating companies.

Table 5.2 shows TELEBRAS's investments in R&D over the period 1977-1984, most of which were directed to CPqD. Again it is important to remember the extreme sensitivity of dollar/cruzeiro exchange rate conversions especially for 1982 and 1983. Total R&D spending over the period (excluding fixed assets) was just under $200m. This figure compares with estimated R&D expenditures by the private sector of $152m during the period 1973-1983.(5) Unfortunately disaggregated yearly expenditures for the private sector are not available, but TELEBRAS's overall spending is clearly reaching the same order of magnitude as that of the MNC subsidiaries and local private enterprise.

The main point to note from Table 5.2 is the relatively low level of R&D investment, both in relation to total investments by TELEBRAS (approximately 3 per cent) and in relation to the gross

Brazilian R&D in Digital Telecommunications

Table 5.2: Investment in Research and Development by TELEBRAS, 1977-1984 (millions of dollars, current prices*)

Year	R&D Expenditure	Fixed Assets**
1977	20.1	5.4
1978	22.0	6.7
1979	31.3	25.0
1980	32.1	22.1
1981	30.8	21.4
1982	28.3	n/a
1983	15.6	n/a
1984	16.0	n/a

(Investments)

* Exchange rates for 1977-1981 as per TELEBRAS rate of January 1981, Cr65.5 per dollar. Exchange rates for 1982 and 1983 calculated as a yearly average from official Central Bank statistics, 1982 Cr183.6 per dollar, 1983 Cr531.5 per dollar.

** Includes land, construction of buildings and acquisitions of real estate and equipment.

Sources: 1977-1981 SSI (1982, p. 53); 1982, Telebrasil (Nov/Dec 1982, p. 78); 1983, Telebrasil (Nov/Dec 1983, p. 4); 1984, Wajnberg (1984, p. 31).

operating revenues of TELEBRAS.(6) TELEBRAS's policy was to invest around 1 per cent of operational receipts in R&D - far lower for example than the major MNCs expect to invest in R&D internationally.(7) If we compare the R&D investment say for 1983 (Cr8.3b) with resources diverted from the telecoms sector to other government activities (Cr150b), finances diverted amount to 18 times TELEBRAS's total investment in R&D.(8) In other words, the actual financial resources allocated to digital telecoms development did not amount to an insupportable resource burden for the telecoms sector, let alone the economy as a whole.

5.3 Indicators of Technological Progress by CPqD

Despite the comparatively low levels of investment in R&D, TELEBRAS developed a substantial base in digital telecoms. In terms of human resources, as Table 5.3

Brazilian R&D in Digital Telecommunications

indicates, by 1983 CPqD employed around 700 staff, with an additional 290 'contracted out' employees. CPqD actually began with a very small number of engineers (approximately 20) drawn from TELEBRAS. As the centre grew in size and began new projects, new employees were drawn from local universities and other institutes, as well as the TELEBRAS service companies. The large majority of full-time employees were Brazilian. Altogether 762 doctors, masters, graduates, technicians and other granted students worked directly on the programmes and projects of CPqD. It would be wrong to suggest that CPqD actually created this base in human resources. What the centre did do was to identify, focus and direct the existing diffuse technological resources within Brazil to meet specific and organised technological targets.

Of course, this does not represent a large R&D institution either in comparison with the huge government R&D centres in the developed countries, or in comparison with the MNC research departments in Europe, the USA, or Japan. However, the strategy of CPqD was very much to remain behind the technological frontier and not to engage in state-of-the-art research until catch-up was achieved. An examination of the achievements to date in terms of programmes and projects suggests that so far the centre has achieved the objectives described above.

Table 5.3: Human Resources of CPqD, circa 1983

	CPqD Personnel Employees	R&D Contracts	Non CPqD R&D Contracts	Total
Doctors	14	06	48	68
Masters	30	03	39	72
Graduates	179	66	38	283
Technicians	67	77	69	213
Granted Students	64	14	48	126
Administrative	175	05	48	228
Totals	529	171	290	990

Source: CPqD, Personnel Department.

Brazilian R&D in Digital Telecommunications

Table 5.4: Major Programmes and Projects under CPqD

Programmes and Projects	Institutions and Firms Involved

1) Digital Exchange Technology
  - Tropico C
  - Tropico R
  - Tropico L
  - Tropico T
	CPqD, EMBRACOM*, Elebra* and P&D Sistemas Eletronicas*

2) Programme of Digital Transmission - MCP 120/480 (PCM 120/480 channels)	CPqD, UNICAM (University of Campinas), Elebra,* Ampere Volt Eletronica Ltda*
- Radi-834 (Digital Radio)	CPqD, UNICAMP, CETUC (Centre of Telecomms Studies, Catholic University - Rio) and LMF (Laboratory of Microelectronics, University of São Paulo)
3) Programme of Data Communications - REXPAX (Experimental packet switching network)	CPqD, FDB (Division of EMBRATEL) and FDTE

4) Programme of Optical Communications
  - ELO-34 (Optic fibre system)
  - Laser and semiconductors
 	
  - Fibre optics
	CPqD and UNICAMP
	CPqD and LPD (R&D Lab. of UNICAMP)
	CPqD, LPD and X-Tal*

5) Satellite Communications Programme - ETP (Public telephone station)	CPqD, EBT, IGB-Control,* AVIBRAS, CETUC and LME
- ERTV (TV receiving station)	CPqD, FBT, IGB-Control,* CETUC, LME, AVIBRAS (Industria Aerospacial S/A)
- LCS (Laboratory of Satellite Communications)	CPqD and EBT
- Other projects including satellite interference, and signal processing and transmission	CPqD, EBT and CETUC

121

Brazilian R&D in Digital Telecommunications

Table 5.4 (contd.)

6) Telecomms Systems Programme
   - Interference between terrestrial
     systems   CPqD, EBT and CETUC
   - Radio-electric systems   CPqD, TELEBRAS

                                          Operations Directorate,
                                          and CETUC

7) Components and Materials Programme
   - Laser and semiconductor   CPqD and LPD
   - Fibre optics   CPqD and X-Tal*
   - Hybrid circuits, thick and   CPqD, CETUC, LME,
     thin film   Laboratory of Elec-
                                          tronic Devices
                                          (University of São
                                          Paulo-LED), Elebra* and
                                          Gradiente
   - Integrated circuits   CPqD, LFD and LMF
   - Electronic grade materials   CPqD and UNICAMP

---

* Private company.

Compiled from various sources including CPqD, TELEBRAS, Assis (1978, pp. 20-21), company reports and interviews.

Table 5.4 is a compilation of all the major projects and programmes conducted by CPqD. Most of the main institutions and larger firms involved are also included. As Table 5.4 shows, the three main telecoms equipment areas are covered, as well as a programme for components and materials and a special programme for optical communications. These programmes involve not only CPqD but a large number of other research institutes, universities and firms. It is useful to examine the progress of some of the major projects to illustrate the overall progress to date in acquiring a base in microelectronic technology.

5.3.1 Exchange technology

By far the largest programme is the Tropico exchange technology programme, which absorbs between 30 per cent and 40 per cent of total CPqD investments. Tropico is a family of digital stored programme-controlled exchanges which utilise the most advanced form of digital technology - TDS. The main objective of the switching programme is to design and develop, in Brazil, digital exchanges of the highest quality suited to the economic, climatic and telephone

122

traffic conditions found in Brazil. In the future it is planned that 50 per cent of Brazil's internal market will be supplied by CPqD exchange technology. The ultimate aim of TELEBRAS is to produce products which are competitive in terms of price and quality with systems on the international market.(9)

CPqD exploited the modularity of digital exchange technology by initially gaining experience in developing small-capacity exchanges. If we trace the progress of exchange development at CPqD it is clear that the knowhow gained during the development of small systems led naturally and gradually to larger switching systems. The initial project, Tropico C, entailed the development of a line concentrator with a capacity of 100 and 200 terminals. (A line concentrator is a device linked to a central exchange which allows a given number of subscriber lines to be 'concentrated' through far fewer lines than otherwise necessary.) Line concentrators are important to Brazil, given the need for low cost expansion of existing exchange capacity, especially in rural areas. CPqD completed the design and development of Tropico C, and successful field tests were carried out in 1982 in Rio de Janeiro. In 1983 the system was contracted out for manufacture and deployment in the TELEBRAS network.

Using much of the same design knowhow, the next project, Tropico R, was the development of a small public exchange with a capacity for 1000 terminals. This type of exchange is especially suited for rural and low density urban use. Again all the development was conducted in CPqD and the same advanced time division switching technology was used. This project also successfully completed field tests and was recently transferred to industry for production.(10) It is interesting to note that the three private companies involved in the later stages of development (see Table 5.4) are all relatively new, wholly Brazilian firms. This illustrates some degree of success in both developing the technology and actually transferring the knowhow to local industry. With some degree of software modification this particular exchange can be increased in capacity to 4000 lines, again illustrating the modularity of the development process.

The development of both these systems testifies to the cumulative nature of technological advance. It also suggests that the design modularity of digital exchanges can provide a mechanism for the gradual learning of skills and knowhow. At the time of writing CPqD intended to deliver a 4000-line exchange in the near future, and to follow on from this with a 10,000-line switching system.

Brazilian R&D in Digital Telecommunications

According to TELEBRAS the next major stage in exchange development is the development of large-scale public exchanges of 50,000 and 60,000 lines under the Tropico L and T programmes. It was recognised that this move into the final phase of high risk, advanced technology described in Figure 5.1 would necessitate a substantial increase in the technological and financial resources allocated to CPqD. The reason for this lies in the relationship between software complexity and exchange capacity. In a given switching system, each line must be able to be connected with every other line at any given moment. In addition, the software programming must account for the timing of each message, subscriber accounting and various other control and operating functions. Even with small exchanges the software programming can prove extremely complex and expensive. As systems grow in terms of capacity the software complexity increases exponentially, and so does the number of software man-hours required to design and 'debug' the final programme. Therefore, for Brazil to achieve the critical mass necessary to move into this scale of development, a great deal of extra financial and human resources would be needed.

Within Brazil in the mid-1980s there were two opposing views as to the feasibility and desirability for CPqD to commit itself to a programme of large-scale switching development. A summary of the arguments for and against helps clarify the issues involved for Brazil and shows that, in general, for DCs there will be a critical trade-off point where it becomes unclear whether the return to additional investments in technology will be sufficient to cover the costs involved.(11)

On the one hand, the international market for central exchange technology is both oversubscribed and fiercely competitive. In the early 1980s 16 major exchange systems had been developed at a cost of well over $6b (Muller, 1982, p. 106). To win export orders it had become almost obligatory for the MNCs to offer extremely cheap credit to potential DC buyers. ITT, for example, in 1982 offered China 25 years' credit at only 1 per cent per annum in order to compete with the French company CIT-Alcatel in switching systems.(12) The large and rising R&D costs of development make entry prohibitive. ITT for example have spent up to $1b on developing their System 12 digital exchange. After investing $100m the Swiss appear to have pulled out of the competition. The British System X, finally developed after many years and at a huge investment cost, now appears unlikely to win any major export orders after losing a large Indian contract to the better-established CIT-Alcatel system. If we compare the magnitude of exchange development costs with Brazil's total investment in R&D per annum of around $20m to $30m, it is obvious that an immediate and massive increase in investment would be essential. Therefore, some argue, why not take advantage of the international competition and simply buy in the necessary equipment, rather than embarking upon a high cost programme of large-scale switching development.

On the other hand, those wishing to proceed with the development of large systems point to the low cost of local engineering effort within Brazil. Although no detailed costings were viewed by the present writer, MINICOM argued that it would be possible for Brazil to develop a large-scale exchange for only $100m. This is due not only to the low cost software expertise available, but also to the strategy of imitating a basic established design and improving and adapting it. In other words Brazil could follow a low cost, catch-up strategy and take advantage of the massive investments by the MNCs. Those in favour of a large-scale Brazilian exchange point to the long-term technological strength this would bestow upon the industry and the capacity of local manufacturers to support the continued rapid expansion of the network into the future. In principle this capability would increase still further Brazil's bargaining power in relation to the MNCs, and allow the option of transferring large exchange technology to local firms, thereby upgrading the capabilities of indigenous industry.

This short digression crystallises the problems facing DCs wishing to take advantage of the divisibility and modularity of digital telecoms and begin local development. Each country faces constraints in terms of market size and absorptive capacity. The benefits of increasing the national level of independent technological capacity must be weighed against the costs and risks of R&D investment. As one progresses up the scale of technological complexity there is a corresponding rise in the financial and technological barriers to entry, as well as the risk of failure. Given that total technological independence is not a viable option and that DCs by definition will pursue catch-up strategies, then there must be a point where the cost of additional investment will not cover the benefit to be gained from that investment.

In the Brazilian case the dispute over the shift to large-scale exchange development seems to indicate that it is only at this very advanced level that the critical point may have been reached (from the perspective of the TELEBRAS administration). To develop large public exchanges, Brazil would be faced with expenditures an order of magnitude higher than those so far invested in technology by CPqD. For DCs with smaller markets and less well-developed technological infrastructure, this critical point would be reached lower down in the scale of technological complexity, perhaps in transmission or peripheral technology. Certainly, in the Brazilian case a great deal of further research would be necessary to venture a judgement on the feasibility and viability of such a project bearing in mind, of course, the severe limitation of investment resources within Brazil - and competing projects of perhaps greater importance.

5.3.2 Other major digital technology programmes

Several other technology projects have reached the production stage following development by CPqD. To illustrate the progress of the centre it is useful to examine some of the major programmes.

First, under programme 2 (Table 5.4), a digital multiplex telephone transmitter (the MCP-30) was developed and put into production by local firms. Two further higher capacity systems, the MCP-120 and the MCP-480, were designed and contracted out for production by local firms. A telegraph and data communications multiplexor, the MDT-101, has also reached the manufacturing stage.(13) The technology used in the packet-switched, public data communications network RENPAC, discussed in Chapter 4, was mastered in the REXPAC project, also noted in Table 5.4. The acquisition of technology in this project enabled local firms to supply over 50 per cent of the value of equipment invested in the network. In the future, TELEBRAS intends to manufacture 100 per cent of the necessary equipment locally.

Second, under CPqD Brazil has become the only country in the Third World to have successfully developed and installed an integrated optical fibre communications system. The ECO-1 system was developed from several of the projects listed above, including the ELO-34 which is a device for transmitting digital signals via fibre optics using lasers. The ELO-34 is currently in manufacture locally, and all the other necessary technology, including industrial grade silicon for the manufacture of optical fibres, has been transferred to industry for manufacture.

Third, the satellite programme is also well advanced and has succeeded in producing low cost receiving stations to link up with the two Brazilian

Brazilian R&D in Digital Telecommunications

telecoms and broadcasting satellites. Other projects are also reaching fruition. The first Brazilian integrated circuit suitable for mass production was produced by the centre and a further four chips were designed and developed. At the time of writing a pilot production line with a capacity of 100,000 hybrid circuits per year was being developed, in conjunction with two Brazilian firms, to be used in the Tropico exchanges. Most terminal and other peripheral equipment such as modems and codec devices were also produced within Brazil with the increasing participation of local firms.

5.3.3 Other indicators of technological accumulation

Two further indicators of technological progress are the number of patents registered by the centre, and the application for these patents by firms wishing to manufacture equipment for the TELEBRAS network. As Table 5.5 shows, since the establishment of CPqD in 1976, 183 official patents were registered at the national directory of patents of the National

Table 5.5: Patents Registered by CPqD, 1976-1984

Product/process	Quantity
Exchange technology	8
Microelectronic circuits and related materials	30
Digital transmission	
(a) general	32
(b) fibre optic/laser technology	12
(c) satellite systems	4
Peripheral/terminal devices	25
Monitoring/testing equipment	37
Other	35
Total	183

Source: Compiled from data collected at the Instituto Nacional da Propriedade Industrial, Rio de Janeiro, (National Institute of Industrial Property), 1984.

Brazilian R&D in Digital Telecommunications

Institute of Industrial Property. It must be pointed out that the above categorisation is very approximate, and in some cases the categories overlap. The integrated circuit category includes other microcircuits such as transistors, capacitors and connectors. General transmission includes digital telecoms and data transmission applications, and microwave developments. Although it was not possible to identify final product innovations separately, the data do indicate that technological output has been achieved in the main areas specified. Unfortunately, during the research it was not possible to gain details of patents registered by the MNCs within Brazil to make a comparison. However, miscellaneous evidence from the National Institute of Industrial Property (INPI) indicated that the leading MNC, Ericsson do Brasil, had registered only 16 patents in total by 1984, and NEC had registered none. Siemens and SESA/ITT, on the other hand, had together registered in the region of 40 or 50 patents. As discussed in Chapter 6, the greater propensity of the two smaller MNCs to patent may be the result of a deliberate technology strategy designed to gain larger shares of the Brazilian market. Overall, however, it appears that patent output by CPqD, together with spending on technology (see section 5.2), outstripped that of the MNCs.

In order to relate patent output to industrial development, a survey was conducted of all patents and technologies applied for and received by firms from CPqD. Table 5.6 presents details of 44 officially registered patent and technology transfer agreements. All contracts were registered after 1981, and some more recent agreements are not yet officially registered, for example in the area of switching technology. Nevertheless, the data give a reasonable picture of the nature of the products transferred by 1984, and the firms involved in the process. Fourteen of the 44 contracts are for the MCP range of digital transmission equipment. Five agreements are related to fibre optic technology, and a further four to the manufacture of satellite receiving stations. The balance is for various types of peripheral and terminal equipment. All products developed are digital semiconductor-based technologies.

According to data from GEICOM, the interministerial group responsible for monitoring telecoms components and materials, total final equipment sales of products originally developed by CPqD reached approximately $65m in 1983, just over 9 per cent of the total market of $700m (Wajnberg, 1984, p. 31). The R&D activities of the centre are therefore

Brazilian R&D in Digital Telecommunications

Table 5.6: Officially Registered Patents and Technology Transfer Agreements by Firms with TELEBRAS

Firm Name	Product/Technology	Year
NEC do Brasil*	MCP-30, MCP-120, MCP-480 digital transmission equipment series	1983
	ELO-34 fibre optic laser transmitter	1984
Standard Electric* (formerly ITT)	Digifone handset	1982
GTE/Multitel*	Digifone handset	1984
	MCP-30, MCP-120, MCP-480	1983
	ELO-34	1983
Elebra	MDT-101B, time division, telegraph/ data multiplex transmitter	1984
	MCP-30, MCP-120, MCP-480	1984
	ELO-34	1984
	CD-2400 traffic concentrator for text	1984
ABC-Telettra*	MCP-30, MCP-120, MCP-480	1983
	ELO-34	1983
Daruma Telecom S/A	Adaptor for public telephone	1982
	Telephone handsets types 78DC, 78MF	1982
	Telephone peripheral device	1983
Splice	Telephone terminals (4 patents)	1983
Icatel	Digifones types 78DC, 78MF	1982
Schause	Epel party line equipment	1983
IGB/Gradiente	Digifones types 78DC, 78MF	1981
X-Tal	Fibre optic technology	1982
	Quartz crystal technology	1982
Antenas Harald	6 metre satellite receiving dish	1982
Avel	MCP-30 digital transmitter	1983
Intelbras	Terminal equipment	1983
Fab/Nac Semiconductors	6 metre satellite receiver	1982
Elma	Terminal equipment	1982

Table 5.6 (contd.)

Amplimatic Telecom	Technology for satellite dish	1983
	Technology for test equipment	1982

*Indicates firm of multinational capital origin.

Source: Compiled from patent data and interviews at the National Institute of Industrial Property of Rio de Janiero, September 1984.

beginning to make a significant impression on the final products sold in the Brazilian market.
  Among the firms applying for CPqD technology, at least four are of MNC origin. The impact of CPqD on MNC activities is discussed in Chapter 6 - suffice it to say here that the transfer of technology from a Brazilian R&D institute to a multinational enterprise represents a considerable increase in Brazil's national technological capacity, and signifies a major shift in technology strategy by some of the leading MNC subsidiaries. The balance of the companies involved is made up of relatively new firms of wholly Brazilian origin.
  In summary, the data suggest that CPqD has made considerable progress in project development and technology transfer in microelectronic telecoms. Despite the relatively low level of resources allocated to R&D, by 1984 CPqD had acquired sufficient human resources and physical infrastructure to generate a broad range of digital technologies to coordinate the activities of other research centres and to transfer the product and process technologies to industry. Although it would be wrong to suggest that these resources were created entirely by CPqD, the centre can claim to have successfully marshalled, directed and applied technological capabilities to the development of digital telecoms. Progress to date in the individual technology projects and in the transfer of CPqD patents and technology to industry testifies to a dynamic and successful process of technological accumulation, not only in peripheral and transmission systems, but also in the complex area of central exchanges and other frontier technologies such as fibre optics and microelectronic components. The following section attempts to show how the technology was acquired and the problems Brazil faced in gaining a base in digital technology from scratch.

5.4. 'Learning' with Digital Technology: The Means and Mechanisms of Technological Accumulation

Since 1976 CPqD has mastered digital telecoms sufficiently well to transfer prototype technologies to industry and, as shown in Chapter 6, sufficiently well to bargain effectively with the MNCs for greater levels of technology transfer. A series of interviews was conducted with those responsible for establishing the original technology objectives and actually implementing CPqD's strategy. The purpose of these interviews was to gain an appreciation of (a) the sources of the technology, (b) the mechanisms of 'learning' involved in the process of converting technological inputs to outputs, (c) the differences between mechanisms of learning with microelectronic and electromechanical technology and (d) the problems encountered by this particular DC in acquiring a base in digital technology. The questionnaires were designed, therefore, to gain a qualitative picture of the learning processes involved at the level of high technology management/coordination and at a more basic engineering level. Two of the main conclusions of the study were (i) that the learning process is intimately linked with the formulation and reformulation of industrial objectives and strategies and (ii) that the mechanisms of learning corresponded to the intrinsic 'character' of microelectronic technology.

5.4.1 National and international sources of technology

Since CPqD began (with a handful of full-time engineers), a large number of domestic and foreign firms, research institutions, government bodies and universities have been actively involved with the centre in developing technology. Table 5.7 lists all the major international and national bodies with which CPqD entered into collaborative technology agreements of various types. International agreements cover a wide range of telecoms activities including satellite development (CIDA), integrated circuit manufacture (ITALTEL, CONSULTEL, AMI), exchange development (UNDP, Bell Laboratories) and fibre optics. In fact, in almost every major area of telecoms technology external collaboration was set up with other research institutes, firms, foreign PTTs and UN institutions. While it is important to recognise the external agreements, the main sources of technology were internal. In terms of technological support, feasibility studies, project development and the supply of electronics engineers, national agreements were of overwhelming importance

Table 5.7: Official National and International Technical Collaboration Agreements* between CPqD and Technology Suppliers

International Agreements:

Institution/Firm	Headquarters	Technology Area	Scope of Agreement
CIDA	Canada	S	TA, KG
CONSULTEL	Italy	ME	TA, KG
ITALTEL	Italy	D, ME	T, KG
CNET/DGT	France	n/a	TA
UNDP/ITU	United Nations	E, S, FO	TA, T, KG
AMI	United States	ME, D	TA, T, KG
SPAR	Canada	S	TA, T
Bell Laboratories	Canada	E, FO, L, DT	TA, T
INTECO	United States	S	TA, KG
International Engineering	Germany	DT, L	T, KG
Scientific Atlantica	United States	S	T, KG, TA

National Agreements:

Universities	Technology Area	Scope of Agreement
LPD-UNICAMP	E, DT, ME	F, GT, PD
LED-UNICAMP	DT, L, FO	F, GT, PD
MGE-UNICAMP	M	GT, PD
USP-S. Carlos	E	GT, PD
UFSCAR-S. Carlos	n/a	n/a
CETUC/PUC-Rio de Janeiro	S, DT	GT, PD
LME-USP-S.Paulo	E, ME, S	F, GT, PD
UFMG-B.Horizonte	n/a	n/a
CETEC-B.Horizonte	n/a	n/a

Other Institutions	
CNPq	TC
SEI	TC
INPI	TC
CEPEL	TC
ITAUTEC	TC
Army (IME)	ME
Navy (DACM/IPqM)	ME

A	
A	
A	
A	
n/a	
GT, PD	
GT, PD	

*Owing to diversity of agreements and technological areas, details of major projects are provided in the text.

Codes	Technology Area		Nature/Scope of Agreement
D	diffusion process	A	administration/collaborative R&D
DT	digital transmission	KG	capital goods supplies/consultancy
E	exchange development	F	feasibility studies
FO	fibre optics	GT	graduate training
L	laser technology	PD	project development
ME	microelectronics components	T	training, at CPqD and elsewhere
S	satellite technology	TA	technical assistance
TC	telecommunications general aspects	n/a	information not available

Sources: CPqD/TELEBRAS, Campinas, San Paulo; INPI (Institute of National Property, Rio de Janeiro) (interviews and documentation collected).

to the establishment and the evolution of CPqD. The institutional links listed in Table 5.7 were the end result of a long-term process of learning by searching, both at home and abroad, for specific technological resources and assistance – before and after the establishment of CPqD. Some of the specific agreements are commented upon in detail to help illustrate the various learning channels and procedures followed by CPqD.

5.4.2 Mechanisms of learning

Learning by searching
The first learning activity engaged in occurred before CPqD was set up and can loosely be termed learning by searching or learning by investigating. The purpose of this largely pre-investment phase was to gain an overall appreciation of the range of technologies available, and to assess if and how any elements of digital telecoms technology could be developed within Brazil for the economic benefit of Brazil. Most of this initial feasibility work was carried out by TELEBRAS using resources within Brazil. In exchange technology a contract was agreed with the University of São Paulo (USP) in 1973 to last for 33 months, to explore the possibility of local development of digital switching systems. By 1976 the university had produced a prototype digital exchange, and this early project (called SISCOM) formed the basis of the CPqD Tropico programme of switching systems. Engineers were also sent abroad for training to the ITU in Europe (part of the UNDP) and to Bell Laboratories in the USA – the world's most advanced centre for telecoms development. At this stage training was designed to assess the state of the art in digital technology and to choose between various options open within the field.

A key feature of learning at this stage was gaining an appreciation of the risks involved in choosing a particular technology. Digital switching technology was still experimental; only ITT and Bell Laboratories were exploring the particular type of switching system (time division switching) eventually opted for by Brazil. The financial risk of investment was large, and in practice the choice of one particular hardware/software layout (or architecture) involved an irreversible commitment to that particular architecture. Given the risk and uncertainty involved it is not surprising that the final architecture of the system was not decided upon until 1980.

This pattern of learning by searching and investigating options occurred across the whole range of CPqD programmes. A parallel project to investigate digital transmission was established at the University of Campinas (UNICAMP). Engineers were sent to Europe and the USA to investigate laser/fibre optic technological developments. In semiconductor component technology Brazilian engineers were sent on research fellowships to American Microsystems Incorporated (AMI). In the special technology required to manufacture hybrid circuits for exchanges, engineers were attached to ITALTEL in Italy to gain the knowhow necessary to manufacture the devices.

This early learning stage involved a continuous reassessment and reformulation of goals and strategies. The state, through TELEBRAS, acted to organise and orientate university research to commercial needs. Even though the government, rather than the entrepreneur, played the leading role, the process was highly 'Schumpeterian' in character involving continuous risk, uncertainty, choice and the promise of economic reward - if successful. The outcome of this learning by investigating was the formulation of a strategy characterised by selective technology substitution and catch-up. Where economically and technologically feasible Brazil would substitute existing technology imports for local development, and by these means attempt to catch up with the advanced countries.

It was clear at this stage that frontier technology research was neither appropriate to Brazil's perceived needs nor feasible in terms of the enormous financial cost and risk involved. The strategy was geared towards (a) gaining an overall appreciation of all the main components of digital telecoms and (b) developing technology locally wherever feasible. It was recognised that, for reasons of scale, technological complexity and cost, some areas of technological development would not be attempted, at least not in the short to medium term. In short the learning process culminated in the technology strategy described earlier.

Learning by setting up electronic capital goods
The next phase of learning involved a complex process of identifying, choosing, purchasing and installing capital goods to develop the products for manufacture. This entailed laboratory designing, the setting up of various support and infrastructure facilities, and establishing the R&D centre itself from capital goods largely purchased from foreign sources. Again, the organisation of these activities was undertaken by Brazilian engineers and managers on the basis of the previous phase of learning by

searching. However, this learning process did not occur in isolation but involved the use of international facilities, organisations and experts. During the microelectronic development programme assistance was hired from the Italian telecoms society, ITALTEL, and a senior engineer in the field was hired from a leading UK manufacturer. The special 'hybrid circuit' project involved designing a process laboratory and purchasing the capital equipment from various sources. These two projects also involved the choice and installation of CAD facilities to enable the circuits to be designed and to produce the physical masks from which circuits are developed.

This phase of the learning process was particularly risk intensive and exploratory. It was discovered, for example, that for reasons of insufficient volume it would not be economically efficient to conduct specific parts of the microcircuit manufacturing process in-house. This mainly concerned the semiconductor diffusion process, where photolithographic and chemical processes are used to etch circuit patterns on specially prepared ('doped') silicon wafers. To overcome this problem agreements were reached with ITALTEL and AMI to carry out these parts of the manufacturing process and to return the semi-finished wafers to CPqD.

In setting up the capital equipment, a continuous learning-by-designing process occurred. According to the engineers involved, one of the main achievements was actually designing and establishing pilot lines to produce equipment and components. In this area of activity confidence was gradually built up through experience. In the case of the laser programme, capital goods were decided upon after the laboratory layout was finalised by CPqD. By the time the laser facilities were established, enough confidence had been acquired to design the laboratory around equipment purchased from abroad from several sources. This is unusual for complex capital goods imports by DCs, where more often than not the plant design is imported wholesale and supplied as a package.(14) In order to achieve the knowhow to unpackage the technology, engineers travelled abroad to Japan and Germany to examine current methods and techniques involved in setting up laser facilities.

It is important to emphasise that the learning process (and the formulation of strategy) did not follow a linear progression based on previously established objectives. The risk and uncertainty inherent in this rapidly changing and advanced technology demanded a continuous process of learning by training, both in the stage of establishing capital equipment and in the later stages of product design and development.

Learning by training and hiring

Learning by training took various forms and occurred inside and outside the country. Some learning by training took the form of organised training courses for Brazilian engineers at international centres of telecoms development. These included courses at the ITU of the UN, at AMI in the USA for microelectronic component production, at ITALTEL in Italy for hybrid circuit development, and at SPAR of Canada where a 51-month contract was signed in 1979 for training and assistance in satellite technology.

Learning by training occurred extensively within the country too. Alongside the university projects mentioned in Table 5.7, special training courses were organised and financed by TELEBRAS. Some of the main university departments involved in graduate training were the Laboratory of Research into Microelectronic Devices (LPD), the Electronics Components Laboratory (LED) and the Group for Research into Electronic Grade Materials (MGE) - all at the University of Campinas in the State of São Paulo. These programmes were designed both to carry out specific industrial related projects and to provide a source of electronics graduates for CPqD and industry. Other major university contracts included the Microelectronics Laboratory (LME) of the University of São Paulo and the Centre for telecoms research (CETUC) of the Catholic University of Rio de Janeiro, financed by CPqD to conduct research and training in the field of advanced satellite communications.

Outside the universities, other research institutes engaged in formal and informal training programmes, including the electronics engineering departments of the army (IME) and the navy (DACM/IPqM), the National Council of Scientific Research (CNPq) and the Secretariat of Informatics (SEI).

The training process involved a substantial degree of hiring of individuals and companies to provide consultancy services. Bell Laboratories of Canada were hired to check certain projects on a two-year contract beginning in 1973. INTECO of the USA was also hired on a two-year contract to provide engineering services and planning assistance for the satellite programme. Scientific Atlantica was hired to help calibrate and manufacture measurement equipment for satellite antennas on an open-ended contract agreed in 1981. Again, these examples are given to show the network of international links established during the development of CPqD. However, the majority of training involved internal institutions, and the momentum and organisation of all external training and hiring was very much a domestic technology effort and reflected the domestic progress in mastering particular areas of technology.

Learning by designing and adaptation of product designs

The 'behind the frontier', catch-up strategy placed great emphasis on learning by adapting and improving existing product designs. This learning process was central to redesigning products to suit Brazilian telecoms conditions and mastering the technology sufficiently well to transfer the knowhow to industry. Within the international telecoms industry the strategy of imitating a new design, the 'fast second' strategy, is common among manufacturers. The aim, of course, is to gain the benefits of imitation whilst avoiding the costs of R&D. In the case of the exchange programme, for example, learning by adapting could be described as the central feature of the overall technology accumulation process. Rather than engaging in high risk, high cost software development, CPqD opted for what appeared to be the most suitable technology and proceeded to develop a small exchange suitable for rural use. As the switching programme developed larger exchanges were developed, again designed to suit Brazil's particular climatic, telephone traffic and geographical conditions.

This process of adaptation of product design occurred throughout the various R&D programmes. Special low cost satellite receiving dishes were designed and the technology was transferred to industry. Brazil's telephone transmission lines are, on average, longer and of lower quality than those of the developed countries and a new 'telephone chip' was designed under the microelectronics programme to meet local demand. The digital transmission programme also succeeded in producing a range of new products suited to Brazil's telephone, data and telex demands. These products were not wholly new products but incrementally improved existing telecoms designs.

Learning by installing information feedback systems

Given the complex task of coordinating the design work of large numbers of engineers, CPqD found it necessary to install computer-coordinated feedback mechanisms. The purpose of computer programming was mainly to synchronise the activities of different software engineers working on the same projects. This allowed for management coordination of the design process of particularly complex tasks such as the TROPICO exchange development programme. As well as coping with the complexity and volume of information being handled, the computer system served to monitor and measure the performance of individual engineers. CPqD developed the software internally and organised regular internal meetings to ensure coordination between the tasks being performed on individual projects.

This process of learning was considered to be extremely important to the management of CPqD's various activities in digital telecoms. With IT, control and monitoring of the design sequence is critically important to the overall success of a particular project. From the computer system a set of manuals was produced to formalise working methods, design specifications, how to write software and so on. In the process of transferring technology to industry these manuals represented the disembodied, codified knowhow upon which training could be given to industial engineers. Within CPqD the formalisation and codification of working practices paralleled the development and expansion of the institute, enabling programmes to be expanded and projects to be monitored effectively.

Summary – the nature of learning, and learning strategies

The nature of the learning mechanisms described here testifies to the inherent risk, uncertainty and choice involved in the accumulation of a new technology. In this case, the government rather than the entrepreneur or corporation assumed the role of risk taker, assessor and investor. Nevertheless, the motivating force was Schumpeterian in character. Acting on behalf of Brazilian industry, TELEBRAS decided to invest in a new technology in order to gain the ultimate economic rewards of such investment – greater market shares and greater profits. In this case the perceived benefits went beyond straight-forward market share and profit considerations, taking into account the external benefits to be gained from greater control over the MNCs, more effective industrial management, and the capacity to supply goods and services to the expanding national telecoms network.

Specific aims and strategies were continuously assessed and reformulated during the process of technological accumulation. The character of the learning mechanisms also changed and evolved during the process of accumulation. From the pre-investment stages of learning characterised by uncertainty and extremely high risk, the centre gradually developed less risk-intensive and more systematic methods of ensuring that technology was accumulated and new products developed. CPqD's experiences conform to the uncertain, difficult and cumulative character of Schumpeterian learning proposed in Chapter 1, and emphasise the critical importance of successful learning in the accumulation and diffusion of new technologies from the developed to the developing countries.

5.4.3 The character of information technology and learning strategies

In the course of the case study of CPqD it became clear that the nature of technological learning was closely associated with the nature of IT itself. As discussed earlier, unlike most microelectronic-based industries the telecoms sector has undergone an almost complete transition from electromechanical technology to microelectronic technology. During the interviews with the engineering and management staff of CPqD an attempt was made (a) to generate a qualitative classification of the two forms of technology and (b) to illustrate the differences in terms of the capabilities required to master the two technologies.

Table 5.8 presents a crude characterisation of the nature of the two technological forms. At the level of product or system, electromechanical telecoms was described as a 'verticalised' technology. Specialised interface parts link up all the components required and each part has to 'fit' perfectly. The task of manufacturing demands a great deal of specialised and, frequently, heavy engineering effort. The highly specialised and complex nature of electromechanical technology means that much of the hardware is manufactured in-house, or by specialised telecoms suppliers. The large manufacturers therefore require support from a network or infrastructure of local components and equipment supply firms. In terms of technological capabilities a broad range of skills is required. Electrical engineering knowhow must be coupled with mechanical engineering skills to produce the complex electromechanical interfacing which characterises pre-microelectronic systems. A broad range of skills is required not only in the early stages of design and development but also in manufacturing, quality control, and operation and maintenance of the equipment, once manufacturing has been completed.

In stark contrast, semiconductor-based, microelectronic technology was viewed as a 'horizontalised' technology. Independent final products are linked together to form a system which is expandable and flexible. The components which form the equipment are largely solid state, microelectronic devices which require no complex interfacing and connection. A single chip carries out the function of several complex electromechanical parts and components. In terms of skill requirement there is a heavy concentration of engineering effort in the research, development and design stages - i.e. the 'brain activities' of the production process.

Figure 5.2 supplements Table 5.8 by characterising the corresponding profiles of technological capabilities needed to design and produce telecoms equipment. Figure 5.2 also compares the capabilities required to install and maintain electromechanical and microelectronic technology. Although, in reality, the picture is far more complex and differs according to the type of equipment concerned and many other factors, the diagram serves to illustrate the contrast between the two technological forms.

With electromechanical technology an extensive range and depth of capabilities are required at the levels of research, design, development, manufacture, installation and maintenance. Hardware development involves specifying the design of various mechanical components and ensuring a correct interface with electrical devices such as motors, relays and connectors. The problem of ensuring the reliability and quality of the equipment carries on into the manufacturing, installation and maintenance stages.

With microelectronic technology the nature and range of skills are entirely different. Instead of a wide range of skills a very narrow range of design-intensive, information-based, software skills is required. This is probably the most distinguishing and central characteristic of semiconductor technology. The nature of the design and development task is a challenge in the management of information rather than physical equipment or hardware.

The hardware is generally purchased from equipment manufacturers in the form of microelectronic components, which then carry out the functions designated by the software. The technological challenge involves such tasks as programme writing, architectural design, the mastery of CAD and, in general, the capacity to manage and manipulate vast quantities of coded information. The narrowness of the range of skills required to develop microelectronic systems applies across the whole range of telecoms product categories. The procedure followed in producing telecoms equipment followed three basic steps: (a) the design of the basic architecture of the system (this involves producing a computerised layout of the hardware and all the component connections in relation to the information flows within the equipment); (b) the design of the logic,

Table 5.8: Technological Characterisation of Microelectronic and Electromechanical Telecommunications

Level of Comparison	Electromechanical Technology	Microelectronic Technology
1. Product/System	- Vertically integrated - Centralised design - Integrated units - Many moving parts	- Horizontally integrated - Modular design - Divisible units - Solid state
2. Manufacturing Process	- Complex/crucial - Intensive fine engineering and electromechanical interfacing - Heavy engineering/capital goods infrastructure - Hardware manufactured in or by specialised telecoms component suppliers	- Simple assembly - Minimal engineering and electromechanical interfacing - Light, clean assembly operation - Hardware purchased from general semiconductor suppliers
3. Technological Capabilities	- Electrical/mechanical - Widely dispersed in production process - Broad range of skills - Telecoms specific, rigid demarcations	- Information intensive - Centralised in design/conceptual stage - Narrow range of skills - Converging with other electronics industries

4. Technological relationship with other industries and products	- Industries traditionally separate - Telecoms-specific skills and knowhow - Product boundaries clearly defined	- Convergence with other micro-electronics industries - Increasingly converging information-based skills - Products converging with other IT goods

Figure 5.2: Technological Capabilities Required in Telecommunications Activities, Electro-mechanical and Microelectronic

Electromechanical/Analogue:

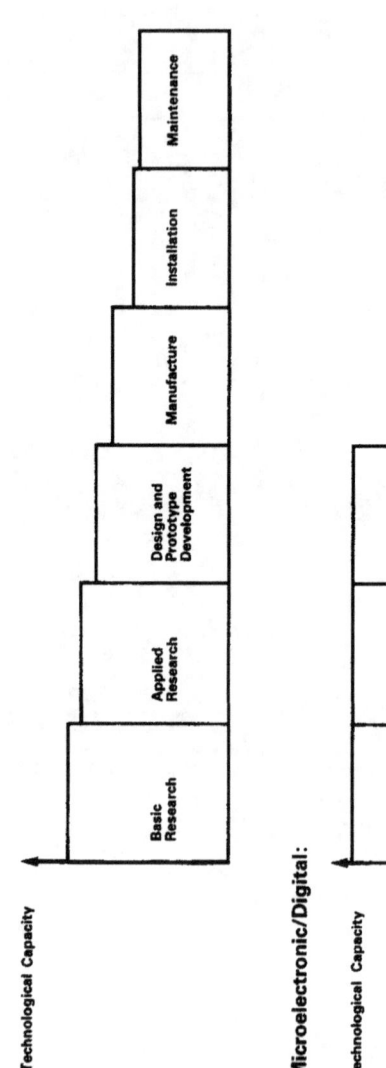

Microelectronic/Digital:

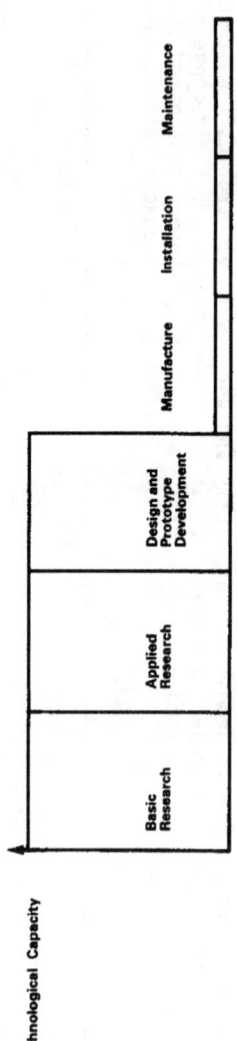

or operational functions, of the system (this involves producing the software necessary to carry out all the information carrying, retrieving and storage tasks required); (c) the assembly of the microelectronic devices onto PCBs which, in turn, are linked together to form the overall system.

Following the design process, the manufacturing stage is a relatively simple assembly-style operation. The boards are assembled, connected up to the input/output devices such as terminals and keyboards, and tested to make sure they operate properly. Given the limited amount of mechanical engineering and electromechanical interfacing, the production is a relatively straightforward, light, clean, assembly operation.

The striking contrast with electromechanical technology continues into the operation and maintenance stages. Microelectronic systems require virtually no technical skill or specialised knowhow to operate and to repair equipment. In most modern systems malfunctions are self-diagnostic, which means that the control computer identifies, locates and diagnoses areas of failure. After the software has completed its design and debugging then, in principle at least, there are extremely few operational malfunctions as there are relatively few moving parts.

These characteristics of IT relate closely to the learning mechanisms identified in Section 5.4.2. The mechanisms described centred almost entirely on the establishment and operation of design facilities. After the search process, electronic capital goods were set up to enable the design of microcircuits, exchanges, transmission systems and so on. Assistance was obtained from design centres abroad, and local laboratories were geared to assisting CPqD to set up its own design facilities. The process of catching up centred almost exclusively on learning by designing, redesigning and adapting information-based designs. Computer systems were installed to facilitate the design of particular projects, and even the management of more complex programmes involved the writing of programmes to monitor and coordinate the design sequence. The information-based, design-intensive nature of modern electronic technology impinges directly on the options facing Third World countries in their efforts to establish R&D facilities in modern telecoms technology.

Conclusions

The nature of digital telecoms and options for developing countries in research and development

There can be no doubt that the Brazilian R&D efforts in digital telecoms have provided the country with a strong dynamic base in digital technology. The indicators of technological progress – patents, product and process developments, human resources and technology transfers – demonstrate that CPqD has already accumulated a significant and independent capacity in microelectronic-based telecoms. Since 1976 CPqD has identified, organised, directed and augmented Brazil's R&D efforts in telecoms. In searching abroad for technology, developing and adapting systems locally and transferring technology to industry, CPqD functioned as a 'system' for the accumulation and diffusion of digital telecoms. Under the financial and management control of TELEBRAS, the various R&D institutes and university groups were organised in such a way as to meet both the long-term government objectives towards telecoms, and the more immediate requirements of the state operating companies.

The activities and programmes of CPqD provide a fascinating insight into both the nature of IT and the options for other DCs aiming to build up capabilities in modern telecoms. The international transition to microelectronic technology presented a range of technological opportunities which Brazil was able to identify and exploit. A key feature of digital IT is the concentration of technological activity in the conceptual, design stage of the production process. This permitted the Brazilian government to centralise technological capacity and authority under one institutional body. In addition, the common nature of the technological process across the various products and processes allowed the pooling and sharing of common technological knowhow, skills and infrastructure. These characteristics of microelectronic-based telecoms enabled one R&D centre, with very limited financial resources, to centralise and apply these conceptual skills directly to the development of commercial products.

With electromechanical technology there was little, if any, possibility of centralising technological resources and applying them to production-related activities in this way. The broad range of complex and differentiated skills and techniques required, not only in design but also in the development and production of electromechanical technology, precluded such an option. The nature of

Brazilian R&D in Digital Telecommunications

electromechanical technology meant that crucial technological capabilities were, of necessity, embodied in the complex industrial infrastructure of the telecoms companies. The necessary mechanical, electromechanical and fine engineering skills were not only diffused across the major firms and their network of suppliers, but also across the specialised engineers and technicians dealing with the complex range of tasks.

The experience of CPqD lends support to the arguments put forward earlier as to the opportunities presented by the modularity and divisibility of microelectronic technology. The modular design of digital systems enabled the R&D centre to begin its activities by developing small, relatively simple telecoms systems and gradually develop the capabilities to advance to higher stages of complexity. The divisibility in manufacture allowed for prototype development and manufacture of various independent products and systems. These two intrinsic characteristics of digital technology presented a further important opportunity - the possibility of fostering the development of new smaller-scale manufacturing firms. CPqD's success in sponsoring Brazilian firms is analysed in Chapter 7. The important point here is that the relative simplicity of the production/assembly task and the possibility of gradual accumulation of technology gave credence to the strategy of supporting the entry of local firms into the market.

Although one cannot present the Brazilian strategy as a definitive model for other DCs to follow, there may be good reasons for other larger countries to establish strategic low-cost R&D centres for digital technological development. The experience of CPqD illustrates that technological assimilation in digital telecoms is a feasible proposition. Governments wishing to strengthen their own local capabilities in this area and prevent a widening of the technology gap - or, more positively, to catch up - may find the strategy followed by Brazil and in particular the mechanisms of technological learning both useful and instructive.

Indeed, the close links between digital telecoms and other fields of IT suggest the possibility of broadening the field of R&D activities beyond the narrow scope of telecoms to strengthen capabilities in other related fields of IT. The convergence of several industries around digital technology and the common features of microelectronics - modularity, divisibility, design intensity - may mean that technological catch-up in other areas of IT is both economically feasible and desirable. While this

Brazilian R&D in Digital Telecommunications

broader prospect needs further careful research, it should be stressed that the success of CPqD, even in strictly telecoms terms, stands in direct contradiction to most research in the field of microelectronics and the Third World.

Notes

1. Dahlman (1982) and Wells (1979) describe, in detail, the general policy changes of this period.
2. The volumes of detailed legislation are presented in the appendices of SSI (1982) and analysed by Assis (1978).
3. The overall success of GEICOM in this area is analysed in Chapter 6.
4. For a full discussion of the institutions involved, see Albuquerque and Waldman (1980, pp. 44-62). For a listing in English see Galli (1982, pp. 35-38).
5. Wajnberg (1984, p. 31). Private sector expenditures on R&D are analysed in Chapter 6.
6. R&D expenditures as a percentage of total investments are calculated as a yearly average from Tables 4.4 and 5.2.
7. Estimates vary between 5 per cent and 10 per cent depending on the corporation.
8. The impact of the diversion of resources from the telecoms sector to other government activities is discussed in Chapter 7.
9. However, it was recognised that initially prices of locally produced equipment would be higher.
10. In July 1982 a national telecoms company, Elebra, was authorised by the Ministry of Communications to begin production of this exchange.
11. In conventional economic language this is the point where the marginal cost of additional investment is equal to the marginal revenue from that investment.
12. Details of the competition for the Chinese and Indian contracts are provided by Electronics Weekly (1983, May 4, p. 11) and Electronics Times (1982, May 20, pp. 1, 10).
13. The technological advance of Brazilian firms is discussed in Chapter 7.
14. Cooper and Hoffman (1981) illustrate this tendency for capital goods imports. Also, as noted earlier, the recent Indian import of telecoms technology involved a 'package' deal.

CHAPTER 6

THE TECHNOLOGICAL INTEGRATION OF THE MULTINATIONAL SUBSIDIARIES

Introduction

After the Geisel government take-over in 1974 the Ministry of Communications was empowered to reduce its dependence on the telecoms MNCs. Within the broader policy towards the telecoms sector MINICOM attempted to 'persuade' the MNCs to locate more technological facilities within Brazil, to reduce their level of imports, and to integrate their technological activities within the industrial infrastructure of the country. As Chapters 4 and 5 showed, the almost complete dominance of the equipment supply sector by the oligopoly of MNCs, and their failure to transfer technology to Brazil, led the government to legislate (a) for the transfer of majority ownership to Brazilian capital and (b) for an increase in the local value of goods produced by the corporations (the so-called Brazilianisation rules). In addition, directive 661 of 1975 stated that the MNCs were to cease the manufacture of electromechanical systems and, as soon as possible, begin the production of microelectronic-based systems.
    The purpose of this chapter is to evaluate the success of the Brazilian strategy, first within the internal objectives of the government, and second within the wider context of the international diffusion of microelectronic technology. To this end an effort is made to explore possible indicators of technological success. The field research concentrated on amassing historical evidence regarding the transfer of ownership to Brazilian capital, and the development of domestic technological and management efforts by the MNC subsidiaries. Section 6.1 begins by stressing the importance of taking a historical perspective of the understanding of the behaviour of the MNCs within this sector (three of whom began their operations at the turn of the

century). Section 6.2 follows with an analysis of the impact of the new technology policy on the transfer of ownership from the subsidiaries to Brazilian capital.

Section 6.3 presents evidence of local technological development and integration of the subsidiaries. This is done by examining R&D expenditure patterns, time series trends in equipment imports and exports, and the responses of the individual MNC subsidiaries to the new policy changes. Particular attention is paid to the case of the market leader EDB, who accounted for roughly 40 per cent of the market over the period examined. As market leader, EDB set the pace for change in the equipment supply industry, and the other MNCs (Siemens, ITT/SESA and NEC) tended to react to EDB and reformulate their own competitive strategies.

In interpreting the evidence we ask whether or not the experience of the MNCs within Brazil's telecoms sector throws any light on the nature of the accumulation of microelectronic technology in the DC context. In particular we ask whether the transition of the MNCs from electromechanical to microelectronic technology conforms to the idea of technological leapfrogging, or to the more difficult, cumulative, process suggested in earlier chapters. The Brazilian experience in bargaining with the MNCs for greater levels of technology transfer also has a direct bearing on whether the destabilising of the telecoms electromechanical oligopoly has, in fact, improved the bargaining position of larger DCs. If this is the case, as argued earlier, then other major DCs may also be able to exploit the changing economic and technological environment to their advantage.

6.1 The Historical Perspective

In order to appreciate the extent of recent changes in the level of industrial and technological integration of the MNCs, it is important to view progress in historical terms. In contrast with Brazilian enterprise in the telecoms sector, the MNCs have operated within Brazil for over 80 years. As Table 6.1 shows, except for NEC of Japan, the MNCs began their operations before or just after the turn of the century by setting up sales offices. As the internal market grew, sales and distribution offices were expanded and greater commercial representation introduced by the parent companies in their competition to supply the local equipment market.(1) The corporations gradually began assembling equipment within Brazil's national boundaries during the 1940s

Table 6.1: Principal Activities of the Major
Telecommunications Multinationals in Brazil - Approximate
Starting Dates

Firm Name	Sales Offices	Import Subsidiaries	Assembly Plants	Manufacturing Plants
Siemens	1895	1905	1958	Late 1960s
Ericsson	Before 1900	1924	1955	1955
Philips*	1920	1925	1949	-
SESA/ITT	Before 1908	1926	1942	1965
NEC	-	1966	-	1969

*Philips were to drop out of the major exchange market during the 1970s.

Source: R.S. Newfarmer, cited by Maculan (1981, p. 116).

and 1950s, spurred on by government import restrictions and inter-MNC competition. Nevertheless, as Chapter 4 showed, by 1973 very little independent technological capacity had been transferred to Brazil, and the subsidiaries were still wholly owned and controlled by the parent companies.

To add to the problems caused by the acute technological dependency of the subsidiaries at the end of the boom period, the telecoms industry, like many other industries in Brazil, faced severe problems of overcapacity, growing financial debt and falling internal demand.(2) It is within this wider economic and technological context that MINICOM formulated its industrial and technological strategy in 1974. Initially the 'Brazilianisation' rules contained in law 661 were resisted by the MNCs who continued with the production of electromechanical exchange equipment.(3) In order to overcome the reluctance of the MNCs to transfer microelectronic-based, SPC exchange technology, TELEBRAS eventually threatened to cancel outstanding orders. By 1977 the four MNCs had begun to comply with the ownership and technology transfer directives in order to win the new orders on offer.

6.2 The Transfer of Ownership to Brazilian Capital

Following the policy changes and threats to cancel outstanding orders, a progressive transfer of voting capital from the MNC subsidiaries to large Brazilian

Integration of the Multinationals

financial groups began. Ericsson, with 40 per cent of the switching market, persuaded two financial groups, Monteiro-Aranha and Atlantic Boavista, to form a holding company, MATEL, to take over their shares. This deal was eventually approved in July 1979, and as a result Ericsson won the largest order on offer and agreed to transfer AXE-10 digital switching technology to Brazil. Siemens, with roughly 14 per cent of the market, sold a majority share to Herring, another Brazilian holding company, forming a new company Equitel. SESA/ITT and NEC, with 38 per cent and 5 per cent market shares respectively, both sold a majority of their voting capital to BRASILINVEST.

Current holdings of Brazilian capital in ordinary shares and total capital of the MNC subsidiaries is illustrated in Table 6.2. Before 1974 there was virtually no Brazilian capital participation in either the major MNCs, or the minor MNCs operating within the country. As a result of the new policy, in all cases a majority of voting capital was transferred to Brazilian companies. In seven out of the ten cases in Table 6.2, a majority of total capital was acquired during the transfer period. In placing orders TELEBRAS did not officially discriminate in favour of 100 per cent owned Brazilian

Table 6.2: Participation by Brazilian Shareholders in Ordinary Shares and Total Capital in Telecommunications Multinationals, circa 1984

	Ordinary Shares	Total Capital
Major Exchange Manufacturers:		
Ericsson do Brasil	74%	31%
NEC do Brasil	51%	17%
Equitel (ex Siemens)	51%	17%
SESA (ex IT)	100%	100%
Minor MNC Equipment Producers:		
ABC-Italtel	75%	75%
ABC-Telettra	51%	51%
Daruma	100%	95%
Multitel (ex GTE)	51%	51%
Siteltra (ex Telefunken)	51%	51%
Sul America Philips	51%	51%

Source: adapted from Wajnberg (1984, p. 22).

Integration of the Multinationals

firms, but did give preference to firms which are engaged in developing technology with CPqD.(4) In practice this policy tends to favour local firms (discussed in Chapter 7). The official policy was geared towards controlling the activities of the MNCs, particularly in terms of local technology developments, rather than gaining complete 100 per cent ownership.

As far as the telecoms subsidiaries are concerned, the monopsony power granted to TELEBRAS was clearly instrumental in persuading the MNCs to transfer company ownership to Brazilian capital. However, the transfer of ownership should be seen within the long-term historical process of Brazil's bargaining with the MNCs for greater domestic involvement and control. Indeed, even after the ownership legislation, the transfer of ownership was not automatic and had to be insisted upon under threat of exclusion from the market. This long-term process of bargaining, with achievements and setbacks, also applied to the transfer of technological facilities to the subsidiaries.

6.3 Evidence of Local Technology Efforts by the Multinational Subsidiaries

Of course, the transfer of firms' voting control does not necessarily ensure the transfer of effective management and technological control. It is quite possible to transfer formal ownership to local capital whilst retaining managerial and technological control within the parent corporation. However, evidence of (a) strategic investments and efforts in local technology, (b) falling technology imports and (c) developments in management and technological organisation at the firm level points to a major shift by the MNCs from the passive subsidiary role under electromechanical technology to a positive technology-developing role under microelectronic technology. To substantiate this argument it is helpful to consider the above three indicators of technological progress in turn.

6.3.1 Research and development expenditure patterns

Table 6.3 presents R&D expenditures for the period 1973-1983 and employment levels for the year 1983 for the leading four MNCs in the telecoms sector. Overall R&D expenditure amounted to $99m, which compares with total government expenditure on R&D of around $200m over the same period. In 1983 employ-

Integration of the Multinationals

Table 6.3: Research and Development Expenditures and Employment by the Major Telecommunications Multinational Subsidiaries, 1973-1983 (millions of dollars, current prices)

Firm Name	(a)Total R&D Expenditure 1973-1983	(b)R&D Expenditure 1981-1983	b/a	R&D Personnel 1983	Total Employed 1983
Ericsson	53	36	68%	559	5598
SESA/ITT	21	5	24%	135	2497
Equitel/ Siemens	18	n/a	n/a	n/a	1700
NEC	7	4	57%	192	2191
Totals	99			>886	

R&D employment includes management and administrative staff involved in R&D.

Sources: Wajnberg (1984, p. 31), Instituto Nacional Propriedade Industrial (Rio de Janeiro) and company interviews.

ment in R&D roughly matches that of CPqD, including engineers under contract to TELEBRAS outside the centre. Excluding Siemens, total R&D spending over the two-year period 1981-1983 amounted to $45m - which is just over half of the total spent by the MNCs over the whole ten-year period. This demonstrates an increasing rate of technology expenditure by the MNCs in the very recent period.(5)

Further evidence indicates that these expenditures reflect attempts by the MNC subsidiaries to organise and develop local technological resources. These efforts were in response to both government pressure and increasing competition between the local MNCs for the new microelectronic exchange orders. Also, variations between firms illustrate the leading role played by EDB in developing technology locally. This is in contrast with the relatively low levels of R&D spending by the Japanese corporation NEC and the former ITT subsidiary SESA.

6.3.2 Trends in equipment imports and exports of the subsidiaries

Before discussing in detail the R&D activities of the individual subsidiaries, a useful aggregate indicator of the level of technological integration of the subsidiaries is the quantity of imports and exports of the supply sector, i.e. the commercial balance of the MNCs. Table 6.4 shows that MINICOM achieved a fair degree of success in reducing MNC imports and increasing the share of local inputs to production. In response to the laws introduced in 1975, imports fell from $249m in 1975 to roughly $48m in 1983. A modest level of exports also helped improve the overall commercial balance of the manufacturing sector from a deficit of $249m in 1975 to $31m in 1983. Evidence from the regulating agency GEICOM shows that the state operating companies also reduced their imports from over $100m in 1975 to approximately $20m in 1983.

By reducing the import value per unit of output, the GEICOM indices of nationalisation increased from 80 per cent in 1975-1976 to approximately 90 per cent in 1983. This simply means that for every dollar of imports the subsidiaries produce ten dollars of local output. Although this is a very crude measure, the telecoms ratio of 1:10 was easily the most successful within the overall electronics sector in Brazil at that time. The consumer goods industry ratio, for example, stood at 1:6.6 and the informatics sector at only 1:3 in 1983. New rules to reduce imports still further were issued in 1983 by CACEX (the department of foreign trade of the Bank of Brazil) with extensions to the list of prohibited imports.

6.3.3 Technological efforts and reorganisations of the individual multinational corporations

Alongside the increased R&D expenditures, and falling imports, there is also evidence of substantial

Table 6.4: Commercial Balance of the Telecommunications Equipment Supply Sector, 1975-1983 (millions of dollars, current prices)

	1975	1976	1977	1978	1979	1980	1981	1982	1983
Imports	249	161	177	68.8	68.5	78.1*	88.9*	79.7*	48.2
Exports	–	1.5	30.7	24.7	33.4	36.9	38.7	21.6	17.2
Commercial Balance (deficit)	249	159.5	146.3	44.1	35.1	41.2	50.2	58.1	31.0

*Increases due to introduction of new digital exchanges.

Source: Wajnberg (1984).

management and technological reorganisation by the subsidiaries, again geared towards acquiring local technological capabilities. The market leader, EDB, took an early lead in these developments. It is therefore useful to examine in detail the case of EDB and then to consider the rival firms' reactions to EDB's efforts to use technological development as a means of competition.

The technology strategy of Ericsson do Brasil
As Chapter 4 showed, the 1970 technology transfer agreement between EDB and its parent company was not only very restrictive but also guaranteed heavy financial payments to L.M. Ericsson in Sweden. Furthermore, the technology actually transferred was limited to the minimum necessary to support local manufacture of the electromechanical exchange equipment. The core technology needed for design, development and adaptation remained squarely in the hands of the parent company. However, the 1975 policy initiative brought about major changes in the organisation of management and technology, and led to a new technology transfer agreement.

In order to win the new contracts for SPC exchanges, and following the transfer of ownership to Brazilian capital, EDB agreed to comply with government wishes and set up a radically new management structure to ensure a genuine transfer of microelectronic technology. Under the new organisation EDB was termed an associate company of L.M. Ericsson.(6) EDB elects its own president while Ericsson appoints a managing director. Not surprisingly several Swedes remain in key positions. The seriousness with which technological development was taken is indicated by the new management organisation which changed from one centred around equipment categories to one based on the different technological activities required to develop and adapt telecoms systems. Figure 6.1 presents the R&D structure of the new technology directorate, together with numbers of personnel employed in technology development in 1983.

The main sub-division employed 354 of the 559 personnel, and is devoted to SPC switching development. The central design of Ericsson's AXE-10 digital exchange remains with the parent company (it cost approximately $500m to develop). However, substantial resources were allocated to design modification and software development. Other key activities include the PABX department and sub-divisions for component development. Much of the local effort is in the adaptation of digital systems to suit Brazil's particular telephone traffic and

Figure 6.1: Ericsson do Brasil: Organisation of Technology Directorate, 1983

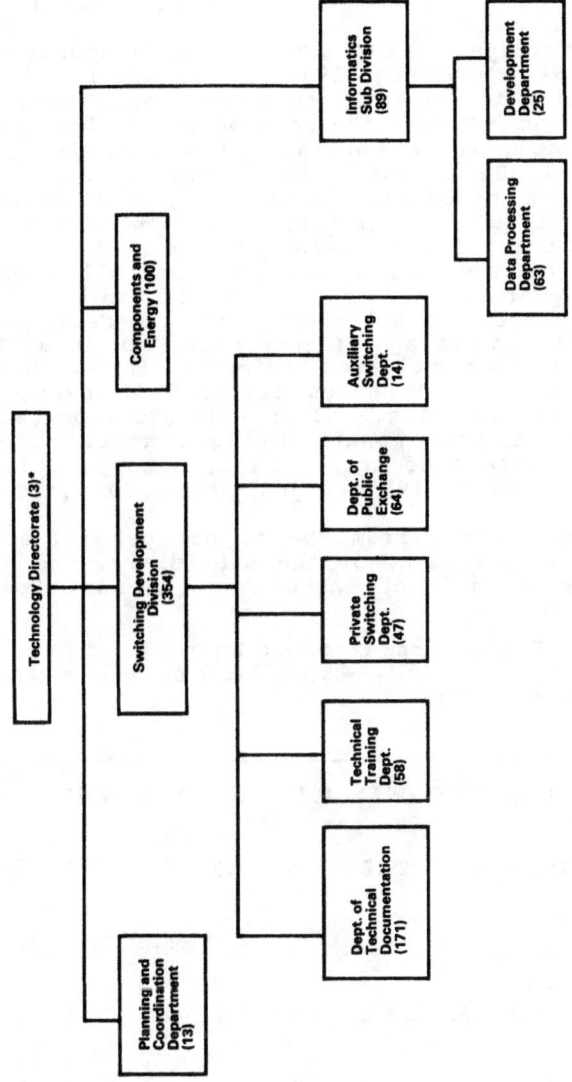

Notes: *indicates employment per department. Total employment 559

Source: Instituto Nacional de Propriedade Industrial (Technology Contracts Division)

Integration of the Multinationals

geographical conditions. A new department was also established for the development of related informatics products.

Over the period 1981-1983 EDB spent approximately $36m on R&D (Wajnberg, 1984, p. 31) which is roughly equivalent to 80 per cent of total government spending on R&D over the same period. Fixed capital in microelectronic capital goods includes 17 CAD stations, 50 terminals for software development, three text processors, and two CAD stations for microelectronic circuit printing. The augmentation of EDB's technological capability is reflected in the success of the company in substantially reducing imports over the period 1975-1983. Table 6.5 shows that over the period 1975-1983 imports declined from $162.3m to an average of just over $22m from 1977 to 1983. Absolute increases in imports in 1981 were due largely to SPC exchanges required to meet infrastructural expansion. After 1981 SPC imports began to decline as local manufacturing capacity increased. As a percentage of total sales, imports fell from 63.8 per cent in 1975 to just under 20 per cent in 1983.

Total exports from EDB do not yet reflect the increased capability of the subsidiary, and do not show any significant increase in trend. However,

Table 6.5: Equipment and Component Imports and Exports by Ericsson do Brasil, 1975-1983 (millions of dollars, free on board, current prices)

	1975	1976	1977	1978	1979	1980	1981	1982	1983
Imports*	162.3	70.6	28.8	9.6	7.3	5.9	7.3	7.8	30.0
SPC Imports	–	–	–	–	–	6.8	26.5	19.0	6.0
Total Imports	162.3	70.6	28.8	9.6	7.3	12.7	33.8	26.8	36.0
Exports	n/a	n/a	7.0	1.8	1.7	3.3	3.2	2.7	2.0

*Excluding SPC exchanges.

Sources: Wajnberg (1984), Brundenius and Goransson (1982).

after 1980, products exported were based on digital technology, and EDB was in a position to offer a range of microelectronic products on the international market. Whether or not EDB succeeds in exporting microelectronic-based products remains to be seen. Nevertheless, the very fact that the subsidiary is capable of offering digital products on the international market marks a significant change in both the previously restrictive policies and the capabilities of the local subsidiary.

The improved technological capability of EDB can also be seen by comparing the contract entered into in 1978 with the previous contract of 1970.(7) The 1978 contract was centred around a new order to supply 800,000 lines of telephone equipment over the period 1982-1986. MATEL, the new Brazilian holding company for EDB, and also TELEBRAS were involved in the negotiations between L.M. Ericsson of Sweden and EDB. The influence of TELEBRAS's purchasing power and growing technological knowhow was almost certainly a major factor in the very favourable conditions obtained by EDB in the negotiations.

Unlike the 1970 agreement, the 1978 contract called for capabilities in product design and process technology to be actually based in Brazil. A brief examination of the terms of the contract supports the view, expressed in Chapter 4, that the earlier agreement was a mechanism for transferring payment to the parent company rather than technology to the subsidiary. The new contract had three main elements - patent, trade mark and product-licensing rights. The first two, patents and trade marks, were granted completely without charge (again unlike the previous contract), substantially reducing the potential cost of the contract to EDB. The third element, product-licensing rights, was not free and contained the provisions for the transfer of technology for the Ericsson AXE-10 digital exchange.

The technology transferred under this agreement can be categorised into (a) disembodied technology, (b) embodied technology and (c) techno/managerial knowhow. Disembodied technology included technical specifications, drawings and other design information. Other technology was embodied in capital goods and, most importantly, people. Extensive training in engineering design, use and adaptation of CAD techniques, equipment installation and all other necessary assistance and advice was included. Techno/managerial knowhow included the expertise and backup information vital for the local development and commercialisation of products. This involved the parent company passing on information concerning machine tool suppliers, procurement sources, and financial and marketing knowhow. In addition, a fairly extensive list of further technical information was supplied on associated IT products, such as office communications equipment and data transmission devices. In short, the contract reasonably covered all the essential hardware and software needed to understand, manufacture and modify the AXE-10 system to suit Brazilian conditions.

To summarise, the evidence shows that during the late 1970s EDB evolved from a position of passivity and dependence on the parent company to a firm with a fairly substantial and growing technological capacity. In historical terms this shift should be viewed as the latest in a series of steps towards industrial and technological integration, beginning with sales and distribution offices, and progressing to assembly and manufacturing facilities. Clearly, this historical process was not automatic at any stage but the result of government pressure on the one hand, and the need to compete with the other MNC subsidiaries on the other. In particular, this most recent phase of acquisition of semiconductor-based technology was the direct consequence of government legislation and TELEBRAS's new centralised purchasing power. The monopsony power granted to TELEBRAS enabled Brazil to insist on the transfer of ownership and of management and technological facilities. Before assessing the facilitating role of microelectronic technology, it is useful to examine the progress of the other major MNCs in integrating their activities within Brazil's industrial infrastructure.

The strategies of Siemens, ITT and NEC
Data collected on Siemens, ITT and NEC also testify to an increasing degree of technological integration partly in response to EDB's strategy. In each case local expenditure on technology increased following the 1975 policy changes, and the overall indices of equipment nationalisation improved, leading to a reduction of imports by the subsidiaries (Tables 6.3 and 6.4). However, corporate responses to the Brazilianisation rules differed across the firms. As noted, EDB took an early initiative in establishing technological facilities to gain a greater share of the market. ITT/SESA effectively withdrew from the market, not wishing to invest in any microelectronic development facilities in Brazil. Siemens/Equitel, although slow to react, began to engage in technology-based competition with Ericsson on several fronts, while NEC appears to have successfully resisted any major changes in technology transfer policy.

Integration of the Multinationals

Beginning with ITT/SESA, the parent company decided it would not comply with the Brazilianisation directives and sold the total of the subsidiary's capital to the financial consortium Brasilinvest. Until 1983 ITT/SESA concentrated on continuing the production of electromechanical parts and components mainly for spares and replacements for the home and, increasingly, overseas markets. In 1983 the company was purchased by a Brazilian entrepreneur and began to reorganise its R&D activities to (a) acquire capabilities in digital transmission, peripheral and PABX equipment and (b) cooperate with CPqD in the public exchange development programme. In 1983 technology was being purchased from abroad, developed in-house and developed in cooperation with the government R&D centre. SESA (the new name for the company) increased expenditure on R&D as shown earlier, and is one of the three authorised manufacturers of CPqD's Tropico family of exchange systems.(8)

Siemens (now called Equitel), having initially lost shares to the market leader EDB, began a technology-based strategy to regain a larger share of the overall market. In response to the Brazilianisation rules, Equitel began introducing technology to adapt private and public exchanges developed by Siemens in Munich. A series of products which were not in the parent company's range were introduced. The subsidiary also began a systematic replacement of imported by locally produced inputs. This involved substantial technology training from Germany to equip the local company with sufficient knowhow to carry out extensive product redevelopment, since direct substitution of imports for local products was not possible. By 1983 approximately 93 per cent of the value of public exchange equipment was of national origin.(9)

Following the local technology training programme a large proportion of the German engineers returned home and were replaced by Brazilian engineers. By 1983 only five engineers at Equitel were German, with none at directorate level. As far as local product development is concerned Equitel participated in a consortium with four other Brazilian-based companies (ABC-Teletra, Siteltra, Induco and Siecom) to develop central exchanges for rural areas. Some of the new products developed by Equitel have been exported to other Latin American countries. Equitel's total exports rose steadily from $250,000 in 1979 to $588,000 in 1981 and $2,623,000 in 1983 (INPI), reflecting the increased autonomy of the subsidiary.

In 1982 Equitel embarked upon a new technology-based strategy to gain a larger share of the central exchange market. This involved a programme of joint technology development headed by the largest Brazilian telecoms firm, Elebra. In January 1983 the two parties signed an agreement, authorised by MINICOM, for the joint development of medium-scale public exchanges in conjunction with CPqD. From the point of view of Equitel, this joint technology cooperation was designed to regain a larger share of the market from EDB.

Evidence for the case of the Japanese corporation, NEC, suggests that the extent of technological integration remained at a much lower level than that of the other subsidiaries, despite some compliance with government policy. Fifty-one per cent of voting capital was transferred, R&D expenditure increased and a new centre for the development of technology was established. NEC claim to have dominated a whole range of digital transmission and peripheral technologies (a list of 37 new products were registered with the Brazilian Institute for Industrial Property), and a staff of 192 were employed in 1982 in R&D. Rising exports also suggest increasing technological capacity. As Table 6.6 indicates, NEC exports rose from $1.2m in 1979 to $5.8m in 1982 and $4.1m in 1983. The main export lines were PABXs, key systems and integrated circuit components. Unfortunately, it is not clear from the data why exports declined in 1983 over 1982 nor what proportion of exports consisted of integrated circuit components.(10)

In absolute terms, the information suggests that NEC increased its local technological capacity. However, in relation to the other MNCs the extent of technological capacity and integration appears to be far less. Table 6.7 presents some rough indicators of R&D 'intensity' for three of the MNCs and the leading Brazilian manufacturer, Elebra, for the year 1983. R&D intensity is used here as an indicator of

Table 6.6: Nippon Electric Company Equipment and Component Exports, 1979-1983 (thousands of dollars, current prices)

1979	1980	1981	1982	1983
1194	2059	3309	5795	4139

Source: INPI, Patents Division, Rio de Janeiro.

Table 6.7: Indicators of Research and Development Intensity of Four Leading Telecommunications Manufacturers in Brazil, 1983

Company Name	(a) Total R&D Spending ($m)	(b) Total Sales ($m)	R&D: Sales (b/a)	(c) Total Employment	R&D Spending Per Employee (a/c)	(d) Total Employed in R&D	Percentage of R&D Staff in Total (d/c)
EDB	18	186	9.6%	5539	3249	559	10.0%
SESA/ITT	2.5	55	4.5%	2497	1001	135	5.2%
NEC	2.0	59	3.4%	2191	913	192	8.7%
Elebra	3.2	29	11.0%	1366	2342	120	5.1%

R&D expenditures for 1983 calculated as an average from the period 1981-1983 (Wajnberg, 1984, p. 31). Data from Siemens/Equitel not available. R&D employment data for Elebra from company interview.

Sources: Wajnberg (1984), INPI, Teleguia (1984) and company interviews.

technological input. As a percentage of total sales NEC spent the least amount on R&D. The three other companies spent more on R&D, both in absolute terms and as a percentage of total sales (b/a). In fact, per unit of sales EDB and Elebra spent roughly three times the amount spent by NEC in 1983. As a percentage of total staff, NEC's R&D employment (d/c) ranked higher than SESA/ITT and Elebra but lower than EDB. Finally, in terms of R&D expenditure per employee NEC spent less than all three other companies, and considerably less than EDB and Elebra. Per employee, NEC spent $913 which was equivalent to 28 per cent of EDB's expenditure ($3249), and 38 per cent of Elebra's expenditure ($2342). While these data cannot be considered conclusive they do suggest that, overall, NEC's R&D effort in quantitative terms was less than the other companies.

In terms of technological integration NEC also appears to have made less effort. In contrast with EDB, SESA and Equitel, no development projects have been entered into with the government R&D centre. In relation to the other MNCs and the large national firms, NEC remained technologically insular, while the other companies began to compete on the basis of highly publicised local technological developments.(11) The reasons for NEC's strategy are not entirely clear; however, interviews with the equipment purchasing division of TELEBRAS indicated that NEC was perceived to embody the most advanced and most suitable digital exchange technology. This perceived technological superiority placed NEC in a stronger bargaining position than the other MNC subsidiaries, as TELEBRAS was keen to acquire NEC's particular system. For instance, despite NEC's resistance to technological integration, the company was awarded a major new contract to supply digital exchange equipment for Rio de Janeiro in 1984, on the basis of their technological lead.(12)

To sum up, the evidence shows that technological investments have become very much a part of the overall competitive strategies of the individual subsidiaries, despite variations between the individual companies. In fact, the Brazilian telecoms sector points to an important and relatively unexplored issue in DC industrial technology studies – i.e. the use of local technological development as a means of corporate competition. This occurred both as a result of the government's policy of insisting on technology development by the MNCs, and the improved capabilities of TELEBRAS which enabled the negotiations with the MNCs to be successful. The events testify to the fact that since the establishment of the MNCs in the equipment sector, they have become more and more 'Brazilian' in character, and are now 'embedded' in the industrial infrastructure of the economy.

It is important to emphasise that these events do not imply a wholesale shift of the locus of innovative activity from parent to subsidiaries. Given Brazil's relatively minor market status in comparison with the USA, Europe and Japan, a relocation of this nature was never considered, either by the corporations or by the Brazilian government. Nevertheless, it is important not to underestimate the changes which have occurred. In response to government pressure the MNCs, for the first time in their historical involvement in Brazil, have accepted that technological advance must be a permanent feature of their operations within Brazilian national boundaries.

Conclusions

The telecommunications multinationals and the developing countries

Since the Brazilian policy changes of the mid-1970s the MNC subsidiaries have substantially increased and integrated their levels of technological activity within the Brazilian economy. From a position of acute technological dependence on their parent corporations, the local subsidiaries are now engaged in a significant measure of technology-based competition within Brazil. Undoubtedly, there remains scope for further development by the MNCs, but the evidence of ownership transfer, local technology expenditures, import reductions, increased value of local input content, management reorganisation and competitive strategies all points to major successes in terms of the policy aims of the government. However, these events should not be viewed in historical isolation. From the very beginning of the MNC activities at the turn of the century, Brazil has, on and off, engaged in a long-term process of bargaining for greater national control over the corporations. The transition to microelectronic technology presented new opportunities for Brazil to bargain for greater levels of technological development by the MNC subsidiaries.

Regarding the nature of technological accumulation with microelectronics, it would be wrong to suggest that the subsidiaries succeeded in leap-frogging older vintages of technology. Rather, the process of technological accumulation resembled a cumulative transition. This gradual transition occurred in two senses. First, the subsidiaries made a transition from a passive technological role to a dynamic, technology-absorbing, role. Second, they made a transition from electromechanical-based technology to microelectronic technology. In both senses of this transition, the new technological form and the new technological role were firmly grounded in the old, and built upon the long-term historical development of the MNCs in Brazil. While one cannot generalise from the Brazilian experience to other DCs, this does imply that success in accumulating an industrial base in microelectronic technology will depend on the existence of industrial and technological infrastructure from which to draw the necessary experience and expertise. Put another way, it seems unlikely that, without a resource base in electromechanical technology, many DCs will be in a position to leapfrog directly to microelectronic technology.

The diffusion of microelectronic telecoms technology to Brazil through the MNC subsidiaries was not automatic, costless or market induced. The Brazilian government, through careful legislation and the use of monopsony purchasing power, succeeded in creating the conditions by which it became necessary for the MNCs to invest in technology. In a sense the policy changes succeeded in creating a Schumpeterian environment within which the subsidiaries were forced to respond. The government, rather than the market, allocated penalties for failure to invest in technology, and rewards for those most successful. It remains to be seen whether the technological momentum created by telecoms administration will continue unabated. However, the evidence does suggest that the seeds of technology-based competition have been sown successfully and the dynamic of advance will continue.

The Brazilian experience highlights one of the crucial developmental issues concerning local technological development and MNCs. Unlike the developed nations where the centres of innovative activity are located and the process of Schumpeterian competition rewards and penalises, in the DCs this environment cannot be taken for granted.(13) By virtue of the size of the Brazilian market, the growing technological capacity of the government R&D centre and the strongly interventionist policy, Brazil succeeded in creating a Schumpeterian environment and the conditions for dynamic technological progress. For other larger DCs wishing to involve the MNCs (pragmatically) in the development of industry and technology, the Brazilian case illustrates the need for a strong domestic policy, coupled with a local technological base, to enable effective bargaining to proceed.

The Brazilian experience strongly suggests that the diffusion of microelectronics throughout the telecoms industry during the 1970s has altered the economic and technological relationships between the MNCs and the Third World. The stable oligopolistic control of the large corporations is no longer monolithic. The restructuring of the industry around microelectronic technology, the increasing international competition for Third World markets and the entrance of new Japanese manufacturers suggest that there are now new opportunities for DCs to reassess their bargaining positions and to exploit the competition among the MNCs. New opportunities to insist on the transfer of industrial and technological capabilities may well present themselves to other large- and medium-scale DCs. Nonetheless, the strong presence of government policy in determining events in Brazil indicates that little will occur without the coordination and determination of telecoms administrations in other Third World countries.

Notes

1. For historical details see Maculan (1981).
2. Again, see Chapter 4.
3. The resistance of the MNCs is documented by Earp (1982).
4. This approach contrasts with the official policy of the Secretariat of Informatics (SEI) which emphasises ownership rather than source of technology. For example, in the microcomputer market SEI insists on 100 per cent Brazilian capital ownership to participate in the market, regardless of the source of technology.
5. Unfortunately, annual rates of expenditure by the MNCs were not available; data on R&D expenditures are from the executive of GEICOM, the organisation responsible for monitoring and controlling technology imports, and contained in Wajnberg (1984).
6. This section uses data from Brundenius and Goransson (1982), updated with evidence obtained from GEICOM and the Instituto Nacional de Propriedade Industrial (INPI), Rio de Janeiro.
7. Full details of both agreements are provided by Brundenius and Goransson (1982).
8. Company interview.
9. Company interview and Telebrasil (Nov/Dec 1983, p. 48).

Integration of the Multinationals

10. A high proportion of integrated circuit exports might indicate that the factory was being used as a cheap labour assembly plant, which would certainly not imply a rising level of technological capacity.

11. More often than not, marketing and advertising stresses the local efforts of the MNCs in contributing to Brazil's domestic technological advance in telecoms.

12. Interview with engineering manager responsible for purchasing policy of Telerj, the Rio de Janeiro operating company. As noted, it was not entirely clear why NEC was perceived to have a technological lead over the other main manufacturers. It may well be that other considerations, such as fast delivery, backup service and price, also influenced the desire of the service company to buy Japanese.

13. With the shift of the locus of innovative capacity in IT increasingly to Japan and the USA, European countries too are recognising that government must play a role in creating the conditions by which innovation and commercialisation will proceed (note the recent spate of government-funded technology programmes in IT discussed in Chapter 2). The problems confronting most DCs are generally of a different character given their relatively small internal markets, poor technological and economic infrastructure, and often far more severe problems of debt, inflation and unemployment.

CHAPTER 7

TECHNOLOGICAL ACCUMULATION AND ECONOMIC CRISIS –
THE EMERGENCE OF A BRAZILIAN TELECOMMUNICATIONS
INDUSTRY

Introduction

The purpose of this final empirical chapter is to examine the growth and development of local industry within the difficult conditions of economic recession and crisis in the post-1974 era. Earlier chapters argued that the intrinsic divisibility of microelectronic technology had opened up new opportunities for entry by indigenous manufacturing firms in the larger DCs. In fact, a key policy aim of the Brazilian government after 1974 was to encourage and support wholly national firms. By direct technological support through the national R&D centre, and by indirect policy measures such as import restrictions and the 'Brazilianisation of production' rules, MINICOM attempted to foster the progress of indigenous industry. The history of Brazil's achievements in this area is therefore of considerable interest to other DCs wishing to enter the production of goods and services in telecoms, and also to the role that government might play in supporting domestic industry.

To understand the significance of local industry it is necessary to view the new firms within the wider context of the telecoms sector as a whole, and in particular, in relation to the MNC sector. Section 7.1 therefore begins by analysing the overall size and growth of the equipment supply sector since the mid 1970s, and tries to assess the impact of the economic crisis and government investment restrictions on the planned growth of the network. Section 7.2 traces the historical growth of national firms within the 20 leading equipment supply firms in order to compare the participation of domestic industry with that of the MNCs.

Section 7.3 presents the results of the substantive research into the emergence and technological evolution of a broad cross-section of Brazilian telecoms companies. Data for more than 200 firms, many extremely small, are presented and analysed to try to comprehend the character of the new companies, the types of activity they undertake, and the technological nature of the goods and services they produce. In the course of the analysis rough estimates are also made as to the total contribution of local firms to equipment and component sales, and to the generation of employment within Brazil.

Section 7.4 addresses an extremely important matter rarely analysed in DC industrial development studies, that is, the costs of locally produced goods in relation to similar products available on the international market. Comparisons are made of Brazilian and 'best practice' international prices, and the total additional cost to the consumer (in this case TELEBRAS) is estimated. Given the symbiotic relationship between the equipment supply sector and the telecoms service sector, these additional equipment costs, we argue, must be viewed within the overall operating costs and revenues of TELEBRAS. Important indicators of the overall economic performance of TELEBRAS are presented to gain an appreciation of the operating performance of the service sector companies since the early 1970s, and the significance of the additional equipment costs to the telecoms sector as whole.

Finally we return to the broader implications of the evidence. We ask whether the experience of Brazilian firms provides any insights into the accumulation process with digital technology, and especially whether the transition to microelectronics, in fact, opened up new opportunities for local firms. Does the evidence support the earlier arguments regarding the gradual process of Schumpeterian learning at the sectoral level? Does the Brazilian experience throw any light on whether the transition to microelectronics has affected the barriers to manufacturing entry for firms in the developing world? For several other DCs the success of Brazilian industry in surviving and competing in this period of severe and prolonged economic crisis may well be of great significance.

7.1 The Brazilian Telecommunications Market: Size, Growth and the Impact of the Crisis

It is plainly impossible to forecast accurately what the size and growth of the telecoms equipment market would have been if the economic crisis had not

Emergence of a Brazilian Telecoms Industry

occurred. However, it is possible to trace the effects of the official cutbacks in planned infrastructural expansion which occurred as a direct result of the post-1973 crisis. From this information one can illustrate the effect on the potential growth of the industrial equipment market in Brazil.

The term 'crisis' refers generally to the recessionary period following the international oil and commodity prices increases of 1973 and 1974. In Brazil this period was characterised by balance of payments problems, accelerating inflation, rising unemployment and extremely low rates of economic growth in relation to the 'miracle' period of 1967-1973.(1) As a direct result of the crisis and, in particular, mounting government debt, the original telecoms expansion plans were cut back considerably, and financial resources were diverted from the telecoms sector to other areas of the economy. In 1975, the overall government planning authority SEPLAN began placing investment restrictions on the telecoms sector. As a result, the level of investment fell from a peak of around $1.8b in 1976 to $1.3b in 1979, and stabilised at around $1.0b from 1980 onwards (Table 4.4, Chapter 4).

In terms of equipment demand, the imposed cuts considerably reduced the size of the market which fell from approximately $1.2b in 1975 to a level of around $0.8b since 1978. The market reductions, illustrated in value terms in Table 7.1, represent a sizeable fall in the numbers of physical lines contracted out by TELEBRAS for manufacture. The market shrunk from around one million lines in 1973 to a level of under 400,000 in 1982. In 1982 and 1983 this level rose to about 500,000 owing to increases in investment over the 1981 and 1980 levels.(2)

Table 7.1: Brazil's Telecommunications Equipment Supply Market, 1975-1983 (billions of dollars, current prices)

1975	1.20
1976	n/a
1977	1.00
1978	0.82
1979	0.89
1980	0.76
1981	0.78
1982	0.83
1983	0.80

Sources: Telebrasil (1983 issues) and Wajnberg (1984).

Emergence of a Brazilian Telecoms Industry

These heavy reductions in equipment demand followed directly on from the rapid expansion of MNC investment during the boom period of 1967-1973, and resulted in a sustained and severe problem of overcapacity after 1975. Telecoms production output over the second half of the 1970s averaged only 55 per cent of installed capacity, reaching around 65 per cent for cable manufacturers.(3) The increased output of 1983 brought about a relatively good performance with overall capacity utilisation of approximately 70 per cent.

As a result of the investment restrictions and overcapacity, employment by the major MNC firms fell by roughly one half over the period 1975-1980, and stood at approximately 10,300 in 1983. Plessey and Philips withdrew from the market and the other MNCs were forced to carry out redundancies and factory closures.(4)

Alongside the enforced investment restrictions, two further means were used to restrict the potential rate of growth of the telecoms network and to divert resources to other sectors. The first relates to the tariff levels imposed by government. While telecoms tariffs remained well below the average rate of inflation over the period 1975-1983, input prices experienced no such restrictions. Extremely high rates of inflation make accurate estimates of the effect of this 'squeeze' very difficult to measure; however, according to the internal telecoms review journal, the effect was a substantial transfer of resources from the telecoms sector to other sectors because of relatively low telecoms price increases. To give some idea of the restrictions placed on telecoms prices, during the period 1973-1983 the basic telecoms subscription rate increased by 25 times, and the price of inter-urban phone calls increased by 35 times (using current prices with January 1973 as a base of 100). During the same period, retail price inflation increased 89 times, industrial electricity prices 120 times, gasoline 118 times and the minimum wage 87 times In a comparison with 12 major public services and products the basic telecoms price remained substantially lower than the average rate of price increase, mainly because of government restrictions on tariffs.(5)

The second method used to divert resources was the direct appropriation of finance from the Brazilian telecoms Fund (FNT), set up in 1973 as a central source of investment funding for the telecoms network. By law, approximately 30 per cent of the price of each telephone call was channelled to the FNT so that MINICOM could expand services into the less profitable regions, thereby cross-subsidising the poorer areas by the more wealthy regions and routings. In terms of the overall importance to telecoms investment the FNT provided roughly 24 per cent of total investment over the period 1973-1981, despite the transfer of resources to other sectors.

After 1975 a large proportion of FNT funds were diverted to another fund, the National Development Fund, to finance other government activities. Between 1975 and 1980 total resources appropriated reached the accumulated figure of Crs43b (approximately $813m.(6) By 1980 the proportion of resources channelled away from the FNT reached 50 per cent. Since 1980 the percentage of the fund actually used for telecoms purposes fell still further. In 1983, for example, of the Crs225b (approximately $424m) received by the fund, only Crs75b ($141m), or 33 per cent of total receipts, were returned for telecoms investment. In 1984 only 10 per cent of FNT receipts were planned to be reinvested in the telecoms sector.

The long-term wisdom of these restrictions on potential investment and expansion of the telecoms network is not an issue which can be dealt with in a sectoral case study, but a matter for overall resource allocation and development planning. It may be that more pressing social and economic needs justify these resource diversions. Nevertheless, the evidence testifies to the scale of the impact of investment cuts on the telecoms sector (the adverse impact on the poorer regions was outlined in Chapter 4). When examining the development of national telecoms manufacturers, it is therefore necessary to bear in mind the continuing economic context of crisis, uncertainty and overcapacity.

7.2 The Major Firms in the Equipment Supply Sector

Table 7.2 ranks the top 20 leading equipment makers by order of 1983 sales, for 1982 and 1983. In 1983 the sales of the top 20 manufacturers stood at $590m - equivalent to around 74 per cent of the total equipment market.(7) Given the wide margin of error involved in exchange rate conversions, the 1982 and 1983 sales data are not significantly different, although total employment fell slightly from 31,244 to 29,657. EDB supplied the largest single share of the market in both years, accounting for approximately 32 per cent of top 20 sales for 1983, and 29 per cent for 1982. The eight former subsidiaries together supplied approximately 70 per cent of the leading firms' sales for both years. In terms of the overall equipment market the MNC subsidiaries

Emergence of a Brazilian Telecoms Industry

Table 7.2: The Top 20 Major Firms in the Telecommunications Equipment Supply Industry, 1982 and 1983 (thousands of dollars, current prices)

	1983		1982	
Name	Sales	Employment	Sales	Employment
Ericsson do Brasil*	185934	5539	177296	6935
NEC do Brasil*	59222	2191	76933	2297
SESA/ITT*	55397	2497	58916	3405
Philips Nordeste*	39881	850	36238	853
Equitel/Siemens*	38637	1700	46976	1765
Elebra	36309	1366	29469	946
ABC-Telettra	36158	6840	22077	6780
GTE/Multitel*	28469	1700E	45237	1768
Siteltra*	22456	759	20540	875
Delta	16949	485	11873	486
Daruma	10915	808	12636	635
Coencisa	10475	326	6681	220
Splice	9821	696	10516	400E
E.E.	8998	149	12920	161
Construtel	7298	1257	6592	1094
Amelco	6532	447	7124	450
Control	5800	480	5344	407
Autel	3796	1200	4674	1230
Fone-Mat	3288	273	6162	217
Unitel	3354	94	11276	320
Totals	589869	29657	609480	31254

In order of 1983 sales. Converted from cruzeiros using official Banco do Brasil exchange rates for 1982 (Crs183.6 per dollar) and 1983 (Crs531 per dollar).

E, estimated.

* Signifies continued foreign capital participation, less than 50 per cent voting capital in all cases.

Sources: Gazeta Mercantil (1983), Teleguia (1984/5), Wajnberg (1984), Anuario Brasileiro de Telecomunicacoes (1983), Visao (1983), and INPI, Rio de Janeiro.

accounted for approximately 51 per cent of sales for both years. In the public exchange market the MNC concentration was far more pronounced: including SESA/ITT (now 100 per cent Brazilian owned), the MNC share of the market was around 98 per cent (Wajnberg, 1982, p. 11).

Since 1974 when there was virtually no significant local participation in the overall market, there has been a consistent and rapid growth of small and, later on, medium-scale firms. In 1976, at the time of the introduction of import restrictions, local firms occupied only 2 per cent of the market. By 1980 this figure had increased to 10 per cent, and in 1981 local firms supplied 17 per cent of the total equipment market (Maculan, 1981, p. 159; Wajnberg, 1982, p. 11). The data for 1982 and 1983 suggest that the share occupied by wholly indigenous firms was approximately 30 per cent of the sales of the leading 20 companies and, as discussed below, an even greater share of the overall equipment market.(8)

It should be said that, in operating within conditions of economic crisis, the MNCs were in a much stronger competitive position than the small- and medium-scale Brazilian firms, for at least four reasons. First, the greater operating scale of the MNCs allows for not only significant cost advantages in production, but also easier access to lower cost financial resources. Consequently, the MNCs were in a better position to withstand short- and long-term liquidity problems, order cutbacks and the general financial constraints intensified by the recession. Second, the size of the corporations and their access to foreign technology allowed easier diversification into other product areas. For example, after 1975, ITT/SESA moved into the production of photographic and computer equipment. EDB began manufacturing components for IBM computers, together with photographic equipment for Kodak. NEC diversified into microwave transmission equipment and parts for mainframe computers. All the larger MNCs broadened their activities into related areas of IT such as intelligent terminals, printers and office equipment.

A third advantage of the MNCs is that the type of equipment they produce, mainly large-scale exchanges, is not subject to the same degree of demand fluctuation and uncertainty as the relatively lower level technology produced by the small-scale Brazilian firms. The longer cycle time allows greater time and flexibility in the planning and organising of production activities. The fourth advantage of the corporations over local industry relates to longer-term investment cutbacks forced upon firms by the recession. If cuts are imposed upon technology investments by the local MNCs, access to parent company technology would, in theory, be available. This is not the case for technology investment by national firms, who depend on their ability to produce technology locally (albeit with government support in some cases).

This final point is extremely important in terms

of the continuing role of Brazilian capital in upgrading and augmenting the overall technological capacity of the telecoms industry. As one of the directors of a medium-size Brazilian company put it, in order for local firms to remain in the market, it is necessary to develop technology as part of their very survival strategy. Without continuously upgrading their capability local firms cannot hope to survive and compete in the highly sophisticated and rapidly changing telecoms market. In other words, dynamic local technological advance is a <u>necessary condition for survival</u> of the new Brazilian firms - this is not the case for the MNCs, who develop technology strategically as a means of market competition and, as Chapter 6 showed, in response to government pressure, but not as a condition for survival.

Nevertheless, despite the economic crisis and the inherent disadvantages of local firms in relation to the MNCs, many companies do appear to have emerged and survived during the decade examined. In order to understand the reasons for, and the extent of, this apparent success it is helpful to examine the nature of the firms concerned and the types of products they manufacture.

7.3 The Growth and Participation of Local Telecommunications Firms

According to the most comprehensive trade journal for the telecoms and informatics industries in Brazil, in 1983 there were approximately 840 firms engaged in IT activities.(9) The firms listed manufactured equipment, components, materials and services for the telecoms industry, the computer and telematics sector, and some consumer IT applications. As the telecoms and computer industries converge around digital technology it becomes extremely difficult to distinguish between telecoms firms and others. Nevertheless, from the 840 IT firms, 206 could be more narrowly classified as either predominately telecoms or as having a sizeable proportion of their sales devoted to telecoms.

Before attempting to interpret the data collected on these firms it is necessary to make the following three cautionary points. First, the actual number of firms is probably a significant understatement, especially among the smaller units, as the journal gathers information on a voluntary basis and presumably does not gain access to 100 per cent of the companies involved. Second, the sales data are not directly comparable with equipment market figures

Emergence of a Brazilian Telecoms Industry

as they include components, material, services and some private telecoms sales, which are not included in the official equipment market information cited earlier (Table 7.1). Third, a comprehensive analysis of the changing role of Brazilian firms should, ideally, include a detailed firm-level investigation with an effort to generate time series data. Unfortunately this type of investigation was outside the scope of the present study and, in the absence of reliable historical information, the survey below was forced to rely on cross-sectional information.(10) Given these caveats, the following should be interpreted as a first step in the assessment of the nature and role of the small-scale domestic telecoms industry.

Table 7.3 presents a profile of the 206 telecoms firms, categorised by sales for 1983. Groups A and A1 include all firms with sales greater than $10m for the year. The data for group A are omitted since to include this group might be misleading. The majority of these companies are large, heavy engineering firms, engaged not only in telecoms but in electricity supply and other heavy infrastructural activities. (They were also largely of MNC origin.) Only a very small proportion of the sales of these firms could be classified as telecoms equipment sales. However, within the 33 companies in groups A and A1, six were identified as relatively new, 100 per cent Brazilian-owned firms, producing mainly telecoms equipment. Group B was a coherent group of 20 Brazilian firms with sales of $5m to $10m. Groups C and D comprised a larger number of smaller companies with sales of $1m to $5m and less than $1m respectively.

As Table 7.3 shows, total sales amounted to around $380m in 1983 and employment was in the region of 25,000. This compares with the total final equipment market of approximately $800m in the same year, and a level of employment of over 30,000. Given the conspicuous absence of Brazilian participation in the early 1970s (11) this represents a surprisingly large number of indigenous firms with a substantial contribution to both sales and employment.

Turning to the individual groups in Table 7.3, sub-group A1 and group B can be categorised together as small/medium-scale firms, engaged largely in the manufacture of finished telecoms equipment. Most of the firms in this category either started up during the 1970s or experienced rapid growth in telecoms sales during the 1970s as a result of TELEBRAS purchasing policy and R&D support. Total sales of the two groups amounted to $230m in 1983, which is

Table 7.3: Size Profile of Brazilian Telecommunications Firms by Sales Groupings for 1983 (millions of dollars, current prices)

Size Group/ Quantity of Firms		Total Sales	Total Employment	Sales per Firm	Employment per Firm
A. >10m	27	–	–	–	–
Sub-group A1	6	94460	3831	15743	638
B. 5-10m	20	135940	8993	6797	450
C. 1-5m	50	117141	8588	2342	171
D. <1m	103	32984	3598	320	35
Totals	206	380525	25010		

Sources: Teleguia (1984/85), Anuario Brasileiro de Telecomunicacoes (1983) and Wajnberg (1984).

equivalent to 38 per cent of the total Brazilian telecoms equipment market.(12) Employment in the two groups stood at 12,824, which compares with total employment by MNC subsidiaries of 22,076 (including firms of MNC origin now 100 per cent Brazilian-owned). This suggests that at least some of the unemployment generated by suppressed demand in the large-scale sector is being compensated for by employment creation in the growing national sector. The nature of the equipment produced was largely peripheral and transmission products based on microelectronic technology, or concerned with interfacing equipment such as keyboards, public and private telephone terminals, modems, key systems and so on.

Together with a high degree of dependence on TELEBRAS for orders, several of these firms benefited technologically from CPqD technology transfer. In 1975 local firms were engaged mainly in manufacturing relatively simple equipment used in HF and VHF radio transmission. In 1980 local firms had progressed to more sophisticated areas of transmission equipment, and to terminal devices for telephones and telegraph. By 1983 some of the larger telecoms firms (particularly Elebra, but also EE, P&D Systems and others) were actively engaged in technological investments and cooperative development with CPqD.

Emergence of a Brazilian Telecoms Industry

The largest national firm, Elebra, although a special case, illustrates the progress of Brazilian capital, the dependence on TELEBRAS for orders, the technological opportunity afforded by microelectronics and the vulnerability of the new firms to fluctuations in demand. By 1983 Elebra had grown to become the sixth largest telecoms firm in Brazil and employed around 1400 people of whom 150 were electronics engineers. In 1982 Elebra invested approximately $2m in R&D or roughly 10 per cent of its annual turnover. At that time Elebra competed with the former MNCs in digital transmission and peripheral equipment. Since the early 1970s the firm invested heavily in exchange technology and was authorised by TELEBRAS to produce small-scale public exchanges. The company has close links with CPqD and develops equipment to suit Brazil's particular telephone traffic conditions. In order to reach this size (over twice the size of its nearest Brazilian rival), the company required substantial financial backing to finance long-term capital investments. Elebra was capable of taking this type of risk as it is part of a group of companies operating under a larger parent company, Docas de Santos. This particular company currently leads a consortium of firms (including one former MNC) in the development of medium-scale switching equipment with CPqD, and intended to manufacture a 4000-line exchange by 1984.(13)

One of the main reasons for Elebra's success in the market was the shift to microelectronic technology and the opportunity this provided in terms of relatively small-scale manufacturing investment. This divisibility in terms of technology and capital also benefited the other firms in groups A1 and B, allowing them gradually to accumulate skills and expertise in peripheral and transmission technology. However, despite the success of Elebra, the company remains highly dependent on TELEBRAS for orders and on CPqD for technology. A large proportion of sales are in digital transmission. Owing to the relatively short manufacturing lead time in this area, cutbacks in equipment orders exert a powerful influence on the company. By entering the exchange technology area Elebra planned to stabilise overall equipment demand and to continue its rapid growth by further diversifying its activities.

Other national firms in groups A1 and B are less fortunate than Elebra in terms of financial backing, and equally dependent on TELEBRAS for orders and technology. Sales of these firms ranged from $5m to $17m and employment averaged just under 500 per firm. Most of the equipment produced was based on, or related to, microelectronic technology. Products transferred from CPqD for manufacture include digital multiplexers (a) for telephone transmission (the MCP-30) and (b) for telegraph and data communications (the MDT-101). Also in transmission a terminal device for digital laser communications (the ELO-34) was in production in 1983, and the optical fibres and silicon materials were being manufactured by Brazilian industry. Various other products were in production including a wide range of public and private terminals, satellite receiving dishes, and other equipment, components and materials. Chapter 5 (Table 5.4) noted some of the leading firms, and some of the products transferred from CPqD for local manufacture. The ability of firms to engage in these activities depended, among other factors, on firm size, financial resources, and technological and management capabilities.

Group C consists of 50 firms employing a work force of 8588. Average sales in 1983 were $2.3m with average employment at around 170. Total sales and employment are, again, not directly comparable with market equipment sales, particularly because this group included a sizeable proportion of technological support services and component production. Sixteen of the 50 firms (32 per cent) registered services, such as network installation and maintenance, as their main activity (although these firms also produced equipment and components). Ten of the 50 firms (20 per cent) quoted components and accessories for telecoms and data communications as their main sales areas. The largest group (24 out of 50, or 48 per cent) were engaged in manufacturing peripheral and transmission equipment for telecoms and data communications. Only four firms were identified as having some links with CPqD. These firms appeared mainly during the 1970s and it is therefore reasonable to hypothesise that they were largely the result of the expansion of the telecoms network and import restrictions placed on the larger telecoms firms. Their emergence is therefore the indirect result of government policy rather than the direct consequence of technological fostering, more common in groups A1 and B. These firms, although small, represent an important and growing base of technological and infrastructural support to the overall telecoms system.

The final group, D, consists of 103 firms, with total employment at 3600 and total sales of $33m. This group is probably the most understated of all four groups given the very small size of the individual companies. Average employment per firm was 35 and average sales stood at $320,000 in 1983.

In terms of composition, firms in group D were similar to group C. The largest section, 61 firms (59 per cent), manufactured peripheral and transmission devices for the telecoms, data communications and consumer markets. A further 30 companies (29 per cent) specialised in various telecoms service activities, including installation, maintenance and other engineering activities. The remaining 12 per cent manufactured components and materials mainly for telecoms goods, but also for other related applications. Few firms had recourse to CPqD technology (only four firms were identified). Like group C, the companies were relatively new and emerged as a response to the new opportunities provided by the emergence of microelectronic technology and the expansion of Brazil's telecoms infrastructure.

7.3.1 Evidence of sectoral learning

At the sectoral level the evidence attests to substantial learning on the part of indigenous industry. New Brazilian firms entered the telecoms equipment market, and existing firms expanded their operations and claimed greater market shares. Over the decade analysed Brazilian industry became a significant contributor to overall sales and employment, and, increasingly, a source of technology for the telecoms network. Indeed, this progressive learning at the sectoral level is reflected in the institutional structures which have emerged to defend the interests of Brazilian firms and to provide flows of information on various aspects of the telecoms market. Accompanying the development of government institutions such as TELEBRAS and GEICOM, local industry has its own representative bodies such as the Brazilian Industrial Association of Electrical and Electronic Suppliers (ABINEE) and the Brazilian Association for Computers and Peripheral Equipment (ABICOMP). These trade associations have developed alongside local industry and reflect and support the development of the network of electronics, computer and telecoms companies in Brazil.

Despite the inherent disadvantages of the small national firms, and despite the economic crisis, many new companies took advantage of the market opportunities presented since 1974. Local firms progressed up the scale of technological complexity and the larger companies are actively engaged in investment in microelectronic technology, sometimes in collaboration with CPqD. By 1984, the main product areas covered were mainly transmission and peripheral equipment. There were signs, however, that the largest of the national firms were moving into the production of small-scale public exchanges. In addition, the new firms played an important role in providing a wide range of components, accessories and services, not only for telecoms but also for other related IT products, systems and services.

Four main reasons appear to explain the entry of Brazilian capital into what was once a rigidly dominated MNC oligopoly: (a) the rapid expansion of the telecoms network during the 1970s; (b) import restriction placed on final equipment manufacturers; (c) the opportunities in terms of divisibility, plus gradual and selective technological learning, made possible by the shift to microelectronic-based telecoms; (d) deliberate government technological support to local industry through CPqD.

7.4 A Note on the Costs and Benefits of Brazil's Investment in Telecommunications Technology and Infrastructure

During the previous chapters an effort has been made to illustrate the financial costs of Brazil's telecoms investments and to relate these to the benefits, both present and future. It is quite apparent that the benefits of installing a modern, efficient communications infrastructure and strengthening local technological capabilities are considerable, if difficult to measure. However, it is also important to consider the narrower costs of developing products locally and sponsoring infant industry. Within this final chapter dealing with sectoral concerns, it therefore seems appropriate to address this difficult issue by comparing the prices of goods produced in Brazil with those produced on the international market. It is also useful to view the additional costs to Brazil in the wider context of the operating performance of the service companies. In other words, to what extent, if any, have relatively high local telecoms equipment costs prejudiced the financial performance of the service providers? And equally important, have the operating companies justified the massive investments in telecoms over the past decade within the narrow economic criteria of financial performance?

Beginning with equipment cost comparisons, Table 7.4 presents details of Brazilian telecoms prices in relation to minimum international market prices. Prices paid for goods produced in Brazil are compared with international prices and the additional cost per unit is calculated. A figure for the total quantity of units sold in Brazil is estimated and used to calculate a hypothetical total international cost for each type of equipment. This total international cost is subtracted from total sales in Brazil to arrive at the total additional cost by equipment item.

It is important to note that the available international price is a minimum for a similar product, and that an exact equivalent may not actually be available on the international market. In addition, the international price does not include freight or import duties. Furthermore, the international price is probably not available to most PTTs in the developed countries who, in general, are obliged to purchase from domestic suppliers and cannot 'shop around'. Given these limitations, the data do give a rough idea as to the difference between domestic Brazilian prices, and 'best practice' international prices.

Sales accounted for in Table 7.4 amount to nearly $400m in 1983, which is roughly one half of the total Brazilian market. Items for which information could not be obtained were (a) transmission wires and cables ($190m) and (b) a wide range of peripheral equipment. The total additional cost to Brazil was $66.2m, approximately 17 per cent of total sales. The largest single item of additional cost was SPC electronic exchanges, which accounted for 47 per cent of the total additional cost. In nine out of eleven cases the Brazilian equipment price was higher than the international price, and in seven cases substantially higher. Even given the limitations of the above data there appears to be cause for concern. Digital exchanges were 40 per cent more expensive in Brazil, multiplex transmission equipment 105 per cent more expensive and digital microwave transmitter/receivers cost 173 per cent more. Only in the area of simple peripheral equipment were Brazilian products price competitive.

Although the information highlights the fact that Brazil pays more for its locally produced equipment, which of course should be a cause for policy concern, it is not possible to draw firm conclusions on costs and benefits from this evidence alone. During the transition to a new technology, and in the process of infant industry development, prices would naturally tend to be high in relation to existing major producers. Relatively low production scales and higher input costs might contribute to higher prices. Also, the fact that the industry is in the early stages of learning suggests that prices will fall as time proceeds. Certainly the main areas of additional cost (digital exchanges, multiplex transmission and electronic terminals) correspond to

Table 7.4: Cost Comparisons of Brazilian Telecommunications Equipment and Internationally Available Similar Selected Major Products, 1983 (average current prices, dollars)*

Equipment Category	Prices in Brazil (per unit)	Int'l Price** (per unit)	Additional Cost (per unit)	Units*** Sold (total)	Total Sales ($m)	Total Int'l Cost ($m)	Total Additional Cost ($m)
Electromechanical exchanges (per line equivalent)	360	330	30 (8.3%)	300000	108.0	99.0	9.0
SPC electronic exchanges (per line equivalent)	420	300	120 (40.0%)	257142	108.0	77.1	30.9
Multiplex transmission, FDM (per terminal point)	820	400	420 (105.0%)	39512	32.4	15.8	16.6
Multiplex transmission, PCM (per terminal point)	380	360	20 (5.6%)	54210	20.6	19.5	1.1
Microwave radio, analogue (per transceiver)	40000	22000	18000 (82.0%)	268	10.7	5.9	4.8
Microwave radio, digital (per transceiver)	60000	22000	38000 (173.0%)	178	10.7	3.9	6.8
Radio UHF (per transceiver)	7500	5000	2500 (50.0%)	933	7.0	4.7	2.3

Radio VHF (per transceiver)	1800	600 (50.0%)	12722	22.9	15.3	7.6
Teleprinters (per terminal)	5050	1850 (58.0%)	7089	35.8	22.7	13.1
Telephone handsets	30	-20 (-40.0%)	925333	27.7	46.2	-18.5
Public telephones	400	-200 (-33.0%)	37250	14.9	22.4	-7.5
Totals				398.7		66.2

* All basic data from GEICOM, presented in Wajnberg (1984), and amended for the purposes of the above calculations.

** This price represents the minimum available price on the international market and excludes other costs such as transportation and import duties.

*** In the cases of (a) exchanges and (b) microwave transceivers, data separating analogue from digital production were not available and an equal division, by value, was assumed. The result in terms of unit output broadly corresponds to actual physical output in the GEICOM data.

the new digital products and technologies. Interestingly, in the areas of electromechanical exchanges and analogue transmission equipment, prices are not significantly higher. Where there is a tradition of equipment production within the country, the local prices are much closer to the international minimum, and in two cases (telephone handsets and public telephone terminals) Brazilian prices are considerably lower than international prices.

Three further factors should also be taken into account when comparing equipment costs in this crude way. First, the cost of importation goes beyond the straightforward equipment price. Chapter 4 described some of the costs involved in dependence on foreign suppliers. These included additional financial payments on technology and expertise, and the loss of control over the management and direction of the domestic supply industry. Second, in terms of technological capacity and the production of appropriate hardware, the equipment industry plays an important role in the overall progress of the telecoms infrastructure, and this important benefit must be taken into account when considering extra equipment costs. Third, in recognition of the symbiotic relationship between the supply industry and the service sector, many countries support their domestic industries with subsidies, technological support and guaranteed orders.

Brazil is certainly not unique in being prepared to pay higher than market prices for locally produced equipment. In the UK, in the early 1980s, the bulk of exchange orders were allocated to domestic manufactures (GEC and Plessey) partly because the system was developed in Britain and partly because of the close relationship between the buyer (British Telecom) and the suppliers. In other words, price comparisons are rarely the only factor considered when deciding to import or buy locally. Similar policies are followed in Japan, Germany and other major telecoms markets which host domestic suppliers (OECD, 1983). It is therefore necessary to view the costs and benefits of local production (a) within the wider context of the important strategic benefits to be gained from a domestic supply industry and (b) in relation to policies followed in other countries.

To place the issue in perspective it is helpful to compare the additional price paid for equipment with service sector revenues and the capacity of operating companies to generate profit. In 1982 TELEBRAS's operating revenues were approximately $2.3b and operational profits stood at $414m. In comparison, the additional price identified in Table 7.4 amounted to $66.2m. Given the close relationship between the supply industry and the service sector, the higher prices paid for equipment might be justified as necessary to the efficient operation and expansion of the network. In other words, the strategic importance of the national industrial and technological base to the service sector must be considered when evaluating the benefits of local equipment production. Certainly for 1982 and, in fact, all other years (see below), relatively high equipment prices did not prevent TELEBRAS from making substantial profits.

To examine the operating performance of the service sector in more detail, Table 7.5 presents selected economic and financial performance indicators of TELEBRAS from 1972 to 1982. In terms of operating revenues TELEBRAS grew from only Crs3.8b (approximately $269m) in 1972 to Crs32.1b ($2.3b) in 1982.(14) This represents more than an eightfold increase in revenues, and establishes TELEBRAS as the eighteenth largest corporation in Brazil (Visao, 1983). Turning to profits, net operating profits are calculated as operating revenues minus operating expenses. Despite fluctuations, over the eleven-year period profits were consistently high in both absolute and percentage terms, never falling below 16 per cent. In absolute terms net profits ranged from a low of Crs1.1b ($77m) in 1972 to a high of Crs8.1b ($574m) in 1979. Profit for the most recent year shown, 1982, was Crs5.9m ($414m). As a result of these extremely high profits, in relation to other major corporations, TELEBRAS ranked as the second largest profit maker in the country in 1982 (in absolute terms), despite being the eighteenth largest in terms of revenues. Given the relatively low tariff rate increases, the relatively high cost of equipment purchases and financial transfers from TELEBRAS to other sectors described earlier, these high rates of profit represent a remarkable achievement.

During the period covered in Table 7.5 TELEBRAS's investments were largely self-financed. The main sources of finance were (a) autofinancing (revenues from telephone sales), (b) profits from international and inter-urban routes and (c) resources from the FNT. Over the period 1973-1977, internal financing averaged roughly 56 per cent per annum.(15) Since 1977 TELEBRAS was almost completely self-sufficient, with internal financing never falling below 94 per cent of total investments. As a result of the performance of TELEBRAS, the company occupies a unique position among Brazilian state enterprises, with extremely low borrowing requirements, price increases below the rate of inflation, rapid growth

Table 7.5: Selected Economic Performance Indicators of the TELEBRAS Telecommunications Operating System(1), 1972-1982 (prices in constant 1977 cruzeiros, millions)(2)

Year	Operating Revenues	Operating Expenses	Net Operating Profits		Annual Investments	Auto-financing(3)		Employment (000s)	Annual Imports	Price Indices, Base 1977=100
1972	3840	2743	1086	40.0%(4)	4397	—		52	n/a	26.25
1973	8945	5577	3369	60.4%	3855	4363	55.5%(5)	60	n/a	30.16
1974	11615	9724	1886	19.4%	14726	3174	21.6%	70	n/a	38.82
1975	14507	12055	2452	20.3%	20516	6125	29.9%	75	1450	49.63
1976	16308	13291	3017	22.7%	25861	5509	21.3%	85	1471	70.10
1977	20290	15929	4361	27.4%	23010	5943	25.8%	86	902	100.00
1978	24737	17982	6755	37.6%	19758	6437	32.6%	92	495	138.70
1979	29230	21046	8116	38.6%	19012	5990	31.5%	94	608	213.50
1980	27083	22987	4097	17.8%	14224	5925	41.7%	97	429	427.50
1981	29403	25352	4052	16.0%	16576	5752	34.7%	100	269	897.30
1982	32096	26237	5856	22.3%	17406	5780	33.2%	101	293	1753.70

(1) TELEBRAS System is under the control of the holding company, Telecommunications Basileira S.A., and is responsible for the operation of 97.3 per cent of total telephones in Brazil.
(2) Converted from current to constant cruzeiros using official Banco Central do Brasil general price indices, as shown in final column. The average exchange rate for 1977 was Crs14.144 per dollar.

(3) Autofinancing refers to resources generated from the sale of rights to telephones to individuals.
(4) Percentage profits calculated as a percentage of operating expenditures.
(5) Autofinancing calculated as a percentage of annual investment.

Data Sources: Telebras Annual Report (1982), DEF-Tendencias (Internal Financial Journal of TELEBRAS) (Oct/Dec 1983), Banco Central do Brasil, Buletin Mensal, (Feb 1984) and GEICOM executive, presented in Wajnberg (1934, p. 29) (import data only).

and high rates of profit. Overall, in terms of private costs and benefits, the costs of the national investments in telecoms are more than compensated for by the benefits.

Table 7.5 also tries to go beyond narrow financial benefits, to illustrate some important external benefits from the service sector investments and the improved technological capacity in telecoms. Employment increased consistently throughout the economic crisis, rising from 52,000 in 1972 to just over 100,000 in 1982. Rising employment was not at the expense of productivity. If we calculate the ratio of employment to sales over the period 1972-1982 (as a rough measure of labour productivity), the data show an almost uninterrupted increase from under 100 cruzeiros per worker in 1972-1973, to over 300 cruzeiros in 1982. Also, imports show a marked reduction, falling from around Crs1.5b ($106m) in 1975 to Crs293m ($20m) in 1982. More importantly though, and outside the scope of Table 7.5, the large investments in telecoms brought about a dramatic improvement in the communications capacity of the country and, as described earlier, laid the foundations for Brazil to meet the forthcoming demands of information technology. From the evidence, there can be no doubt that benefits from Brazil's commitment to telecoms infrastructure and technology vastly outweigh the costs involved.

Conclusions

Microelectronic change and opportunities for manufacturing entry

Since the early 1970s Brazil has witnessed a surge of new, often very small, firms entering the production of telecoms equipment, components and services. Many of these firms fall outside the realm of direct government support and organised technology transfer. They are the consequence of opportunities presented by the rapid expansion of Brazil's communications infrastructure, the shift to microelectronic technology, and the determination of the government to control imports and give support to national technology. Despite the economic crisis and the cutbacks in planned telecoms investments, by the early 1980s these firms supplied a significant proportion of telecoms equipment demand and contributed substantially to the overall expansion and upgrading of the telecoms infrastructure.

The evidence indicates that local firms progressively **learned** with microelectronic-based technology, allowing the largest companies to graduate up the scale of technological complexity. Moving from basic peripheral devices, Brazilian firms gained the knowhow to produce more complex transmission equipment and, very recently, exchange technology. Although by 1984 the industry as a whole was still in its infancy it already constituted an important source of employment, as well as an additional source of technology for the telecoms network.

In some respects the policy of telecoms expansion and import restrictions acted to insulate the emerging Brazilian companies from the worst effects of the crisis. However, this pattern of rapid growth in IT industries is a worldwide phenomenon. As the transition to digital technology proceeds, it is at the centres of gravity in IT - in fields such as telecoms - that the greatest opportunities lie for economic growth and expansion. For other DCs, the success of Brazilian firms in entering the market and providing goods and services indicates strongly that there may well be opportunities for other countries to enter the manufacture of telecoms equipment. More generally, the evidence suggests that policy makers should seriously consider the prospects for manufacturing entry across the whole spectrum of electronics telecoms and IT industries.

Turning to the theoretical context, outlined in Chapter 1, this sectoral evidence lends further support to the argument that the diffusion of a new technology is not mechanistic, effortless or costless. The learning process underlying the diffusion of digital telecoms in Brazil was the result of specific technological investments and efforts by leading firms. The success demonstrated by specific firms in gaining market shares and entering the field of microelectronic telecoms led other firms to imitate the leaders and try and gain the rewards from successful market entry. While the Brazilian telecoms industry, as a whole, is still in the very early phase of the diffusion cycle and the future remains to be seen, the evidence attests to the difficult, specific and cumulative nature of technological learning.

Finally, the experience of Brazilian firms supports the argument made earlier that the transition from electromechanical to microelectronic technology has destabilised the traditional economic relations of dependence and dominance in this sector. The divisibility of the new technology has opened up new opportunities for selective manufacturing entry and the gradual accumulation of capabilities in specific areas. The shift of the locus of technological effort away from manufacture towards design

Emergence of a Brazilian Telecoms Industry

and development means that the technological control exercised by the large MNCs over the production process is becoming less and less of a barrier to entry. If the arguments presented here are correct and the design capabilities in telecoms (and possibly other fields of IT) can be centralised and accumulated at a low cost, then the possibilities for manufacturing entry, reducing imports and locating value added within national boundaries, should be placed centrally on the policy agenda for developing countries.

Notes

1. For an analysis of, and different views on, the cause of the crisis see Wells (1979) and Balassa (1979). The terms 'crisis' and 'recession' are used interchangeably here.
2. Information from Revista Telebras (various issues) and Wajnberg (1984).
3. Data from GEICOM, presented in Wajnberg (1982, p. 6).
4. It should be noted that the equipment supply sector accounts for only a small proportion of total telecoms employment in Brazil as elsewhere. Overall telecoms employment continued to rise during the crisis (see below).
5. In 1983, for example, retail price inflation was 223 per cent and telecoms tariffs were only permitted to rise by 175 per cent, or 78 per cent of the average rate of inflation (Teleguia, 1984/5, p. 78). For historical details of relative price increases see Telebrasil (Nov/Dec 1983, pp. 7-8). See also Revista Telebras (Sept 1981, p. 72) for an earlier study which broadly confirms these findings.
6. Telebrasil (Nov/Dec 1983, p. 3).
7. The leading firms' output is not strictly comparable with the total (official) telecoms output of roughly $800m for two reasons: (1) firms' output includes some proportion of non-telecoms production, mainly related IT products and (2) the official telecoms market estimate probably understates the growing private telecoms applications area. Nevertheless, the data on firms' total output do give a good indication of the overall concentration in the industry.
8. It must be stressed that these comparisons are very approximate and subject to the wild fluctuations of the cruzeiro/dollar exchange rate, inaccurate records and the absence of available time series data. Accepting these limitations, the figures do demonstrate the increasing importance of local firms in the market.
9. Teleguia (1984) - the Brazilian guide to the telecoms and informatics industries. Evidence for this section was also gathered from Anuario Brasileiro de Telecomunicacoes e Telematica (1983), and other trade journals including Revista Telebras (various issues) and

Telebrasil (various issues), and from interviews with GEICOM, TELEBRAS, CPqD and INPI.

10. A detailed historical study of the surprisingly large number of new national telecoms and information technology firms - their emergence, their current role and participation in the market, and their technological importance to the overall telecoms sector - could be the subject of a complete, separate, study.

11. According to an earlier study by Maculan (1981) Brazilian firms accounted for just 2 per cent of total sales in the early 1970s.

12. As mentioned, this percentage is not the actual proportion of telecoms final equipment supplied by Brazilian firms as some other products, components, materials and services are included in the sales figures. Nevertheless, the value of sales of these firms, in relation to the total equipment market, is a useful indicator of the relative size of the various sub-sectors.

13. Company interview and Companhia Docas de Santos Annual Report (1982).

14. All prices are in constant 1977 cruzeiros. The average exchange rate for 1977 was Crs14.144 per dollar.

15. TELEBRAS Annual Report (1982). Note that internal financing includes profits from international and inter-urban routes and resources from the national telecoms fund, as well as 'autofinancing', which is defined as revenues from the sales of rights to telephones.

CONCLUSIONS

In order to generate a useful working methodology to carry out the study of Brazil's telecoms industry an attempt was made to integrate the empirical and conceptual findings of the developmental 'learning' school with diffusion theory. Within diffusion theory it was possible to extend the learning approach from the strictly microeconomic level to include the Schumpeterian style learning which occurs between firms, as well as at the sectoral, governmental and macroeconomic levels. This extension was put forward in order to explore how a developing country such as Brazil might acquire and successfully diffuse a new, 'foreign', technological form. The general argument was made that, because DCs are dislocated from the international centres of innovative activity, dynamic learning at these various levels is the main mechanism by which technological accumulation and advance occurs in the Third World.

This notion of Schumpeterian learning integrated naturally with existing diffusion studies. Diffusion theory offered a theoretical framework within which the concept of technological learning could be properly understood and developed. In carrying out this task it became clear that the concept of Schumpeterian learning added a valuable new dimension to diffusion theory; that is, a methodology for understanding how the diffusion process occurs. Indeed, this dynamic learning could be viewed as one of the principal mechanisms of technological diffusion between firms, sectors and ultimately whole economies. Different types of learning paralleled and explained the shape of the diffusion cycle, overcoming the tendency in diffusion theory to treat technological accumulation as a mechanistic and automatic process. This dynamic concept of learning also promised to differentiate between technological forms and to provide a means for understanding how a

Conclusions

new paradigm - such as IT - could be absorbed by, and diffused within, a developing economy.

It is unnecessary to repeat all the findings of the Brazilian case study as these are presented in detail in the conclusions of Chapters 4 to 7. However, it is worth focusing on some of the most important findings which have relevance beyond Brazil and beyond the confines of the telecoms sector. The evidence shows beyond doubt that the transition to microelectronic technology presented a range of important technological opportunities to Brazil. These were identified early, seized and exploited. None of Brazil's achievements were automatic, costless or the result of market forces. They were the consequence of creative government policy and a strong commitment to a modern communications infrastructure, as well as indigenous industry and technology. Technological change was therefore a necessary, but not sufficient, condition for success.

In terms of infrastructure Brazil succeeded in leapfrogging several generations of electromechanical telecoms technology, and now has installed a sophisticated, microelectronic-based communications network. The modernised public telecoms network in Brazil provides a wide range of IT services beyond conventional telephony, and the overall communications capacity of the economy has expanded considerably. Other DCs too may benefit from their lack of commitment to previous technological forms. In fact, in countries currently installing and expanding their basic telecoms network there is little choice but to leapfrog older vintages of technology. There can be little argument for installing obsolete, more costly and less efficient technology.

Central to Brazil's success both in infrastructural expansion and industrial development was the government R&D centre in digital technology - CPqD. At very low cost, CPqD was able to galvanise Brazil's technological resources, design digital systems suited to local conditions, and add substantially to the country's bargaining power in relation to the multinational corporations. The case study of CPqD showed that in a relatively short period of time the centre was able to accumulate a substantial dynamic base in digital technology. This was achieved through the application of a range of design-intensive, information-based learning mechanisms, specific to digital technology. This type of enterprise could not have been achieved with electromechanical technology. On the one hand the modular divisible nature of microelectronic technology permitted the gradual technological accumulation and selective development of digital systems. On the

Conclusions

other, the shift towards information-based, design-intensive technology allowed for the centralisation of common telecoms facilities under one roof, and the application of local scientific and intellectual skills to the task of productive development.

On the industrial front, Brazil moved from a position of deep and costly technological dependency to a position of technological advantage and integration. The multinational subsidiaries responded to government pressure by reducing imports, locating more production in Brazil and investing in technology. New local firms entered the market producing relatively simple equipment and gradually expanded their technological expertise and market shares. Again, technological change provided the opportunity for these very significant advances to take place. The intense international competition destabilised the historically cemented economic relations between Brazil and the MNCs, and the Brazilian telecoms administration was able to exploit the corporate rivalry by insisting on the transfer of technology as a condition for remaining in the market. At the same time the intrinsic design modularity of the new technology enabled a progressive upgrading of the capabilities of the subsidiaries.

National industry made substantial inroads into the equipment market and at the time of writing looked set to continue its development. Despite the conditions of economic crisis many new small- and medium-scale Brazilian firms entered the production of telecoms goods and services. The evidence indicated a substantial degree of Schumpeterian learning at the sectoral level, leading to the consolidation of an independent national base in the new technology. Over the period examined local industry contributed significantly towards overall production and employment and provided a new source of technological support for the national telecoms network. Again, microelectronic innovation was a necessary condition for these advances, but not a sufficient one. The progress of national industry also depended very much on the growth of the telecoms network and government technological support for the larger firms.

Unlike infrastructural developments, industrial progress could not be described as 'leapfrogging'. What occurred in Brazil was a progressive transition to microelectronics, involving a gradual process of investment, risk and uncertainty. In the MNC sector, firms faced the difficult and costly task of making the transition from electromechanical to digital technology (or ran the risk of being completely

Conclusions

excluded from the market). Also, the MNC subsidiaries were forced to make the transition from a passive subsidiary role to one of far greater independence in the realm of technological and management activities.

The notion of industrial leapfrogging implies that firms, and perhaps whole economies, can move directly to a new technological form - in a similar way, say, to installing a modern telecoms network - gaining the benefits of the new technology and by-passing older generations of less efficient technology. However, in the sphere of industrial technology, to enter the production and development of microelectronic equipment and ultimately to compete internationally, it is actually necessary to build a substantial innovative capacity into the industrial infrastructure of the economy. As the Brazilian case showed, this process was difficult, gradual and costly. Rather than leapfrogging, the absorption of microelectronic capability rested on the ability to extend and transform existing resources and endowments. At the firm, sectoral, government and national economic levels, Brazil gradually acquired and internalised the technological capabilities crucial to market entry. Rather than leapfrogging, Brazil slowly and painfully 'learned' its way along the diffusion curve, gradually and selectively progressing up the scale of technological complexity. Further investments and risks will undoubtedly be needed to sustain and continue the technological momentum curently in progress.

In the wider international context the Brazilian case did not suggest that a wholesale process of industrial and technological leapfrogging by developing economies to IT or any other new form of technology, is highly likely. The notion of leapfrogging implies an ease of movement and transition, and an avoidance of previous technological stages. Certainly, this was not the case in Brazil. Here, the process of technological accumulation was a struggle characterised by investment, effort, creative policy intervention, gradual and complex industrial learning, and the mastery of complementary technologies. As future international patterns of industrialisation unfold, it may well be that, selectively, other NICs will successfully enter and compete in the IT industries. However, the Brazilian case suggests that the successful newly industrialising economies will first find it necessary to accumulate substantial innovative capabilities within the industrial infrastructure of their economies. Rather than leapfrogging, this process will be achieved by the gradual process of

Conclusions

technological learning at the levels of firm, sector, government and nation.

Future Research - Information Technology and the Developing Countries

One critically important finding which arose from the international section of the study is that in the areas of telecoms and the other information-intensive service industries, there exists little, if any, 'breathing space' for DCs to react to the current microelectronic-induced industrial and technological change. Unlike many industrial applications of IT, microelectronic technology has already dramatically transformed the telecoms, computer and informatics industries. This is not surprising. Historically, IT is the first technology uniquely suited to coherently and efficiently processing information. The closer an industry is to information processing and retrieval the more receptive the industry will be to technological advance based on IT. What is surprising is that research has focused largely on the impact of microelectronic technology in 'conventional' industries, much further away from the poles of diffusion and transformation in IT. In these industries it is widely accepted that massive changes are still to come, and the pattern, pace and consequences of these changes are very uncertain and unpredictable.

Given the pace of change in the IT industries, DCs have wrestled with decisions regarding modern computing and telecoms technology for many years. Yet, there exists little research into the social and economic effects of these technologies, and the failures and successes of government policies in different countries. This is not to say that research in other fields of microelectronics and DCs is unimportant. However, there is an urgent need to redress the balance of research and to deal with the question of how the use of these technologies has already affected Third World economies, and the opportunities and problems faced in building up technological capabilities and, in some cases, manufacturing capacity. Research into these matters might provide insights into how the application of computing and IT has already affected productive efficiency, employment, social and economic organisation and so on.

To undertake research into the impact of microelectronics into the IT industries is practical, urgent and potentially very useful. From the historical point of view it would not be necessary to

Conclusions

rely on speculation as to future trends, as most research to date into conventional industry has been forced to do. Several DCs, large and small, already have valuable stories to tell in the fields of digital telecommunications, informatics and computer applications. The urgency of this work lies in the fact that policy makers are currently facing decisions on the installation of telecoms infrastructure and the use of computing technology throughout the Third World. The experiences of different countries in these fields might help others avoid serious mistakes, gain any benefits the new technology has to offer, and plan the development of the IT infrastructure in a way best suited to the countries' needs and problems.

A better understanding of the need for, and the feasibility of, developing technological capabilities in IT, especially in the smaller and medium-scale DCs, might prevent a further widening of the technology gap as the diffusion of digital technology proceeds. Some important insights and lessons were learned from Brazil's experience in telecoms. However, as stressed throughout, Brazil is a very special case among the DCs and cannot be used as a policy model for other countries. Research is urgently needed into the groups of smaller, poorer DCs, with limited absorptive capacity and small local markets. Some of these countries are already critically dependent on IT for communications, electricity supplies, tourism, commerce, banking and so on. Where to strike the balance between importation/local manufacture, technological reliance/local capabilities is an important and researchable topic. To fail to acquire technological capabilities and to simply remain a user of IT may run a serious risk of failing even to be an efficient user of IT in the long term. Research could help to avoid this danger by providing information as to potential ways smaller DCs may be able to acquire the capacity to use IT efficiently, and adapt systems to suit their specific needs and circumstances.

For the smaller and poorer DCs, research into telecoms is especially needed. Quite apart from the crucial role telecoms plays in economic progress, it is unique among the IT industries for at least two strategic reasons. First, in contrast with other areas of IT, all purchasing is normally centralised under one administration. This can bestow a considerable degree of monopsony power into the hands of the DC governments. Second, to be in possession of international telecoms facilities imposes a certain degree of cooperation between telecoms administrations in different countries. These two

Conclusions

special characteristics of telecoms suggest there might be possibilities for regional cooperation between smaller DCs in the areas of technology development and, perhaps, in bargaining together for improved technology transfer terms from the MNCs.

In terms of purchasing, it may be feasible for the smaller countries within regions such as Latin America and Africa to insist on the location of manufacturing facilities within particular national boundaries. This improved bargaining power might also be applied to 'persuade' the MNCs to cooperate with the long-term telecoms development plans of groups of countries. Another feature of telecoms, discovered in the Brazilian case study, is the feasibility of centralising R&D facilities and using shared infrastructure to gain knowhow and experience in a wide range of telecoms products and processes. Under the previous technological regime, these technological activities and processes were distributed across a wide range of firms, institutions and individuals, and could not be centralised in this way. Can cooperation in R&D help groups of countries gain a 'foothold' in modern telecoms technology at low cost as in the case of Brazil? Or do existing regional conflicts and political differences outweigh the degree of cooperation imposed by international communications links?

We saw, too, that a telecoms R&D centre potentially had many useful linkages to other areas of IT activity. As the telecoms and computer technologies continue to converge around digital technology, shared R&D facilities may be one mechanism to acquire technology in the informatics and telematics industries. Groups of countries, and some specific larger DCs, may be able to exploit this technological convergence by using telecoms facilities for developing capabilities in fields such as product development, process development, the use of CAD, high technology management, engineering training and software engineering. Only detailed investigation can illustrate if and where these technological opportunities lie, and whether institutional divisions within countries and political divisions between countries rule out imaginative responses to the challenge of IT.

IT, above all, is a design-intensive technology. It is a technology uniquely suited to the application of thinking activity to the production of commercial goods and services. Brazil succeeded in applying its university resources and other academic research institutions directly to commercial, production-related activities. In a sense, the national R&D centre acted as a bridging institution between the academic sector and the industrial sector. Other countries, too, may be able to exploit relatively marginalised scientific and technological resources in this way. Research can help us understand how and if the existing scientific and technological systems, which have developed over many years in the Third World, can be directed to the urgent problems posed by IT. The changing relationship between science, technology and production in IT is a little understood phenomenon. Research in this area promises to reveal practical insights, not only into the industries discussed here, but into the other industrial and non-industrial sectors which are further behind in the cycle of diffusion of IT.

A final issue which demands investigation is the most recent developments in IT which threaten to make obsolete even the most advanced present forms of microelectronics. As industry undergoes transformation and restructuring around microelectronics, it should not be forgotten that IT itself is rapidly changing and developing. In response to the recent Japanese announcement of research in a new generation of electronic technology - the so-called fifth generation - governments throughout Europe have begun to invest massively in R&D programmes to prevent themselves being left behind in the rapidly growing IT industries. New semiconductor techniques promise to process data in parallel, which will vastly increase the speed and computing power of future generations of IT products. New software engineering tools are being developed to automate the software development process to transform the design of IT systems from a slow human craft-based activity to a massively more efficient, faster process. 'Artificial intelligence' or 'knowledge-based systems' also promise to expand the efficiency and capacity of computing, and to provide a wide range of new digital technologies for use in many social and economic activities.

Many extravagant claims are made about the revolutionary effect these advanced forms of IT will have on the international economy. It is, of course, in the interests of those involved in the R&D laboratories and industries concerned to 'hype up' the potential impact of these technologies. One only has to turn to the massive literature on artificial intelligence to confirm this point. Nevertheless, it is important to try and understand the real economic implications of these trends for the IT industries. Is the technological frontier really advancing so quickly as to impinge on the possibilities for DCs to manage the technology gap and to prevent even countries as advanced as Brazil from keeping up with

Conclusions

technology change? Or are these technologies possibilities for the future with little real imminent prospect for accelerating industrial and social transformation?

For the developing world sober investigation into the claims of the technologists, and especially the evidence of diffusion of advanced IT in the DCs, might help clarify the picture for the DCs. Again, this is an area entirely ignored by economists in development economics, technology and development, and even in the research literature narrowly concerned with microelectronics and the Third World. Hopefully, the evidence of Brazil's remarkable achievements in managing the technology gap in digital telecoms will draw more attention to one of the most important modern economic challenges facing the developing world.

APPENDIX 1

Glossary of Technical Terms

Analogue   Electromagnetic wave form analagous to a continuously variable quantity such as temperature. Digital, on the other hand, is transmitted in discrete, separate pulses using techniques such as PCM (see below).

Coaxial (Cable)   A cable used for trunk (long-distance) telecoms transmission. The coaxial outer sheath and central coil are both electrical conductors, separated from each other by an insulating material. Expensive to install in comparison with alternative systems such as microwave relays, optical fibres and satellites.

Codec (Coder decoder)   Coverts analogue speech into digital form for transmission and back again for reception.

Crossbar   Near obsolete electromechanical exchange used as an intermediate technology between Strowger and fully automatic electronic exchanges.

Digital   A discrete or discontinuous signal transmitted in intervals. Modern computer and telecoms technology is based on digital technology because of its superiority over analogue in terms of speed, reliability and low cost per bit of information. The term digital is often used to describe the technological basis of modern telecoms equipment. (Also see Microelectronic and Semiconductor.)

Distributed Switching   A digital exchange system which employs decentralised control and switching functions throughout the hardware, allowing more flexibility and reliability than centralised systems.

Appendix 1

Electromechanical   Semi-electronic, incorporating moving parts (and analogue-based), unlike solid state, digital, microelectronic technology.

Exchange or Switching technology is the technological 'heart' of a telecoms network. All messages are controlled, routed and switched within and between networks by a stored programme in electronic exchanges, and by electromechanical connections in Strowger and Crossbar exchanges.

Fibre Optic   see Optical fibre.

Frequency Division Multiplexing (FDM)   A means of digital transmission which allows many messages to be simultaneously transmitted by 'interleaving' samples of each signal, thereby increasing the capacity of a coaxial or microwave network.

Informatics   Automated digital data processing systems (or networks) incorporating two or more computers, involving data storage, manipulation and transmission.

Information Technology (IT)   The term used for the whole range of telecoms, informatics and telematics systems (and industries) based on digital technology and allowing the storage, transmission and manipulation of data at low cost and great speed. In effect, a coherent technology for handling information.

Information Technology (IT) Industry   The industry which provides the equipment and services based on IT. In this book a distinction is made between the information-intensive industries (the IT industries) and the industrial application of microelectronics, for example, to the automobile industry. Sometimes IT is used to describe all applications of microelectronic technology.

Integrated Circuit   Any microelectronic component with more than one functioning element. Also known as a 'chip', a microelectronic device or a semiconductor component. A circuit is designed using CAD and a miniaturised physical pattern, or 'mask', is produced. This is then 'etched' onto silicon wafers using a complex photolithographic/chemical process. The wafers are then divided into thousands of individual circuits which are 'mounted' onto plastic or ceramic packages and tested. The latest very large scale integration (VLSI) technology allows for a million or more circuits to be condensed on one tiny chip.

Appendix 1

Integrated Services Digital Network (ISDN) The concept of a wide range of fully interlinked IT, communications and broadcasting services, utilising the most advanced digital techniques to achieve low cost, fast, integrated communications, data processing and broadcasting services.

IT see Information technology.

Microelectronic The term used to describe the technological basis of IT, and the actual, miniaturised, component inputs (see integrated circuit).

Microwave Very short electromagnetic radio wave used in telecoms transmission. Within the overall wavelength spectrum of long, medium, short, infrared, ultraviolet, X-ray and gamma rays.

Modem A device used for 'modulation and demodulation' of telecoms signals. In other words, it takes an analogue electrical signal and converts it into a digital signal for transmission, and vice versa.

Multiplexer A device which interfaces with a central exchange and converts analogue into digital signals, and then transmits them using PCM techniques. Many thousand telephone conversations and other signals can be simultaneously transmitted by 'interleaving' samples of each signal, thereby increasing the capacity of existing coaxial or microwave networks. Also, the different types of signal can be 'multiplexed' together without interfering with each other.

Optical Fibre Used for telecoms signal transmission; made of silica which is much cheaper and more readily available than copper, which is used in conventional cables. Advantages over coaxial cable are larger capacity, resistance to corrosion (but not to transmission signals – therefore fewer signal regenerators, or 'boosters', required). In addition, optical fibres can be installed using existing infrastructure such as coaxial ducts or railway lines.

PABX, Private Automatic Branch Exchange A self-contained, usually digital, telephone exchange used in private institutions and separate from the public telecoms network.

Packet Switching Used in data communications systems. Information is stored in binary digits until line capacity is available for transmission. The resulting data stream is termed a 'packet' (it

Appendix 1

has been called 'an electronic post office').

Pulse Code Modulation (PCM) Digital transmission of information by modulation according to a pulse (see Analogue and Digital).

SDS Space Division Switching - see TDS, Time division switching.

Semiconductor The principal material used in the production of microelectronic cicuits, having special electrical conducting properties suited to the mass production of microelectronic circuit components.

Solid State No moving parts, fully electronic, as opposed to electromechanical.

SPC see Stored programme control.

Stored Programme Control An electronic exchange with internal functions performed by programmable software, rather than electromechanical controls.

Strowger The first automatic telephone exchange. Invented in Kansas in 1889 but still in wide use. Based on banks of rotary switches connected in series. Slow, inflexible and costly in comparison with digital, solid state exchanges.

Switching see Exchange.

TDM see Time division multiplexing.

Telecommunications (telecoms) See text.

Telematics Sometimes known as teleinformatics, represents all those computer services based on digital technology which process data and employ the public telecoms network, for switching and transmission, thereby gaining the cost advantages of using existing capital equipment. In many cases telephones and TV sets are used to request and view information.

Time Division Multiplexing A digital transmission mechanism by which various types of data, including speech, can be simultaneously transmitted by interleaving samples of each signal. Different signals are 'multiplexed' together without interfering with each other (not possible with analogue).

Time Division Switching TDS is the most recent SPC exchange technology. Signals are transferred from one point to another by sending samples down

Appendix 1

different paths, depending on their desired destination. At exactly the right time a particular 'gate' opens and allows the signals down a specific path. TDS is more economical than conventional space division switching (SDS) where the physical path is permanently connected.

BIBLIOGRAPHICAL REFERENCES

Albuquerque, J.P. and Waldman H. (1980) Pesquisa e Desenvolvimento em Telecomunicações: Um Panorama Geral, CNPq: Conselho Nacional de Desenvolvimento Científico e Tecnológico; Coordenação de Informática e Comunicações - CIC - Superintêndencia de Desenvolvimento Industrial e de Infra-Estratura, Outubro, Brasilia

Allen, G.C. (1972) A Short Economic History of Modern Japan, Third Edition, George Allen & Unwin Ltd., London

Anuário Brasileiro de Telecomunicações (1983) The Brazilian Telecommunications Directory, Year 2, no. 2, National Review of Telecommunications, São Paulo, Brazil

Arrow, J.K. (1962) 'The Economic Implications of Learning By Doing', Review of Economic Studies, vol. XXIX, pp. 155-73

Arthur D. Little (1983) World Telecommunications 1980-1990

Assis, M.S. (1978) Desenvolvimento Técnico - Científico no Setor de Telecomunicações, Universidade Federal do Rio de Janeiro

Balassa, B. (1979) 'Incentive Policies in Brazil', World Development, vol. 17. pp. 1023-49

Baranson, J. (1978) Technology and the Multinationals: Corporate Strategies in a Changing World Economy, Lexington, Massachusetts

Barron, I. and Curnow, R. (1979) The Future with Microelectronics, Frances Pinter, London

Behrman, J.N. and Wallender, H.W. (1976) Transfer of Manufacturing Technology Within Multinational Enterprises, Ballinger, Massachusetts

Bell, R.M. (1982) Learning and the Accumulation of Industrial Technological Capacity in Developing Countries, Science Policy Research Unit, paper prepared for the International Workshop on Facilitating Indigenous Technological Capability, Centre for African Studies, Edinburgh University, May

Bell, R.M. and Hoffman, K. (1981) Industrial Development with Imported Technology: a Strategic Perspecive on Policy, first draft, unpublished, Science Policy Research Unit,

Bibliographical References

University of Sussex
Bell, R.M., Scott-Kemmis, D. and Satyarakwit, W. (1980) Learning and Technical Change in the Development of Manufacturing Industry: A Case Study of a Permanently Infant Enterprise, Mimeo, Science Policy Research Unit, University of Sussex
Bessant, J. (1983) 'The Diffusion of Microelectronics' in S. Jacobsson and J. Sigurdson (eds.) Technological Trends and Challenges in Electronics. Dominance of the Industrialised World and Responses in the Third World, Research Policy Institute, Lund, Sweden
Bessant, J.R., Bowen, J.A.E., Dickson, K.E. and Marsh, J. (1981) The Impact of Microelectronics: A Review of the Literature, Frances Pinter, London
Boon, G.K. (1982) 'Some Thoughts on Changing Comparative Advantage' in R. Kaplinsky (ed.) Comparative Advantage in an Automating World, IDS Bulletin, March, vol. 13, no. 2
Braun, E. (1982) 'Electronics and Industrial Development' in R. Kaplinsky (ed.) Comparative Advantage in an Automating World, IDS Bulletin, March, vol. 13, no. 2
Brewer, A. (1980) Marxist Theories of Imperialism: A Critical Survey, Routledge, London
Brundenius, C. and Goransson, B. (1982) Swedish Technology Transfer in the Telecommunications Industry - A Case Study of Ericsson do Brasil, Research Policy Institute, Lund, Sweden
Business Times Malaysia, 17 May 1985
Clark, J., Freeman, C. and Soete, L. (1981) 'Long Waves and Technological Development in the 20th Century', Klett-Cotta Sonderdruck, Ernst Klett, Stuttgart, Germany
Clippinger, J.H. (1977) 'Can Communications Development Benefit the Third World?', Telecommunications Policy, vol. 1, no. 4, September
(1977a) 'Datanets and the Third World' Telecommunications Policy, vol. 1, no. 3, June
Companhia Docas de Santos (1982) Annual Report, 1982, Rio de Janeiro, Brazil
Cooper, C.M. and Hoffman, K. (1981) Transactions in Technology and Implications for Developing Countries, Mimeo, Science Policy Research Unit, University of Sussex, March
Cruise O'Brien, R. and Helleiner, G.K. (1980) 'The Political Economy of Information in a Changing International Economic Order', International Organisation, Autumn, vol. 34, no. 4, pp. 445-71
CSE Microelectronics Group (1980) Microelectronics - Capitalist Technology and the Working Class, Blackrose Press, London
Dahlman, C.J. (1982) Foreign Technology and Indigenous Technological Capabilities in Brazil, paper presented at the University of Edinburgh Workshop on Facilitating Indigenous Technological Capability, May

Bibliographical References

Dang Nguyen, G. (1985) 'Telecommunications: A Challenge to the Old Order' in M. Sharp (ed.) Europe and the New Technologies, Frances Pinter, London

Davies, S. (1979) The Diffusion of Process Innovations, Cambridge University Press, Cambridge

Dosi, G. (1981) Technical Change and Survival: Europe's Semiconductor Industry, Sussex European Research Centre, University of Sussex, European Papers, no. 9.

(1982) 'Technological Paradigms and Technological Trajectories: A Suggested Interpretation of the Determinants and Directions of Technical Change', Research Policy, vol. 11, no. 3, June

(1984) Technical Change and Industrial Transformation: The Theory and an Application to the Semiconductor Industry, Macmillan, London

Dosi, G. and Orsenigo, L. (1984) Market Processes, Rules and Institutions in Technical Change and Economic Dynamics, Mimeo, Science Policy Research Unit, University of Sussex

Earp, F.S.A. (1982) Serviços de Telecomunicações no Brasil, Tese Submetida ao Corpo Docente da Coordenação dos Programas de Pós-Graduação, como Parte dos Requisitos Necessários para a Obtenção de Grau de Mestre em Ciências, Universidade Federal do Rio de Janeiro/Faculdade de Engenharia COPPE/UFRJ

Edquist, C. and Jacobsson, S. (1984) Trends in the Diffusion of Electronics Technology in the Capital Goods Sector, Technology and Development Discussion Paper no. 161, Research Policy Institute, Lund, Sweden

Electronics and Power - November/December 1985, and other issues

Electronics Times - No. 174, 20 May 1982, pp. 1 and 10, and other issues

Electronics Weekly (1983), 4 May 1983, p. 11, and other issues

Enos, J. (1984) 'Government Intervention in the Transfer of Technology: the Case of South Korea' in IDS Bulletin, Developmental States in East Asia: Capitalist and Socialist, April, vol. 15, no. 2

Fels, R. (ed.) (1984) abridged edition of: Schumpeter, J.A., Business Cycles: A Theoretical, Historical and Statistical Analysis of the Capitalist Process, McGraw-Hill, New York

Financial Times - various issues

Forester, T. (ed.) (1980) The Microelectronics Revolution, Basil Blackwell, Oxford

Fransman, M. and King, K. (eds.) (1984) Technological Capability in the Third World, Macmillan, London

Freeman, C. (1974) The Economics of Industrial Innovation. Penguin Books Ltd., Harmondsworth

(1979) 'The Kondratieff Long Waves, Technical Change and Unemployment' in Structural Determinants of Employment and Unemployment, vol. 11, pp. 181-96, OECD,

Bibliographical References

Paris
(1980) The Diffusion of Technology in the Economic System, paper prepared for the 60th Anniversary of Netherlands Electronics and Radio Society, May 1980 (published in the journal of NERS)

Freeman, C. (ed.) (1984) Long Waves in the World Economy, Frances Pinter, London

Freeman, C., Clark, J. and Soete, L. (1982) Unemployment and Technical Innovation: A Study of Long Waves and Economic Development, Frances Pinter, London

Galli, E. (1982) Microelectronics and Telecommunications in Developing Countries, UNIDO/ECLA Expert Group Meeting on Implications of Microelectronics for the ECLA Region ID/WG.372/4 V.82 25601

Gazeta Mercantil (1983) Balanço Anual, 1983, Ano.VII no. 7, São Paulo, Brasil

Griliches, Z. (1957) 'Hybrid Corn: An Exploration in the Economics of Technological Change', Econometrica, vol. 25, pp. 501-22

Hardy, A.P. (1980) 'The Role of the Telephone in Economic Development', Telecommunications Policy, vol. 4, no. 4, pp. 278-86

Hobday, M.G. (1982) The Role of Telecommunications in Economic Development: A Review of Recent Literature and an Alternative Interpretation with Special Reference to Policy Issues, Mimeo, Science Policy Research Unit, University of Sussex

(1985) Telecommunications and Information Technology in Latin America: Prospects and Possibilities for Managing the Technology Gap, Report prepared for UNIDO

(1986) Digital Telecommunications Technology and the Third World: The Theory, the Challenge, and the Evidence from Brazil, D.Phil Thesis, Science Policy Research Unit, University of Sussex

Hoffman, K. (1985) 'Microelectronics, International Competition and Development Strategies: The Unavoidable Issues - Editor's Introduction', World Development, vol. 13, no. 3, pp. 263-73

Hoffman, K. and Rush, H. (1985) Microelectronics and Clothing the Impact of Technical Change on a Global Industry, ILO, Geneva

Hudson, H.E., Goldschmidt, D., Parker, E.B. and Hardy, A. (1981) The Role of Telecommunications in Socio-Economic Development A Review of the Literature, Information Gatekeepers Inc., Brookline, Massachusetts

International Business Week (1983) Telecommunications: The Global Battle, Special Report, October 24

International Telecommunications Union (1984) The Missing Link, Report of the Independent Commission for Worldwide Telecommunications Development, ITU, Geneva

Jacobsson, S. (1983) 'Numerically Controlled Machine Tools - Implications for Newly Industrialising Countries' in S. Jacobsson and J. Sigurdson (eds.) Technological Trends

Bibliographical References

and Challenges in Electronics: Dominance of the Industrialised World and Responses in the Third World, Research Policy Institute, Lund, Sweden

Jacobsson, S. and Ljung, T. (1983) 'Electronics, Automation and Global Comparative Advantage in the Engineering Industry' in S. Jacobsson and J. Sigurdson (eds.) Technological Trends and Challenges in Electronics: Dominance of the Industrialised World and Responses in the Third World, Research Policy Institute, Lund, Sweden

Jacobsson, S. and Sigurdson, J. (eds.) (1983) Technological Trends and Challenges in Electronics: Dominance of the Industrialised World and Responses in the Third World, Research Policy Institute, Lund, Sweden

Jequier, N. (1977) 'International Technology Transfer in the Telecommunications Industry' in D. Germidis (ed.) Transfer of Technology by Multinational Corporations, Development Centre of the OECD, Paris

Kaplinsky, R. (1982) Electronics, Comparative Advantage and Development, a UNIDO study, Frances Pinter, London
 (1982a) 'editorial' Comparative Advantage in an Automating World, IDS Bulletin, March, vol. 13, no. 2
 (1984) Automation: the Technology and Society, Longman, Essex

Katz, J. (1980) Domestic Technology Generation in LDCs: A Review of Research Findings, Working Paper no. 35, IBD-ECLA Programme, CEPAL Offices, Buenos Aires
 (1984) 'Technological Innovation, Industrial Organisation, and Comparative Advantages of Latin American Metalworking Industries' in M. Fransman and K. King (eds.) Technological Capability in the Third World, Macmillan, London

Keynes, J. M. (1973) The General Theory of Employment, Interest and Money, Macmillan, London

Kondratieff, N.D. (1978) 'The Long Waves in Economic Life', Lloyds Bank Review, July, no. 129, pp. 41-60 (first published in 1936)

Krugman, P. (1983) 'New Theories of Trade Among Industrial Countries', AER, Papers and Proceedings, pp. 343-47

Lall, S. (1975) 'Is Dependency a Useful Concept in Analysing Underdevelopment', World Development, November/December
 (1982) Developing Countries as Exporters of Technology: A First Look at the Indian Experience, Macmillan, London

Leff, N.H. (1980) 'Some Welfare Effects of Telecommunications Investments in Developing Countries', Graduate School of Business, Columbia University, Mimeo

Leontief, W. and Duchin, F. (1983) Military Spending: Facts and Figures, Worldwide Implications and Future Outlooks, Oxford University Press, New York

Leppan, E.D. (1983) A Literature Survey and Partially Annotated Bibliography on the Impact of Microelectronics on the Third World, paper prepared for the Meeting on the Impact of Microelectronics, Mexico City, Dec 14-16, 1983. Jointly Sponsored by the Ministry of Industry,

Bibliographical References

Government of Mexico and the International Development Research Centre, Ottawa, Canada

Lockwood, W.W. (1968) The Economic Development of Japan: Growth and Structural Change. Princeton University Press, New Jersey

Luedde-Neurath, R. (1984) 'State Intervention and Foreign Direct Investment in South Korea', Developmental States in East Asia: Capitalist and Socialist, in IDS Bulletin, April, vol. 15, no. 2

Maculan, A. (1981) Processo Decisório No Setor de Telecomunicações, Tese de Mestrado Apresentada ao IUPERJ, como Requisito Parcial para Obtenção do Grau de Mestre em Ciência Política, em dezembro de 1981. IUPERJ, Rio de Janeiro, Brasil

Magdoff, H. and Sweezy, P.M. (1977) 'Keynesian Chickens Come Home to Roost' in H. Magdoff and P.M. Sweezy (eds.) The End of Prosperity, Monthly Review Press, New York

Mansfield, E. (1961) 'Technical Change and the Rate of Imitation', Econometrica, vol. 29, no. 4, pp. 741-66

Mattos, H.C. (1983) Speech of the Brazilian Minister of Communications, International Telecommunications Union, International Forum on Telecommunications, Geneva

Maxwell, P. (1980) Technical Change and Organisation in Steelplants: an Argentine and a Brazilian Case, Simposio de Analisis Organizacional, 16-18 de Otubre de 1980, Buenos Aires

(1981) Technology Policy and Firm Learning Efforts in Less-Developed Countries: A Case Study of the Experience of the Argentine Steel Firm Acindar S.A., D.Phil Thesis, University of Sussex

Metcalfe, J.S. (1981) 'Impulse and Diffusion in the Study of Technical Change', Futures, vol. 13, no. 5, pp. 347-59

Metcalfe, J.S. and Soete, L. (1983) Notes on the Evolution of Technology and International Competition, paper presented to Workshop on Science and Technology Policy in the 1980s, University of Manchester, (in M. Gibbons and P. Gummett (eds.) Science and Technology Policy in the 1980s and Beyond, Longman, London)

Mitchell, J.L. (1978) 'The Appropriateness of Satellite Communications for the Third World', Media Asia, vol. 5, no. 2, pp. 90-103

(1978a) 'Seeking a New International Order of Information: A Stalemate', Media Asia, vol. 5, no. 1, pp. 14-20

Mlawa, H.M. (1983) The Acquisition of Technology, Technological Capability and Technical Change: A Study of the Textile Industry in Tanzania, D.Phil Thesis, Science Policy Research Unit, University of Sussex

Mowery, D. and Rosenberg, N. (1979) 'The Influence of Market Demand Upon Innovation: A Critical Review of Some Recent Empirical Studies', Research Policy, vol. 8, pp. 102-53

Bibliographical References

Muller, J. (1982) *Government Policy and the Telecommunications Equipment Sector: an Assessment of the Major Issues in the Face of Changing Technology*, SERC, unpublished mimeo, University of Sussex

Nelson, R.R. (1959) 'The Simple Economics of Basic Scientific Research', *Journal of Political Economy*, vol. 67, pp. 297-306

Nelson, R.R. and Winter, S.G. (1974) *Neoclassical vs Evolutionary Theories of Economic Growth: Critique and Prospectus*, Mimeo deposited at the Science Policy Research Unit, University of Sussex

(1977) 'In Search of a Useful Theory of Innovation', *Research Policy*, vol. 6, 1977, pp. 36-76

(1982) *An Evolutionary Theory of Economic Change*, Belknap Press, of Harvard University Press, Cambridge, Massachusetts

Newsweek (1983) 'Special Report on Telecommunications', May 23

O'Connor, D.C. (1985) 'The Computer Industry in the Third World: Policy Options and Constraints', *World Development*, vol. 13, no. 3

OECD (1982) *Telecommunications Equipment: Even a Growth Industry Can Have Structural Problems*, OECD, Observer, November 1982, pp. 12-18

OECD (1983) *Telecommunications: Pressures and Policies for Change*, OECD, Paris

Oshima, K. (1984) 'Technological Innovation and Industrial Research in Japan', *Research Policy*, vol. 13, no. 5, pp. 285-303

Pavitt, K. (1979) 'Technical Innovation and Industrial Development, 1. The New Causality', *Futures*, December

(1980) 'Technical Innovation and Industrial Development, 2. The Dangers of Divergence', *Futures*, February

(1984) 'Sectoral Patterns of Technical Change: Towards a Taxonomy and a Theory', *Research Policy*, vol. 13, no. 6, pp. 343-73

(1984a) *Chips and Trajectories: How Does the Semiconductor Influence the Sources and Directions of Technical Change?*, Mimeo, Science Policy Research Unit, University of Sussex

(1985) *International Patterns of Technological Accumulation*, paper prepared for the Prince Bertil Symposium on Strategies in Global Competition, Stockholm School of Economics, 7-9 November 1984

Pavitt, K. and Soete, L. (1981) 'International Differences in Economic Growth and the International Location of Innovation' in H. Giersch (ed.) *Emerging Technologies: Consequences for Economic Growth, Structural Change and Employment*, J.C.B. Mohr (Paul Siebech), Tübingen

Pelton, J.N. (1981) *Global Talk: The Marriage of the Computer, World Communications and Man*, Harvester Press, Netherlands

Bibliographical References

Perez, C. (1983) Structural Change and the Assimilation of New Technologies in the Economic and Social Systems: A Contribution to the Current Debate on Kondratiev Cycles, Science Policy Research Unit, Mimeo (paper presented at Royal College of Art Seminar on April 14, London)
 (1985) 'Microelectronics, Long-Waves and World Structural Change: New Perspectives for Developing Countries', World Development, special issue on Microelectronics, vol. 13, no. 3, pp. 441-63
Perez, C. and Freeman, C. (1986) The Diffusion of Technical Innovations and Changes of Techno-economic Paradigm, paper prepared for the Venice Conference, March 1986 (Science Policy Research Unit, University of Sussex)
Phillips, A. (1966) 'Patents, Potential Competition, and Technical Progress', American Economic Review, vol. 56, pp. 301-10
Rada, J. (1982) 'Technology and the North-South Division of Labour' in R. Kaplinsky (ed.) Comparative Advantage in an Automating World, IDS Bulletin, March, vol. 13, no. 2
Rempp, H. (1981) Flexible Manufacturing Systems not yet Economic, Fraunhofer-Institut für Systemtechnik und Innovationsforschung, November 16, Karlsruhe
Revista Telebras, various issues
Rogers, E.M. (1962) Diffusion of Innovations, Free Press, New York (First Edition)
 (1976) Communication and Development, Sage Publications, Beverly Hills, California
 (1983) Diffusion of Innovations, Free Press, New York (Third Edition)
Roobeek, A.J.M. (1984) Changes in the Structure of the Telecommunications Industry, Universiteit van Amsterdam, Research Memorandum (Vakgroep bedrijfseconomie) no. 8417
Rosenberg, N. (1976) Perspectives on Technology, Cambridge University Press, Cambridge
 (1982) Inside the Black Box: Technology and Economics, Cambridge University Press, Cambridge
Rosenberg, N. and Frischtak, C.R. (1984) 'Technological Innovation and Long Waves', Cambridge Journal of Economics, vol. 8, pp. 7-24
Saunders, R.J., Warford, J.J. and Wellenius, B. (1983) Telecommunications and Economic Development, A World Bank Publication, Johns Hopkins University Press, Baltimore
Schiffer, J. (1981) 'The Changing Post-War Pattern of Development: The Accumulated Wisdom of Samir Amin', World Development, vol. 9, no. 6, pp. 515-39
Schmookler, J. (1966) Invention and Economic Growth, Harvard University Press, Cambridge, Massachusetts
Schumpeter, J. (1971) 'The Instability of Capitalism', in N. Rosenberg (ed.) The Economics of Technical Change: Selected Readings. Penguin Books Ltd., Harmondsworth
Soete, L. (1978) Inventive Activity, Industrial Organisation and International Trade, D.Phil Thesis,

Bibliographical References

Science Policy Research Unit, University of Sussex
(1981) 'Technological Dependence: A Critical View' in D. Seers (ed.) Technological Dependence: A Critical Reassessment, Frances Pinter, London
(1981a) Technical Change, Catching Up and the Productivity Slowdown, paper prepared for the Joint CRSTE/RPI/SPRU Conference on Technological and Industrial Policy in China and Europe at the Research Policy Institute, Lund, Sweden, June
(1983) Long Cycles and the International Diffusion of Technology, Mimeo, Science Policy Research Unit, University of Sussex
(1985) 'International Diffusion of Technology, Industrial Development and Technological Leapfrogging', World Development, special issue on Microelectronics, vol. 13, no. 3, pp. 409-23

Soete, L. and Dosi, G. (1983) Technology and Employment in the Electronics Industry, Frances Pinter, London

Soete, L. and Turner, R. (1984) 'Technology Diffusion and the Rate of Technical Change', Economic Journal, vol. 94, September, pp. 612-23

Spero, J.E. (1977) The Politics of International Economic Relations, George Allen and Unwin, London
(1982) 'Information: The Policy Void', Foreign Policy, no. 48, Fall

SSI (1982) Transborder Data Flows and Brazil: The Role of Transnational Corporations, Impacts of Transborder Data Flows and Effects of National Policies, Special Secretariat of Informatics of the National Security Council of the Presidency of the Republic of Brazil in Cooperation with the Ministry of Communications of Brazil, 19 August 1982, 82-23079

Stoneman, P. (1981) 'Intra-Firm Diffusion, Bayesian Learning and Profitability', Economic Journal, vol. 91, June, pp. 375-88

Strassman, W.P. (1968) Technological Change and Economic Development: The Manufacturing Experience of Mexico and Puerto Rico, Cornell University Press, New York

Sylos-Labini, P. (1969) Oligopoly and Technical Progress, Harvard University Press, Cambridge, Massachusetts

Tavares de Araujo, J. (1982) Technical Progress and Forms of Competition: A Case Study of the Glass Industry, PhD Thesis, University College, London

Taylor, P. (1985) 'AT&T in Telephone System Venture with Ricoh', article in the Financial Times, 31 July 1985

Teitel, S. (1981) 'Towards an Understanding of Technical Change in Semi-Industrialised Countries', Research Policy, vol. 10, pp. 127-47

TELEBRAS (1984) Research and Development at TELEBRAS: Ten TELEBRAS Years, internal TELEBRAS journal, Brazil

Telebrasil: Revista Brasileira de Telecomunicações, (internal telecommunications journal of TELEBRAS), various issues

Bibliographical References

Teleguia (1984/85) 'Teleguia: O Guia Completo das Telecomunicações na Empresa', Telepres, São Paulo

Tigre, P.B. (1982) Technology and Competition in the Brazilian Computer Industry, D.Phil Thesis, Science Policy Research Unit, University of Sussex
(1983) The Mexican Professional Electronics Industry and Technology, Report prepared for UNIDO, ST/MEX/80/002/11-61/62.4.2

UNCTAD (1982) 'The Impact of Electronics Technology on the Capital Goods and Industrial Machinery Sector: Implications for Devloping Countries', Problems and Issues Concerning the Transfer, Application and Development of Technology in the Capital Goods and Industrial Machinery Sector, UNCTAD, Trade and Development Board, TD/B/C.6/AC.7/3 GE.82

Visao (1983) 'Quem e Ouem na Economia Brasileira', 31 de Augosto, no. 35a

Wade, R. (1984) 'Dirigisme Taiwan-Style', in IDS Bulletin, April, vol. 15, no.2, Developmental States in East Asia: Capitalist and Socialist

Wade, R. and White, G. (eds.) (1984) Developmental States in East Asia: Capitalist and Socialist, IDS Bulletin, April, vol. 15, no. 2

Wajnberg, S. (1982) 'A Indústria Eletrônica Brasileira Situação em 1982', Suplemento Técnico Telebrasil - 1, Junho, Telebrasil, Rio de Janeiro, Brasil (Official Report of the Executive Secretary of GEICOM)
(1984) 'A Industria Eletrônica Brasileira - Situação em 1984', Telebrasil, Suplemento Técnico, Telebrasil, Rio de Janeiro, Brasil (Official Report of the Executive Secretary of GEICOM)

Warren, W. (1980) Imperialism Pioneer of Capitalism, NLB Verso, London

Wellenius, B. (1977) 'Telecommunications in Developing Countries', Telecommunications Policy, vol. 1, no. 4, pp. 289-97

Wells, J.R. (1979) 'Brazil and the Post 1973 Crisis in the International Economy' in R. Thorp and L. Whitehead (eds.) Inflation and Stabilisation in Latin America, Macmillan, London

Wilmott, R. (1985) 'Wanted: An Industry that is World Class', article in the Financial Times, 26 June 1985

INDEX

absorptive capacity 28, 62, 76, 77
analogue
   telecommunication systems 38
AT&T 47, 50, 55

Brazil
   MNC investments in 91-3
   new communications infrastructure 88-109
   technology transfer to 93-5
Brazilian economic crisis 9, 169, 170-3, 191
Brazilian informatics
   services provided 104-5
Brazilian IT producers 176
Brazilian National Development Fund 173
Brazilian R&D in telecoms
   activities 111-48
   exchange technology 111-48
   policy objectives 111
   see also CPqD
Brazilian Telecoms Fund 172-3
Brazilian telecoms industry
   costs and benefits of 182-90
   development of 95-7, 169-92, 196
   employment in 178-9
   equipment manufacturers 173-81
   market size and growth 170-3
   MNC integration 149-67
   MNC ownership of 96

origins 88-90
   policy objectives towards 112-4
Brazilian telecoms infrastructure
   evidence of leapfrogging 97-105
   policy objectives towards 97-8
   role as IT infrastructure 101-5
   service sector reorganisation 90-1
Brazilian telematics
   services provided 104-5
China 6
comparative advantage 60
CONTEL 90
convergence
   industrial 45-56
   and microelectronics 44-5
   technological 7
   in telecoms 38-41
CPqD
   achievements of 111-48, 195
   and diffusion of technology 111
   human resources 120
   and local firms 178-9
   objectives of 111
   philosophy of 116
   programmes and projects 121-2
   technological progress 119-39
   see also Brazilian R&D in

Index

telecoms
Crossbar 38, 43

DCs
   and telecommunications
     1-5, 8
   see also Third World
dependency theory 12
developing countries
   see DCs
development economics 3
diffusion
   curve 25
   cycles 21, 194
   of information technology 11
   inter-firm 17, 30
   intra-firm 17
   and learning 29-32, 191
   mechanisms of 21
   theory 6, 14-24, 194
digital 2, 3, 108, 113, 170
   see also microelectronics, IT and semiconductor
divisibility 42-3, 73, 84, 169

EDB 93-6, 156-60, 163
Elebra 162, 178-9
electromechanical
   oligopolies 63
   technology 3, 4, 6, 9, 84-108
   see also leapfrogging
EMBRATEL 90
Equitel 161-2, 163
   see also Siemens
Ericsson do Brasil
   see EDB
European equipment manufacturers 50-3
exchange systems
   barriers to entry 74-5
   and informatics 39-40
   investment in 38-9, 72
   see also switching equipment

fifth generation technology 201-2
Fujitsu 49

GEC 186

GEICOM 128
Geisel Government 113, 149
government policy
   in Brazil 108, 112-4, 169
   and learning 27
   role of 5, 10, 195

Hitachi 49

IBM 49, 50
India 6
informatics services 39
information technology
   see IT
innovation
   adoption of 16-21
   diffusion of 16-21
   and economic growth 13
   rewards from 14
   supply and demand of 17-21
Integrated Services Digital Network
   see ISDN
international
   diffusion of technology 21-4
   economic environment 7
International Telecommunications Union
   see ITU
ISDN
   and telecoms infrastructure 67
IT
   character of 140-5
   and developing countries 198-202
   and economic development 2, 197
   infrastructure 67
   and learning strategies 140-5
   service provision 39
   and skills 57
   and social activities 2
   and telecoms markets 55
   see also microelectronics and digital
ITT 47, 89, 160, 161
ITU 1

Japan
   catch-up growth 22

Index

multinational corporations
of 7, 58

Kondratieff long waves 16

Latin America 8, 47, 68,
77-85
leapfrog/leapfrogging 3, 6,
7, 9, 10, 60-85, 108, 195,
196-7
learning
approach 6, 11, 194
and CPqD 112
by designing 138
and developing countries
24-5
and diffusion theory
24-32, 65, 191
and digital technology 131
and feedback systems
138-9
and government policy 27
mechanisms of 134-40
pre-investment 25
by searching 27
sectoral level 27, 181-2,
190-1
by setting up capital
goods 135-7
sources of 131-4
strategies 139-40
technology adoption and 25
and technology transfer 27
by training and hiring
137-8
see also Schumpeterian
learning
L.M. Ericsson 47, 55, 89
logistics curve 17

Malaysia 6
microelectronics
and CPqD 112
and developing countries
35, 60, 61-6, 190-2,
198-202
diffusion of 2, 58, 64,
166
divisibility of 42
and employment 63
innovation 7
labour-saving nature 62
opportunities 7, 84, 190-2

technology 2, 4-5, 9, 43,
57
and telecommunications
35-58
transition to 5, 170, 191,
196
see also digital
technology, IT and
semiconductor
MINICOM 5-6, 90-2, 113, 172
Ministry of Communications
(of Brazil)
see MINICOM
MNCs
advantages over local
firms 175-6
in Brazil 6, 155-67, 196
competition 8, 73, 74,
83-4
and economic development
2, 165-6
expenditures on R&D in
Brazil 153-4
policies towards 113
reliance upon 8
subsidiaries in Brazil 9,
113, 151-3
technology efforts in
Brazil 154-67
modularity 42, 73, 84
monopsony power 166
multinational corporations
see MNCs

NEC 49, 50, 150, 160, 162-4
neoclassical economics 3, 11,
16
neo-Schumpeterian
theory 3, 6, 12
see also Schumpeterian
learning
neotechnology theory 12-16
see also neo-Schumpeterian
northward drift 8

OECD 1, 49
Oki 49
Organisation for Cooperation
and Economic Development
see OECD

peripheral equipment 37, 40,
75

220

Index

Plessey 55, 186

R&D
    activities of TELEBRAS 113-48
    centre 8, 9
    costs 50
    by MNCs in Brazil 162-5
research and development
    see R&D
rural telecoms in Brazil 106-8

Schumpeterian competition and DCs 166
Schumpeterian learning 7, 11, 24-32, 170
semiconductor
    industry 65
    paradigm 35-6
    technology 7
    see also microelectronic, digital and IT
Siemens 47, 55, 160, 161
STC 55
Strowger 38-43
switching equipment 37
    see also exchange systems

telecoms
    commercial balance in Brazil 155
    competitive strategies in 47-8
    and economic development 68-70
    equipment costs 170
    equipment industry 36-8, 48
    equipment suppliers 49-56
    infrastructure 1, 35
    international industry 35-8
    investment restrictions 172, 173
    as IT infrastructure 67
    and IT markets 55
    joint ventures 51-6
    'leading-edge' technology 2
    network 3, 9
    options for DCs 146-8
    production process 41-3, 57
    purchasing power 199-200
technology
    accumulation of 9, 127, 166, 170, 194, 197
    convergence 7, 38, 44-5
    and dependence 4, 8, 62, 151, 196
    gaps 7, 8, 10, 60, 62
    imitation 15
    international diffusion of 21-32
    leaders 23
    leads and lags 15, 23-4
    opportunities in 15, 85, 146-7, 170
    paradigms 14, 23, 35
    strategies of MNCs 149-67
    theories 11-32
    and trade 15
    trajectories 14
    transfer 4, 8, 27
    transfer to Brazil 93-5
    see also convergence
TELEBRAS
    administration 8, 126
    demand for telecoms equipment 171-2
    investments in R&D 118-9
    operating performance 186-90
    organisation 91-2
    patents registered by 127-30
    purchasing policy 177
    R&D activities 111-48
telecommunications
    see telecoms
Third World 8, 50
    see also DCs
transmission equipment 37, 40

UN 1
United Nations
    see UN
US Government 51

Vargas government 89

World Bank 1

221

For Product Safety Concerns and Information please contact our EU
representative GPSR@taylorandfrancis.com
Taylor & Francis Verlag GmbH, Kaufingerstraße 24, 80331 München, Germany

www.ingramcontent.com/pod-product-compliance
Lightning Source LLC
Chambersburg PA
CBHW061442300426
44114CB00014B/1793